SMUGGLER
A MEMOIR

ALSO BY RICHARD STRATTON:

Smack Goddess
Slam: The Book (editor, with Kim Wozencraft)
Altered States of America: Outlaws and Icons, Hitmakers and Hitmen

SMUGGLER

A MEMOIR

A TRUE STORY OF **MARIJUANA**,
THE HIPPIE MAFIA AND ONE OF
AMERICA'S MOST WANTED
INTERNATIONAL DRUG TRAFFICKERS

RICHARD STRATTON

ALLEN&UNWIN

First published in the United States as *Smuggler's Blues* in 2016 by
Arcade Books, a division of Skyhorse, Inc.

First published in Great Britain in 2017 by Allen & Unwin

Allen & Unwin
c/o Atlantic Books
Ormond House
26–27 Boswell Street
London WC1N 3JZ

Phone: 020 7269 1610
Fax: 020 7430 0916

Email: UK@allenandunwin.com
Web: www.allenandunwin.com/uk

A CIP catalogue record of this book is available from the British Library.

Trade paperback ISBN 978 1 76029 380 2
E-book ISBN 978 1 92557 507 1

Printed and bound by MBM Print SCS Ltd, Glasgow
10 9 8 7 6 5 4 3 2 1

MIX
Paper from
responsible sources
FSC® C117931

A smuggler works from inclination, from passion. He is on the one side an artist. He risks everything, runs terrible dangers; he is cunning, invents dodges and gets out of scrapes, and sometimes acts with a sort of inspiration. It is a passion as strong as gambling.

—Fyodor Dostoyevsky, *The House of the Dead*

CONTENTS

AUTHOR'S NOTE

Smuggler is based on my fifteen-year career as a player in the so-called hippie mafia, importing and distributing marijuana and hashish. Some of the names, locations, and the timeline of events have been altered to protect the identities of those who were never captured and may still be active in the marijuana underground.

This book is dedicated to those unjustly tried, convicted, and sentenced to prison for trafficking in a God-given plant. Free the prisoners of the War on Plants.

SMUGGLER
A MEMOIR

1

NORTHERN EXPOSURE

Phillips, Maine, April 1980

DAWN COMES EARLY this time of year. Particularly up here in the North Country. It's four in the morning. Bright stars still visible in deep velvet skies tinged crimson along the eastern horizon. *Red sky in morning, smugglers take warning.*

The GMC dually rumbles into motion down the gravel driveway. I love this truck; with the plush, roomy crew cab, it's like driving along the road in your living room. I always buy American, patriot that I am, and my motto is: When in doubt, buy a truck. Hit the play button on the stereo. Neil Young's "Powderfinger": *Look out, Mama, there's a white boat comin' up the river* blasts from six speakers. I substitute my own lyrics: *Look out, Mama, there's a big bird comin' up the river . . .*

Or maybe not. You never know how real anything is in this business. Be prepared, that's the Boy Scout motto. Not that I was ever a Boy Scout; got kicked out of Cub Scouts. The pack leader was a pervert, and I called him on it. None of the adults believed me. Still, my Yankee WASP work ethic, drilled into me by my maternal grandmother, Ethel Lowell Burnham—Ba Ba, we called her—demands that I do my job to the utmost of my ability even if everyone around me is fucking up.

"Anything worth doing," Ba Ba would tell me, "is worth doing right." And she was always right, lived long enough to know.

It's a short drive from the farm down Wheeler Hill and along Toothaker Pond Road to the river. My big white Alsatian shepherd, Karamazov, doesn't like rock music as much as I do. He sticks his head out the window and lets the soft spring air fold back his ears. I need the music loud. Most people in this part of the world are still asleep and I've already taken a couple of hits off the oily, resin-soaked roach I left in the ashtray on the kitchen table back at the farm. To say I'm high and nervous doesn't come close to describing how I feel. I'm plagued by fear. Terrified. Freaked-the-fuck-out. Just the way I like it.

Not simply fear of arrest, though that is always with me. Not fear of failure, either. No, it is a deep-seated dread that everything they have always said about me is true: *You're a bad kid, Rickie Stratton. A trouble-maker. A juvenile delinquent. You may even be a sociopath. And that shit you smoke, that music you listen to, is only going to make you worse.* They being the Authorities: adults, teachers, principals, probation officers, cops, judges, and shrinks. Lawyers. My big fear is that I am proving them right. I am a failure at everything except crime. The only way I know to soothe this runaway fear is to keep assuring myself *they* are wrong and what I am doing is right.

My ground crew is bivouacked at the lodge, set on a low hill beside the trout pond a stone's throw from the river. Who would have expected that a place like this exists only a few miles down the road from the horse farm I own with the novelist Norman Mailer? Yes, that Mailer. The enfant terrible of American literature. Who lately has been calling himself Aquarius. One could argue it's all his fault. When I read his work in college, I sensed he was writing about me. Mailer bought the farm with Channing Godfried, a former Kennedy speechwriter and whiz kid who quit the Johnson administration over the Vietnam War. That was ten years ago. They paid twenty grand for the house, ramshackle barn, and 160 acres of land on the side of a rocky hill with a view of Mount Blue across the valley. I was living in Provincetown,

Massachusetts, with Anaïs, my wife, renovating a home, waiting for a load. There I met and became friends with Mailer. He heard I had access to good weed. Mailer and Godfried hired me to fix up the farm. When I began to make serious money, I bought them out.

My mouth is cotton dry from nerves and reefer. There is a spring beside the private road that leads into the lodge. I stop the dually. Karamazov and I get out. He laps up the water with his long pink tongue, and I fill a jug, take several cool swallows to soothe my throat and drown the butterflies in my belly. This is the best water I have ever tasted, gurgling up from deep in the ground, fresh, clean, full of minerals, and uncontaminated by human technology. It's Mother Earth offering up her vital liquid to wash clean the stain of civilization.

The lodge was vacant and run down when we took it over. A relative by marriage, fellow scammer—I call him by his nickname, Jonathan Livingston Seagull—a pilot, discovered this place while out trail-riding on a motorcycle. He came back to the farm and said, "You'll never guess what I found down by the river." Local lore has it that the lodge and airstrip were built back in the 1940s by John Fox, a self-made millionaire from South Boston, former owner of the long defunct *Boston Post* newspaper. Fox was a friend and business partner of Joseph P. Kennedy, father of JFK. Gloria Swanson supposedly stayed at the lodge occasionally while she was having her affair with Joe Kennedy. At one point Fox owned 7,000 acres of land in this valley. He carved out the mile-long airstrip in the woods beside the river so he could fly up from Boston on weekends. Across the river he built a fourteen-room lodge on a spring-fed pond he stocked with trout. When we discovered the place, it was owned by a shady New Jersey developer who had fallen on hard times and wanted to sell. My partners and I bought the property in the name of a company that is wholly owned by a shell offshore corporation. Amascontee Lodge and Flying Club we call it, named after the Native American tribe that hunted these woods before the white man came.

I suffer from *agoramania*—an uncontrollable urge to acquire real estate. Property. Land. Homes. Buildings. As if anyone can really own any part of God's creation. We lease it at best. But it gives me some assurance that I actually exist. I bought a 6,000-acre ranch in the Texas Hill Country where I stride around the boundary like James Dean in *Giant* and lie to myself: *This is mine*. Knowing it was all paid for with black market money, knowing the IRS is already hot on my trail, poised to take it all away. It's a fool's paradise I live in, but I tell myself it beats a life of quiet desperation.

The ground crew for this operation consists of two ex-Marines, Vietnam vets. Father Flaherty, who looks like a priest, got his nickname while driving a motor home we bought from a Texas outfit known as Global Evangelism Television. We left the logo—a picture of a camera and a cross—painted on the outside of the motor home and posed as evangelists while transporting loads of reefer up from the ranch in Texas. Father Flaherty's partner has been working with me for years. I call him JD or Jimmy D. He's as loyal as Karamazov but with some strictly human habits that are in evidence as I walk into the front room of the lodge: empty bottles of tequila, beer bottles, a Ziploc bag of weed, roaches, and cigarette butts. JD got smashed in the mouth with a rifle butt during a fight with a fellow Marine and has never bothered to have his front teeth replaced. He's passed out on the sofa, though there are plenty of bedrooms upstairs. Karamazov pads over and nuzzles him with his wet snout.

"Rise and shine," I say when JD rolls over and looks up. He grunts in response.

Jimmy D and Father Flaherty have enlisted a couple of rookie helpers. One is a local guy, a carpenter who did much of the finish work up at the farm and has been renovating the lodge—call him Mild Bill. He's quiet, bearded, looks like Abraham Lincoln. The other guy is JD's old lady's brother, nicknamed Dangerous Dan, who's been in and out of jail a few times but is known to hold his mud. The fifth wheel is Cal, a big, laid-back dude from San Diego who came with the scam.

He works for a rich neophyte dope dealer out of Kansas City who is attempting his first importation—five tons of primo Colombian gold reefer.

The men load into two big Ryder box trucks. We caravan across the bridge and along the road beside the town dump to the airstrip. Father Flaherty has set up a VHF-AM ground-to-air radio in the log cabin beside the runway. The trucks park midfield beside the wind sock— hanging limp in the early morning lull. JD and I get out and walk the length of the field. Karamazov bounds along beside us, or he takes off into the woods in pursuit of deer.

"It's soft," I say as my boots sink into the sod. "Way soft. I don't know about this." Jimmy D grunts in response, flicks the butt of a Camel into the wet grass. He has never had much faith in the reality of this trip.

The strip is situated beside a long bend in the river, which makes it easy to spot from the air, and is positioned to take advantage of prevailing winds. But it's mushy after the winter thaw and spring rains. We've been using a single-engine Cessna to smuggle small loads of weed and hash to our northern neighbors. The Canadian border is only fifty miles away by air. We can deliver a three- or four-hundred-pound load into Quebec, drop it off, and be back with a bag full of money in a couple of hours and on one tank of fuel. On any given day, I might make ten grand before lunch. Not bad work if you can get the merchandise. That's always the problem in this business: merchandise; supply, also known as product. America consumes upwards of ten tons of weed a day. Canada smokes another two tons of pot a day and at least half a ton of hash. It's an importer's bonanza. With a five-thousand-foot airstrip in a state that has a long coastline pocketed with deepwater coves and a sparsely populated foreign border, we are well situated in a smuggler's paradise. During Prohibition rumrunners made use of these same routes and methods. I have an air freight catch at Logan Airport in Boston, known in the trade as a patch, where we smuggle in regular shipments of high-quality hashish from Lebanon. At the ranch in

Texas, we land planeloads of Mexican and Jamaican reefer, ship it back east in motor homes and horse trailers for distribution in New York, Boston, Toronto, and Montreal. Meanwhile my partners and I are putting together a mega-load of hash, the mother lode that will make us all seriously wealthy.

The past few weeks have been one of those insane periods in the business. It's either feast or famine. At times we may be sitting around for months on end waiting to bring in a load that never materializes, or three trips happen at once. We sometimes subcontract loads for scammers who need our services. A smuggler named Jimmy Chagra, a heavyweight Lebanese American out of El Paso, Texas, has a Panamanian freighter loaded with thirty tons of Colombian pot off the Maine coast. Chagra's off-load fell apart after the ship had already set sail. For the past ten days, I've been organizing lobstermen and fishing boats, lining up tractor trailers and drivers, renting stash houses, hiring people to sit on the load. For this Chagra has agreed to pay me a fee of five dollars per pound.

Before the offload goes down, I get a visit from a pilot I call by his radio handle: Yogi Bear. He shows up at the farm with the Kansas City Kid, a gentle, good-looking greenhorn dope dealer in his twenties feeling the first flush of free money. Yogi looks like his nickname. He's big and burly, with a potbelly, a beard, and bushy black hair. These guys claim they have a plane, a DC-6 they bought in Kansas. The reefer is somewhere on the Guajira Peninsula in Colombia. Yogi Bear is going to fly the weed in using the DC-6. What they don't have is a place to land the load.

It's hard to tell how serious this trip is at the time of their visit. These guys are party animals. Yogi is a good pilot, but smuggling is a sideline. He's a gadget freak who runs a successful business setting up live video feeds for high-profile events. He informs me the trip has to happen quickly as he's preparing to shoot some big beauty contest in Atlanta—maybe even the Miss America pageant—so he only has a small "window of opportunity" in which to make this happen. I get the feeling Yogi may be trying to move the Kansas City Kid for some down-payment money.

We ride down in my four-wheel-drive pickup to take a look at the strip. Yogi doesn't even get out of the truck. After we drive the length of the field, clock it at just over a mile, he pronounces it "perfect." I warn him that even though there is a deep gravel base under the sod surface, and drainage into the river is adequate, the field can be soft this time of year. We've never landed anything close to the size and weight of a DC-6 carrying 10,000 pounds of weed and who knows how much fuel on this field.

Yogi says, "Don't worry about it. We'll be fine." The kid from Kansas City wants to know if I can supply a ground crew and trucks to deliver the weed to his distributors in Chicago.

"Sure," I say, "for a fee." We work out the deal over shots of tequila, joints, and lines of coke. Kansas City gives me fifty grand in cash, tells me his man, Cal, will show up in a week or so with more money and a timetable. We party into the wee hours; they split the next day. I hear nothing from them for a week. Meanwhile, I'm meeting with Chagra's people to facilitate the offload. I've almost forgotten about Yogi and his pal when I get a call from Kansas City. I make the fifteen-minute drive from the farm to the nearest pay phone and call back.

"My man is checked into room 122 at the Holiday Inn in Augusta," Kansas City tells me. In his room at the hotel, Cal has got more money and a brand-new ground-to-air radio he has no idea how to operate. He tells me Yogi is supposedly in Santa Marta, but no one has heard from him in a few days. There is some concern he may have split with the money he was supposed to give the Colombians for the pot. This whole scheme seems harebrained to me, but I'm committed. Besides, this is what turns me on—a new adventure. I call in JD and Father Flaherty, who were staying on the coast helping set up the offload. Father Flaherty figures out how to operate the radio. We hire the rest of the ground crew, rent trucks, and wait.

Now it's on. Or not. No one seems to know for sure. Communication with Colombia has been sketchy. Yogi is either in the Guajira with the load ready to go or he is MIA with the money. We have been preoccupied with the Panamanian freighter off-load, which I know for certain is happening. Big Cal, who has been staying at the Holiday Inn in Augusta, drives over to the farm and tells me the DC-6 left Colombia and will be here at dawn—at least, that is what he heard from his friend in Kansas City.

There are parts of the field where the gravel has been exposed that feel pretty solid. If Yogi follows the river and comes in low over the trees, near the east end of the field, and drops in tight, he should be all right. And he'll be light going out, so that shouldn't be a problem. Father Flaherty is monitoring the radio. Everyone is tense.

As the sun breaks in the east, low clouds scud in over the mountains. The wind is light, right down the runaway. To the north, a darker mass of clouds looks ominous. There is an undercurrent of feeling this whole thing may be a fool's errand. JD is convinced Yogi Bear scammed the Kansas City Kid and in a couple of hours we'll drive out of here empty and pissed.

"Hey, *jefe*!" Father Flaherty shouts and comes running from the log cabin. "We have radio contact!"

"Karamazov!" I call to the dog, and we lope down the field to the cabin. The last thing I want is for him to get hit by an airplane.

"This is Yogi Bear to Groundhog. Do you read me, Groundhog?"

"This is Groundhog. We read you loud and clear, Yogi," Father Flaherty speaks into the transmitter. He looks up at me and grins.

Over the crackle of static, Yogi says, "Can you see your shadow?"

Father Flaherty gives me a puzzled look. "What the fuck does that mean?"

Even before I can answer, I hear the distant drone of four powerful Pratt & Whitney engines becoming louder by the second. Now we are all skittish with the excitement that comes from imminent danger. We run out to the strip. I tell the drivers to start their engines.

After a moment, before we can see the plane, the roar of the engines is impossibly loud. The trees seem to shake and the hills vibrate with noise. The air is dense with sound—a sound foreign to these parts—as the monstrous machine descends rapidly into this peaceful valley. In my mind I see farmers and woodsmen all over Franklin County waking up and wondering if it's time to head to the air raid shelters. *The Russians are coming. . . .* But there is no time to think, no time to imagine what the locals might be thinking, for there is the plane coming in loud, coming in huge and hot, landing like a giant, fat-winged locust chewing up the scenery. I suddenly realize how foolish, how insane it is to have attempted to bring a 50,000-pound behemoth with a 10,000-pound payload to earth on this patchy sod-and-gravel field.

Yogi Bear is an expert STOL—Short Take Off and Landing—pilot. But he's either asleep at the yoke or the strip comes up too fast for him because he overshoots the end of the runway, drops hard, touches down too far into the field. I'm afraid he's going to crash into the trees at the far end of the strip. The rear wheels hit ground, the nose levers forward and the front gear digs into the sod like the blade of a plow. Grass and mud sprout in ribbons, clogging the gear, causing the plane to buck then dive and belly flop with a screeching metallic wail heard over the scream of reversing engines.

Yogi kills the engines as propeller blades hit the ground and fling grass and dirt in the air like shit hitting the fan. The plane is skidding now, burrowing its nose along the ground like a dog sniffing for scent. The rear gear folds under, the plane is wheel-less, landing more like a seaplane. I catch a quick glimpse of Yogi in the cockpit as the plane slides by. He appears remarkably composed, working the controls, trying to slow the plane before it hits the trees. We watch dumbfounded, helpless, fascinated. One wing tip strikes ground, the plane twists on its axis, does an about-face, slides, slides closer to the end of the runway and the riverbank. Now I'm afraid it's going to slip into the river. Or burst into flames. The shriek of the metal on gravel is like the cry of a wounded beast. The other wing tip smacks into a tree and topples it like the fell swoop of an axe.

Then—silence. The six is lying at the tree line, its tail teetering on the river's edge, looking like nothing so much as a giant bird of prey shot from the sky. I hear the rapid patter of footfalls and look over to see the two rookie helpers running off into the woods.

"Whoa! Where the fuck're you goin'?" JD shouts. "Let's get this bird unloaded!"

The cockpit door pops open. Yogi Bear, dressed for the occasion in a khaki jumpsuit and safari vest, hops out, followed by his terrified Colombian copilot. "I hurt my knee," Yogi says, limping over to me. "Get me out of here. I've got an appointment in Atlanta."

"What am I supposed to do with that?" I ask, indicating the crashed plane.

Yogi shrugs, cracks a smile, and says, "Turn it into a disco."

2

THE GOOD SAMARITAN

THE NEAREST COP shop is half an hour away from our tranquil valley. In less than twenty minutes, we have five tons of reefer in the trucks and on the road. The plane is clean, no residue of controlled substances, no seeds or shake, no paperwork to connect it to anyone except the phony Bermuda corporation to which it is registered. No evidence of a crime per se. Just a big, abandoned machine, a relic of the War on Plants, it will recline at the end of the strip for some time, though never open as a disco. Yogi and his Colombian copilot get soused in the bar at the airport in Portland before boarding a flight to Boston, then on to Atlanta.

After that, the freighter off-load, if not exactly anticlimactic, is more like a precise military—or naval—operation. The weather is our only obstacle. Fishing boats rendezvous with the mother ship off the coast in high winds and rough seas. Loaded tractor trailers head down the interstate toward Boston, New York, and points west in sleet and freezing rain. The second day into the off-load, I'm driving around overseeing the inventory, weighing, marking, and transshipping hundreds of bales of compressed Colombian pot. I have a half ton stashed waiting to go to my friends in Canada. It looks like a good 15 to 20 percent of the load is no good, soaked in diesel fuel and bilge water. The Colombians will demand to see it, but that is not my problem—except where to store it. My immediate problem is getting the rest of the load on the road, headed out of the state, and then getting paid.

A late-season Nor'easter leaves a few inches of fresh snow on the ground in the high country. I hook up with a coke dealer I call Fearless Fred Barnswallow. Breaking one of my cardinal rules—never trust a coke fiend—and against my better judgment, I have enlisted Barnswallow to help line up stash houses for some of the load. It isn't only that cokeheads are unreliable; people who deal and use a lot of coke attract weird, often negative energy. It's the devil's candy, true, but I have a soft spot for Fearless Fred. I feel partly responsible for the latest coke binge he's been on since he met Maria, my Colombian former girlfriend over Halloween in Aspen, Colorado. I suspect she has been supplying him with kilos of blow. I hope that making a few honest bucks in a crooked sort of way will enable Fred to pay off his coke bill with the Colombians, leave the nose powder alone, and get back to doing what made him rich in the first place—helping me move weed into Canada.

Fred has a plane, a single-engine Beechcraft, and a hangar he leases at a municipal airport that has a 4,000-foot paved runway. He lives in a hilltop log cabin mansion he shares with two or three gofers, his pilot and communications expert, a couple of strippers, and Bear, his German shepherd. The Barnswallow's roost is party central. I try to spend as little time as possible at Fred's because I'm certain he must have picked up local Heat. He's got an attic full of pot plants under grow lights. Lately he's become obsessed with weapons. He's got an Uzi, a Mini-14, two or three handguns. Yet any kind of violence is totally alien to his character. He's a gentle soul with a generous nature. He's supporting half the little town he lives in—including, he tells me, a corrupt cop.

This morning, his place smells like a morgue: a cold chemical smell I'm certain comes from smoking cocaine base. Fred denies it up and down, but his looks betray him. His skin is pasty and sallow; his eyes are sunk deep in his head and have dark circles around them like a raccoon's. His long black hair is lank and oily. He reminds me of Keith

Richards without the talent. I drag him down to a local diner and get him to eat some breakfast. The way he wolfs down the food tells me it's the first real meal he's had in days. It's impossible for me to dislike this guy—but at the same time I don't trust him. Not that he's dishonest; he would never cheat me or anyone else. But he's weak. He's a casualty of the drug war. I want to clean him up, lock him in a room for two weeks in some kind of forced rehab. But right now I need him and his people to hold some of the tons of weed I've got floating around the state.

"You should meet this guy," Fred tells me.

"What guy?"

"My friend, Arnold . . . the cop."

"I don't want to meet any cops," I tell him. "I don't want to meet anyone."

"He's cool," Freddy says. "I bought a gun from him last week."

"Great. Whatever you do, don't tell him about any of this."

"Where's all this weed coming from, anyway?"

"Colombia," I say. Fred's on a need-to-know basis.

After looking at a couple of placcs and making arrangements with the people who live there, we are in my four-wheel-drive truck with a camper cap on the bed, heading up the steep hill back to Fred's home when we see a sedan that has slid off the road and is stuck in a ditch. I pull over, Fred and I get out and look over the situation. I offer to pull the guy out with my truck. We attach a towrope, get him back on the road; he thanks us, we shake hands and—the man gazes at me curiously with his clear blue eyes. There is a glimmer of recognition that unnerves me. He's clean cut, with short, light-brown hair, and he's wearing a tan windbreaker. He looks like a college football coach. *Do I know this guy? Does he know me?*

"You ever see that guy before?" I ask Barnswallow when we pull up at his house.

"Uh uh," Fred says. "You comin' in? Some girls're comin' by later."

"I can't, man. Too much to do . . . Listen, Freddy. Put the pipe away. Clean your shit up. Take care of yourself."

"Yeah. I will."

"You can make a lot of money. How much do you owe the Colombians?"

He gives a start. "Huh?" Like I'm not supposed to know.

"Maria's people. What's your tab?"

"I don't know . . . fifty . . . sixty grand."

"You can put that together in a week. But not if you're sitting in your room sucking on the devil's dick."

Fred nods, brushes his hair back from his eyes. "Thanks, man. I hear ya."

He gets out. I watch him shamble toward his home. He's got terrible posture. He wears black canvas high-top sneakers even in the dead of a Maine winter. Bear, his big black-and-tan shepherd, comes up, wagging his tail, happy to see his master. It's comforting how our dogs love us no matter how fucked-up we may be.

Over the next couple of days I sleep no more than a few hours a night in different hotels and motels as I finish dispersing the load. The spoiled bales are stashed in an old barn, waiting for the Colombians to come inspect them. Some friends from San Francisco trade me their brand-new white Oldsmobile Toronado in exchange for my four-wheel-drive pickup. They remove the cap, buy a camper, attach it to the truck, fill it with bales of pot, and head back to the West Coast.

With the load almost entirely gone, I'm ready to chill for a few days. It's been an exhausting two weeks but I've made a lot of money—if I can collect it, never a sure thing in this line of work. As I get closer to the farm, I become increasingly paranoid. Something doesn't feel right. It's nothing I can identify, but when you've been in the business a while, you learn to pay attention to your gut. I worry someone might have spotted the Toronado with California plates somewhere it shouldn't have been, and that I might draw Heat to my home. There is already enough fallout around the farm and the lodge from the busted-up DC-6 lying at the end of the airstrip. People know who owns the lodge and airstrip even if there is no way to tie it to me. I'm seeing agents lurking in the shadows. So I decide to spend the night at a motel in Farmington, the nearest town of any size to the farm.

Oh, anonymous me. I get the best rest when no one knows where I am. And no place is too shabby for me to hang my hat. I like a Red Roof Inn or a Super 8 when I'm in the middle of a trip. The lower budget the motel, the better. Park the car around back away from the main road. Check in under an alias and blend in with the rest of the traveling salesmen. The room smells of disinfectant, damp, cheap carpet, and plastic wall covering. The windows don't open. I make no calls from the room. I've got a sack full of quarters for the pay phone, a paperback book about Meyer Lansky, some personal stash, and an overnight bag. Nothing to connect me to any of the frantic importation and distribution of enough weed to satisfy North America's enormous demand for a few days except a few scraps of paper with my coded phone numbers and financial records.

I delude myself that this is how I prefer to live—solo. There is no one checking up on me, no one to answer to except myself. My wife, Anaïs, left me a year ago. We're still on pretty good terms, but she grew tired of the smuggler's life. She lives in Toronto and still works with our group laundering money. I don't need to call anyone and explain where I am or what I'm doing. I'm an outlaw. I live by a set of values and morals that are unique to my chosen calling. Together with my far-flung network of smugglers and dealers, we provide a quality product for a reasonable price. Nobody dies from smoking the shit. We don't steal or extort money from neighborhood shopkeepers. No, and we don't kill or maim people who don't pay their bill. We simply stop doing business with them. We don't smuggle or deal heroin or cocaine. Or do we?

Now I know why I'm feeling threatened. Fearless Fred. Maria and the Colombians. The Lebanese. Jimmy Chagra and the organized crime people I work with in Boston and New York. These people have no such scruples. I'm a hypocrite if I pretend I am not complicit in whatever they do. That is the nature of the underground. This fear comes bubbling up from the knowledge that I am violating my own principles. I feel vulnerable. So I drown my shame in a bottle of red wine and pass out watching TV.

Early the next morning, I am up smoking my morning joint and compiling my list of things to do. I go for coffee and to use the pay phones at a restaurant up the road from the motel. I am well known in the area, especially to local law enforcement. The sheriff sometimes hangs out at my farm, drinking, playing poker, singing *I shot the sheriff, but I didn't shoot no deputy* after we polish off a bottle of Patrón Silver. One night he left his hat there and I kept it as a souvenir. I spend a lot of cash money in the county, employ locals who can't get other work, and rely on innate Yankee hostility for outsiders and big government.

When I walk into the restaurant, I spot a couple of county deputies having coffee. I'm about to go over and say hello when I pick up on their vibe. Something is definitely wrong. Now all my antennae are keen. I sense weirdness going back to the day I helped the blue-eyed stranger stuck by the side of the road near Barnswallow's pad. But that's the thing with paranoia—you never know how much of it is well founded, particularly when you smoke a lot of weed. I learned to pay attention to these flights of fear, follow them to their logical—or illogical—conclusion, hunt down the dread, and ferret it out like a wild animal running loose in the attic of my brain.

The deputies want nothing to do with me. They quickly turn away, glance down at their coffee, and pretend they have no idea who I am when I look over and nod. I take the cue and keep walking past their booth. At the door to the restroom, when I turn back to look, they are huddled in tense conversation.

I stare at my face in the men's room mirror. "Stratton," I say to my reflection, "you are about to get popped." Quickly, I go through my pockets, tear the slips of paper I have with phone numbers and records of the load into pieces, dump the bag of personal stash, and flush it all down the toilet.

There is still a dusting of snow on the ground as I walk out of the restaurant, keep walking past the Toronado with the California plates, walk along the road and past the motel where I crashed the night before. I walk a mile up the highway to a shopping mall and into a drugstore where I know there are pay phones and a few video games in the back. *Paranoia, paranoia, great destroyer*, I say to myself when no army of agents leaps out of the shadows to pounce on me. Let me play a few games of Gorf, one of my favorite video games, call the farm in an hour or so, and have JD come over and pick me up. We'll come back for the Toronado later. I'll have him drive me to the airport, get out of town. Go to Spanish Wells in the Bahamas and hide out until things cool down.

I am into my third or fourth game of Gorf, racking up one of my all-time high scores, with a few local kids standing around watching, when I look up and see them: DEA agents, maybe half a dozen of them, dressed like thugs, with their guns drawn. They swarm into the drugstore and make straight for where I stand. I take my hands from the video game controls and raise them above my head.

"Richard Stratton! You're under arrest!" says one of the agents.

"Wow! Cool," says a kid behind me.

And then I recognize the DEA agent. It's him, the blue-eyed way-laid traveler who was stuck in the ditch at the side of the road on fearless Fred Barnswallow's hill. And now the fucker is pointing a gun at me.

The federal agents hustle me outside and drive me to the local jail at the Farmington police station where I am locked up in a tiny, dark, filthy cell. I make my one phone call to my personal attorney, Channing Godfried. Since I bought out the horse farm we've become friends over the years. He now owns a farm near my place and lately he's been acting as my counsel, dealing with an ongoing IRS investigation. When I reach him at his home in Cambridge, he tells me he will call a criminal defense lawyer he knows in Portland, Maine, and see what he can find out.

What impresses me about being arrested is that it is exactly that—you are arrested, stopped in your tracks, locked up in a small space.

You are no longer in control of where you go or what you do except within the confines of the cell and your body and mind. Life becomes at once remarkably simple, focused and internal. There is nothing I can do about whatever might be going on out there in the larger world. It is all happening right here in my head and in this dark, cramped space. I must hunker down, go within, and compose my mental and emotional attitude. Find my inner peace and dwell there. Keep telling myself *I can handle this. They missed the load.*

The cell is so small I can barely sit down. The cops tell me they have been instructed to keep me isolated, and this cell, not much bigger than a phone booth, is all they have available. There is a clogged drain in the middle of the floor with what looks like puke and piss puddled around it. I dance from foot to foot for eight hours consoled by the thought, *They missed the load.*

Finally, they come for me in the person of Special Agent Bernard Wolfshein of the Drug Enforcement Administration. An unlikely federal dope cop if ever I met one (and I have met a few), Wolfshein apologizes, says he was detained while they searched the farm. He explains it is against agency policy for him to transport a prisoner without backup. But, if it's okay with me, he will make an exception in this case. Otherwise we will have to wait several more hours.

"You won't try to escape on me, will you, Dick? They call you Dick?" Wolfshein asks.

"No. Richard."

"Richard. Right, right. Richard. You won't try anything crazy? I know you're not that kind of guy. Right, Richard?"

This guy's a trip, I'm thinking, Special Agent Bernard Wolfshein with his dark, wavy hair and Brooklyn accent. He seems out of place in the wilds of western Maine. Reminds me of Columbo, the TV cop played by Peter Falk. He even looks like him. And he affects an absent-minded or preoccupied manner that does little to hide his obvious intelligence. He shuffles into the jail wearing a rumpled trench coat, horn-rimmed glasses. He checks his weapon and fills out the forms to remove me to federal custody. His gun, I notice when he picks it up on the way out, has white adhesive tape wrapped around the handle. It looks like something salvaged from a yard sale.

Two Farmington cops escort me outside to Wolfshein's fed car.

"See what I'm sayin'? What're we gonna do, here, Rich?" Wolfshein asks me. "Geeze, I don't know. I hate to . . . Well, if I cuff you behind your back . . . I mean, it's a long ride—how long is it?"

The cops shrug. "In this weather?"

It has started to snow again. Late April and it's snowing. Big, fat flakes like floating tufts of cotton. "I could put you in the backseat," he says. "No, that's no good. I'll put you up front with me where I can keep an eye on you. But I'll have to—look, I know it's gonna hurt, it'll be uncomfortable—I hate to do it, Rich, but I'm gonna have to cuff you behind your back."

"It's okay," I tell him.

"You sure? I mean, you say that now but—"

"What else can we do?"

"Exactly," Wolfshein agrees. "What else can we do? Nothing. We gotta do what we gotta do. Yes? But it'll be all right? I mean, because I know you're not the kind of guy who will try anything crazy, am I right?"

"That's right."

"Good. Good. I thought so," Wolfshein says and nods. He pushes his glasses up over the bridge of his nose and opens the car door. I sit in front, hands and arms wrenched behind my back, turned sideways in the seat so I'm not sitting on my wrists. Wolfshein climbs in behind the wheel. He seems as concerned about my discomfort as I am. "You know," he says, "later on, if you wanna stop and get out and move around. Go to the men's room . . . I don't know. See, this is the problem. This is why I shouldn't be doing this without, you know . . . I shouldn't be transporting you by myself, I mean, without backup. But we'll make it, Rich, you and me. And I'm sure you were ready to get out of that place. Am I right?"

"Right again."

He chuckles and starts the car, and we drive off into the snowy night.

Wolfshein warns me that anything I say can and will be used against me. "They read you your Miranda rights? When they arrested you? And you called your lawyer? What's his name? Pretty famous guy, huh? Used to work for JFK. Godfried. You're his only client. That's impressive."

He smiles, shakes his head. "But not as famous as the other guy, the writer. Norman Mailer. Wow, now there's a great writer. I mean, I may not always agree with everything he writes, but the way he puts it, his writing, you gotta hand it to him, right, Rich? That man can write."

"He's a great writer," I agree.

"Great guy too, no? He's your friend, Mailer. How long have you known him?"

"A little over ten years."

"How did you guys meet? He's from Brooklyn, isn't he? I'm from Brooklyn."

"I never would have guessed."

Wolfshein laughs. "Listen. You don't have to say anything. We'll keep it strictly off the record—I mean, if you feel like talkin', you know, we won't talk about . . . I don't know. I can't even call it a case. I'll be perfectly honest with you, Rich. I think we were a day late and a dollar short."

It's the first good news I've heard all day.

Wolfshein continues, "I mean, I was there. We searched your place . . . all day. You own that place with Mailer, don't you?"

I don't answer, don't feel I need to. I get the impression Wolfshein knows the answers to his questions before he asks them.

"You know what we found? I mean, we had guys in there from head-quarters in the DC office with these machines, checking the walls and the floors, looking for hidden compartments . . . stashes or whatever. I kept trying to tell them: This guy is not about to keep anything serious where he lives. He's smarter than that. He's old school. Been doin' this since he was . . . what? A college kid? High school selling ounces? You and I know, a guy like you, Rich—you're not gonna be keepin' any real weight where you live. No way. So they searched the barns, the horse stables—you got some nice horses there Rich . . . We walked all around the property. You've got a lot of land there too, you and what's his name, the writer. Searched the place high and low. You know what we found?"

"No, what did you find?" I'm nervous as hell because I know there is extremely incriminating evidence at the farm—if you know where to look.

"Nothing. Two ounces of marijuana." The way he pronounces marijuana, there's no question it's an alien controlled substance. "It was sitting right out in plain sight. On the kitchen table. I didn't bother to enter it as evidence. I mean, possession of two ounces in this state isn't even a felony. You're looking pretty good on this one, Rich. I don't know if there's even enough to indict you. You know?" He shrugs. "I mean, I'm not a lawyer but what do we have?"

Relief. Momentary.

"Oh, and one other thing that confused me," Wolfshein says and I'm tense all over again. "We found a sheriff's hat. Huh?" He smiles at me. "You wanna explain that one to me, Rich?"

"I'd rather not," I say. "It's a long story."

"I'm sure it is," Wolfshein says and gives me a quick nod and smile. "But I'm glad I was there, when they went to your place, I mean. I wanted to be there because I didn't want anything to happen like what happened when they went to that other guy's place. What's his name?" He uses Fearless Fred Barnswallow's real name.

"That was stupid. Senseless," the agent says. "I mean, no need for that at all."

Wolfshein stops talking, looks over at me. My stomach is knotted up all over again. "I don't know what gets into these guys," he says after a moment. "I've been on this job, what? Fifteen years now? Never fired my gun once. That's the truth. Some of these other guys, well—they're cowboys. They can't help themselves."

He hesitates, lets this sink in. I'm wondering, *What's he talking about? What the fuck happened?*

"They shot the dog," Wolfshein says and shakes his head. "Killed the guy's dog. Nice dog too. German shepherd. No need for that at all. That's why I wanted to be there when they went to your place. I didn't want them to kill your dog."

I don't know what to say. "Thank you," is all I can come up with. In my mind I'm seeing Fred's big, friendly-but-protective dog, Bear, lying in the snow in a pool of blood. "Shit," I say. The thought of them killing Bear is bad enough. I'm also afraid of what I'm sure they found when they searched Fred's home: guns, cocaine, money, records, pot plants. But how can they connect it to me . . . unless Freddy rolls?

Stupid motherfucker, I'm thinking. *You brought this on yourself.*

Wolfshein is not finished playing games with my head. Out of the blue, he starts talking about Lebanon. He reminds me of a Middle East Airlines flight from Beirut to Paris I was on a year earlier. We had engine trouble and had to make an emergency landing in Athens. How the hell does he know about that? I'm wondering. And how much more does he know? He keeps asking if I'm hurting, if I'm uncomfortable sitting with my hands cuffed behind my back. Of course I'm uncomfortable. I feel like telling him it's nothing compared to what he's doing to my state of mind:

"I don't suppose you know anything about that plane that crashed up near you, huh, Rich? Big plane. Hold a lot of marijuana in a plane like that."

He laughs, shakes his head and looks over at me, pushes his glasses up his nose. "Ever hear of a guy named BR?" He uses Yogi's real name.

"Doesn't ring any bells."

"No? Big guy. Pretty good pilot from what I hear. I think he's out of Toronto. He may have had something to do with that plane."

What the fuck is this guy's game? He knows way too much. How long has he been on us? Have they got Yogi in custody somewhere talking? Is Wolfshein trying to flip me, get me to roll over and rat out my friends?

I decide to turn the tables and ask a few questions of my own. "Who are you?" I ask.

"Just a guy . . . doing his job."

"In Portland, Maine?"

"No, I'm out of Boston. DC, really. Headquarters. Up until a few months ago . . . more than that. Maybe even close to a year now. I was acting liaison between Congress and DEA. Spent my days trying to explain to senators and congressmen why we need more money . . . to go after guys like you." He chuckles. "Then they sent me back out into the field. I'm kind of a floater. I go where—well, where you go."

Now I know he's bullshitting me. No way is my trip worthy of a guy like Wolfshein. "Right now I just want to go home and go to bed," I say.

"I know what you mean," says Wolfshein. "I'm beat too. Which home? You lead a pretty nomadic lifestyle, Rich."

This is too weird. I'm beginning to feel like Raskolnikov sitting with Detective Porfiry. Better keep my mouth shut before I say something I'll regret.

"You've had a good run," Wolfshein says at last. "Most guys in your business don't last half as long as you have. I mean, you've had your ups and downs, am I right? There was that load that went south at the airport in New York. You and your pal there got locked up on that one. But you were never indicted, right?"

"Right."

"What happened? They couldn't produce the evidence?"

I can't let this go unanswered. "I heard DEA agents stole it."

"Really? I heard that too. You know that for a fact?"

"That's what I was told, by my lawyer. And when they brought us before the judge, they couldn't explain what happened to the evidence, supposedly two or three tons of hash. It was a mystery. The judge threw the case out. I heard the hash was sold on the streets of New York. Jack Anderson wrote a column about it in the *Washington Post*."

Shut up, Stratton. You're talking too much.

Wolfshein shrugs. "Could be," he says. "What can I say? Some of these agents . . . Well, it's a dirty business, on both sides."

"It's ridiculous," I blurt out, unable to contain myself. "The whole thing is fucked up. Your so-called War on Drugs. It's a war on the American people. And it's crazy. A waste of time, money, people's lives. For what? You can't stop people from doing what they're going to do."

"It's the law," says Wolfshein.

"Big deal. That doesn't make it right. It used to be illegal for blacks and women to vote."

"It's my job."

"C'mon, that's no excuse. That doesn't make it right, either. You're a Jew, right?"

"Yeah."

"It was the Nazi's job to kill Jews. Does that make it right?"

"We're not talking about killing Jews."

"No, you're right, we're not. We're talking about locking people up—many of them young Americans—in cages, human warehouses for years *for trafficking in a plant*. Something God created. That's also a form of persecution, wouldn't you say?"

"No." Wolfshein shakes his head. "I think you're exaggerating. It's a crime. People who commit crimes need to be punished."

"Okay. So what if it became the law to kill pot smugglers? Just herd them all up and execute them. No trial or anything. Hang 'em in the town square. Like in Iran. Isn't that what some of these wackos you work for advocate? What if that became your job? Shoot 'em on sight. Would that make it right? Like if it was your job to kill me right now. Would you still do it?"

"No, of course not," Wolfshein says. "But that's not gonna happen. Not here. This is America."

"Oh, yeah, right. I forgot."

He is silent for a moment. "Drugs ruin people's lives."

"C'mon. People ruin people's lives," I say, thinking of myself. Mentally kicking myself in the ass for working with Fearless Fred.

Wolfshein glances over at me. "You okay? You want me to stop? So you can get out and move around? I know you won't run."

Why does he keep saying this? I'm wondering. Where the hell am I going to run with my hands cuffed behind my back? The man has a gun, even if he's never shot it. There's always a first time. I may be crazy, but I'm not stupid.

"I'm all right," I answer, but I'm not. This guy has me all freaked out.

"Interesting," Wolfshein says. "I can see you've given this a lot of thought. So, it's . . . political with you. I mean, you're not in it just for the money."

"In what?" I have to smile. "Who said I was in anything?" I say. "We're just having a philosophical conversation here. Right?"

Wolfshein laughs, nods. "Right, Rich. That's right."

THE LOCAL LAWYER Godfried called is waiting at the Cumberland County Jail in Portland when Wolfshein deposits me.

"Good luck," the agent says, and offers me his hand once the cuffs have come off.

"Thank you," I say and shake his hand. "It was good talking to you. And thanks again for not letting them kill my dog."

He nods, gives me a long look. "You know, I gotta tell you, there's some truth to what you say. Maybe there's no way we can stop people using drugs. But not everyone looks at it the same as you, Rich. There are some very bad people out there making a lot of money smuggling drugs. Somebody's gotta stop them."

It's nine o'clock at night, but the attorney has arranged for me to go before a federal magistrate for a bail hearing. I'm being held on what is known as a criminal complaint. No formal charges as yet. My lawyer convinces the magistrate I am not a flight risk since I own considerable property in the state. He makes the point that no evidence of any crime was found on my person or at my home. There is virtually nothing to connect me to whatever it is the government agents seem to think went down. The magistrate agrees to accept the deed to the farm in lieu of a cash bond.

I spend the night in the county jail. In the morning Jimmy D drives down with a copy of the deed. No one seems to notice that the property is in my name *and* Mailer's. His name is still on the deed. I'm thinking he would be required to sign the bail bond as well, but I'm not about to bring this to anyone's attention. I sign the papers and walk out into the streets of Portland, once more in control of the space in which I move.

3

FOOL'S PARADISE

THEY MISSED THE load. They had me—for a minute. They impounded the Toronado with California plates. (I call my friends in San Francisco, who tell me not to worry. It's registered to a dead guy.) They searched the farm over the course of a workday while I sat in the local lockup. All they came up with was an unindictable couple of ounces and the sheriff's hat. Not only did they miss the load—they missed my stash.

It seems almost too good to be true, and it is because there is also the Fearless Freddy factor. I don't even want to contemplate what they found when they raided the Barnswallow's nest. You name it. And phone numbers. Financial records. Paperwork connecting him to a plane and hangar. People—strippers and gofers—who know way too much about Fred's operation. And they shot and killed his loyal companion, Bear, the one true friend Fred had.

Shit. Poor Fred. And me—what an asshole to have involved him in the first place. How many times have I told myself and the people I work with to stay away from anyone who uses or deals cocaine? Then I turn around and do exactly what I tell others *not* to do. Fucking brilliant. I violate my own principles. If that isn't self-sabotage, I don't know what is.

Now I'm in damage control mode. There is a little over $200,000 in US and Canadian currency, and maybe fifteen Mason jars full of different strains of cannabis, plus my financial records and business phone numbers—exactly the kind of evidence Wolfshein would have salivated over—hidden in the stash. It's built into a space in the central chimney that comes up through the middle of the old farmhouse and supports two fireplaces, one in the dining room and the other in the living room. In my study there is a bookcase built against what appears to be a solid brick wall, but is actually the chimney. I'm told the settlers who built these old farmhouses left a space between the fireplaces, a kind of alcove in the center of the chimney, where they would hide in case of an Indian attack. That may be apocryphal; the space may be designed for storing firewood. But to the untrained eye, looking at that wall, you would think that the bricks continue all the way down behind the bookcase, through the floor, and onto the granite foundation in the basement. If you remove the books and adjust one of the shelves, the wooden back of the bookcase slides open to reveal my stash.

There it is. Relief. The money, in ten thousand-dollar stacks in vacuum-sealed plastic bags, I pack into my suitcase and load into the trunk of a rental car parked out front. The financial records and business phone numbers I put in my briefcase. I grab a couple of jars of weed and close the stash back up. Karamazov never leaves my side. He knows something is wrong. Strangers with weapons invaded his home. His boss has been gone for days. And he understands the signs: suitcases, strange cars, a lot of hurried activity. I'm leaving, going away— again. I take the dog for a long walk on the property, beside the brook up the steep hill behind the house, where he often disappears chasing bears. Sometimes he comes home whimpering with a mouth full of porcupine quills.

Today there is a mystical tranquility to the hills and valley below. I sit among a pile of boulders deposited here millions of years ago when the glacier carved these mountains and rivers and valleys, and I feel the history of the place coursing through my veins like the ageless water bubbling in the brook by my side. There is a town twenty miles from here, on the way to the Canadian border, named Stratton. My great-great-great-great grandfather, Hezekiah Stratton, came to this part of Maine in 1768. He cleared a farm in the primeval forest on the banks of the Sebasticook River near a small settlement called Kingsfield. Besides being a farmer, good Hezekiah was a hunter and trapper. In the fall of 1775, during the Revolutionary War, Benedict Arnold and his troop of 1,000 soldiers, chosen from the ranks of the Continental Army in Cambridge, marched through these parts on their way to fight British forces encamped in Quebec. Hezekiah Stratton was asked to join the expedition as its guide.

When Mailer and Godfried offered me the farm, I knew nothing of my ancestral connection with this part of the land. I was born in Boston, grew up in suburban Wellesley, Massachusetts. Maine meant little more to me than Vacationland—stamped on the license plates—a place where kids went off to summer camp, and lobster. It's cold up here; my blood draws me nearer the equator, to Arizona, Texas, Mexico, and the Caribbean islands. My plan was to spend maybe a year here fixing up the place, then decamp for warmer climes. But the border held me in thrall. There are places near here where you can drive across old logging roads into Canada and never encounter a customs and immigration checkpoint. When I first came to Maine a decade ago there were only two DEA agents in the whole state. The coast, with its deepwater coves and active fishing and lobstering industries, became popular with seafaring smugglers after the Coast Guard clamped down on South Florida and the Mid-Atlantic states. Like Hezekiah, I was something of a pioneer here. The crash landing of the DC-6 was certainly a first for Franklin County. Now it feels like time to move on.

In my meditative state, I'm time traveling. Tramping along beside the river with Hezekiah and General Arnold. Flying up the river with Yogi Bear in the danger bird. Indians and British troops are massing at the frontier. Federal agents and state cops sniff around the valley trying to pick up my trail. Is it all coincidence that I am here now, traversing these same routes? Putting myself in harm's way? Or is there no such thing as time? It's a man-made construct. All that ever really changes is the outward appearance of things. We repeat myriad patterns ad infinitum.

One thing I know for sure: As soon as they are able to regroup, Wolfshein and the federal drug cops are going to be all over us. Their investigation is ongoing. They will need more evidence to secure an indictment and conviction. Wolfshein is smart, he knows he doesn't have enough on me, and he is a formidable adversary, nothing like how I imagined my DEA counterpart. I never expected to like the guy, and I am grateful to him for not letting them kill Karamazov. Still I know his professional purpose is to lock me up for a long, long time. And who knows how many others within our outlaw family?

This is where the kernel of my guilt lives like a cyst, in the small hard horrors of this life. An estranged wife. A broken home. A dead dog. Jail is merely the arrest of movement, a halt in the frantic activity that distracts me from contemplating failure and regret. Some time ago I sent a guy who worked for me to Houston. Euvelga Rebofat, we called him, a sad, handsome drunk. Curse of the Irish. He brought his girlfriend with him. She was a beautiful young woman not involved in the business. They had only been there a month when she was brutally murdered. It had nothing to do with me or with why they were there. It was a random killing, and the murderer was caught and ultimately executed. But I could not help thinking that I had participated in her death and in her killer's execution.

Shit happens, I tell myself and stand and stretch. Today, all I know is I must and will give Bernard Wolfshein and his men with the DEA a worthwhile good run for their time and energy. It's the game, after all, the chase, the matching of wits and the energy I get from danger that drives me. I could be selling insurance, like my father, taciturn Emery Stratton. Neglecting my family, like my father. Playing golf and cribbage with harmless, time-bandit friends at the country club, instead of engaged in a life-threatening game of catch-me-if-you-can with armed federal agents.

I'm miserable as I tie the great white Karamazov to one of the three maple trees in front of the house to keep him from chasing after me. His big, majestic head is held high, watching me go. The caretakers will take good care of him. But he's no pup. I have a melancholy inkling I may never see him again. Or this farm. My fool's paradise.

* * *

BOSTON, THE ATHENS of America, a city upon a hill with limpid blue skies arched above the gold dome and cupola of the State House. In the spring this town is a feast for men's eyes. Nature bursts forth in flower. Everything is in bloom. Trees blossom along Commonwealth Avenue and in Boston Common gardens. The streets are full of budding coeds. Females shed their winter wraps and reveal their inner beauty. The air is fresh off the Atlantic. Pheromones carried on the soft breeze like pollen arouse my desire for something more than adventure. I want tenderness. I want stability, someone to hold me and assure me that I am a good man with a purpose and not just a wandering criminal.

As much as I love Boston, I have always felt confined here, trapped by the past. As a teenager I was drawn to the anonymity of New York City. All my life I have been running away from what was expected of me: Go to school, get good grades. Go to college, get a good job. Marry a local girl, preferably a white Anglo-Saxon Protestant. Have two kids. Move into a home in the suburbs. Buy a station wagon and shop at the mall—Shopper's World, actually, one of the first malls in America. It's the American way. But I flipped the script and became an outlaw. I ran away from all that, escaped the air-conditioned nightmare. And I am still running, looking over my shoulder. As I move about the city, I sense the ominous presence of a thick miasma of federal law enforcement bureaucracies—IRS, DEA, FBI—weighing on my spirit.

I check into a pyramid-shaped hotel on the banks of the muddy Charles River in Cambridge and consider that my phony identification is probably blown. It's time to become someone else. I make a few calls, go from pay phone to pay phone. The residential phones I've been using—my parents' home phone in Wellesley; my local partner, Benny's phone; the phone at my office and crash pad in Cambridge; the office phone at a body shop we own in Lowell—from now on it's best to assume they are all tapped. At the body shop, I pick up my vehicle—a black GMC Suburban with tinted windows like the Feds drive. My friend scans it to make sure DEA has not installed a tracking device. The car has a built-in stash under the rear seat, where I hide most of the money. That is one rule I adhere to religiously: Protect the money.

My first meeting is at a hotel with a mysterious character known as the Wizard of ID. He manufactures and sells false identification. I leave the Suburban parked in the hotel garage, call the Wizard's room on the house phone. "Come on up," he tells me. "I want to show you something." He's a slim blond in his thirties with big teeth, a lantern jaw, and a paranoid, suspicious nature. He insists on patting me down. "Nothing personal," he says. "It's business." Then he leads me into an adjoining room where he has one of those photo machines used by the Department of Motor Vehicles.

"Have a seat," he tells me and points to the photo machine. "I can make you as many licenses as you need while you enjoy a beverage from the minibar. Then I meet my contact at the DMV, I give them the information, they enter it into the computer and . . . you're good to go." He flashes me a toothy grin.

"How much?"

"Ten grand each. Three for twenty-five. I take care of my person at the DMV." He shows me one of the licenses, a perfect Massachusetts driver's license. "It will hold up under any kind of traffic stop. You need passports, birth certificates, I have matching birth and death certificates . . . for $15,000 a set."

The Wizard brings out a three-ring binder with several clear plastic inserts holding birth and death certificates. "We find some guy who would be around your age if he hadn't died as a child. . . . Here's one.

Canadian. We like Canadians. Good passport, especially in the Middle East." He grins. He has been pressing me to set him up with my connection in Lebanon. He says he has a catch—a secure method of entry—at the Port of Miami, and he and his Miami-based partners want to bring in a big load of hash. Tons.

Another rule of thumb in the dope-dealing trade I have violated at my own disadvantage is: Keep your contacts to yourself. People have a way of jumping connections. The Wizard wouldn't turn me on to his guy at the DMV. It doesn't make sense for me to hook him up with my people in Beirut. I offered to broker him a load in Lebanon if he could assure me of the money and the security of the catch.

"With these documents, there is no cross-referencing," he explains, referring to the birth and death certificates. "You assume the identity of the dead guy. You get a Social Security card. Driver's license. Credit cards. Establish a residence where you can receive mail, then apply for a passport. Take you a few weeks. Maybe a month or two. But by then you'll have new ID that will hold up under anything short of an FBI fingerprint check."

I opt for the three-license package deal and one set of birth and death certificates. After I sit for my photo, the Wizard tells me to wait for him downstairs in the restaurant while he makes the licenses and meets with another client. "Where are you parked?" he asks.

"In the garage."

"So you're cool. Take me fifteen, twenty minutes. We'll grab lunch. Talk about our other business. You got the money?"

I give him four packs of ten grand each and head down to the lobby restaurant.

The one thing that rankles, as I sit having coffee waiting for the Wizard to appear with my new identities, is that he knows who all these phony people really are. He could always sell or trade that information to the Feds. Ordinarily I would not do anything this risky with someone I don't entirely trust. But the urgency of the situation demands that I make my move now.

I met the Wizard through my longtime local partner, Benny, a fellow Wellesley guy I've known since high school. Benny first ran into the Wizard at his chiropractor's office. They struck up a conversation after being introduced as having "a lot in common." Benny usually paid his chiropractor's bill with bags of weed. Benny handles all our Boston-area wholesale distribution and has a thriving retail business. Before long he was showing the Wizard samples of Lebanese hash. The Wizard wants to do quantity. He says he and his people can handle multiton loads of quality hashish. Benny bought some ID from him. I met with the Wizard in New York and Miami; he introduced me to his partners, and I sold them a couple of hundred kilos of hash. So far, so good. I have no reason to suspect him other than my highly paranoid state and a slightly creepy vibe he gives off.

There is no fault to be found in his work. He's a perfectionist. The licenses he hands me as we sit together in the restaurant are faultless. I am now three new people with a fourth about to be resurrected from the dead. "So," he says after I inspect the licenses and return them to the manila envelope with the birth and death certificates, "when do we leave for Beirut?"

"I didn't know that was part of the deal."

"C'mon, man. Share the wealth. There's more hash over there than you can handle."

"I tell you what. I'll go over and put together a load for you. Give me the money and the particulars of how you want it sent."

"No, no. We don't do anything unless we know who we're dealing with."

I tell him, "You're dealing with me."

We finish our lunch and part company.

"I'll get back to you," he says, with an enigmatic smirk. "Enjoy your new selves."

It's his skull-like smile that unsettles me. I don't know his real name or where he lives. Pierre, he calls himself lately, but he switches identities like most people change clothes. His partners in Miami are cocaine cowboys—a French Canadian from Montreal and a Colombian from Medellín. But the Wizard is from no discernible location, has no identifiable roots. All I have on him is a phone number for an answering service. When I ask him where he's from, he blows me off. He has one of those broad American accents like a newscaster. From his appearance I would guess that he is a WASP. There is a preppy aspect to the way he dresses: loafers with no socks, a pastel sweater draped over his shoulders, pleated slacks. He looks like he would be more at home at a garden party in the Hamptons than drifting from hotel to hotel selling phony ID. But who am I to talk? I am as much of an anomaly as the Wizard.

My people on both sides of the family come from old New England stock dating back to before the Revolution—a dying breed. I should have been a lawyer or a banker, a pillar of the community. Yet from an early age I was drawn to the dark side. Too much TV. Watching episodes of *The Untouchables*, I wanted to be Al Capone, not Eliot Ness. The Lone Ranger, Robin Hood, ex-con detective Boston Blackie, enemy to those who make him an enemy, friend to those who have no friend. These were my heroes.

Not that I could have been a bank robber or even a bookmaker. That seemed like real crime to me. Had pot not been illegal, I probably would have gone straight. Wolfshein was at least partly right when he remarked that it is the politics of the drug war—and particularly the War on Plants—that engages me intellectually. That and the rush of getting over on the Man. I try to assure myself that what I do is in defense of the American notion of life, liberty, and the pursuit of happiness. As an American, I tell myself, I have a moral obligation to defy tyrannical authority and break the laws that are wrong. After all, it is a plant we are talking about, created by God, and what should be an inalienable right in a free society: to alter our consciousness as we please so long as we do not harm others. With this reasoning I attempt to console my restless conscience. Yet there is the nagging suspicion that what really moves me is the glamour of being an outlaw.

In the parking garage, I slip the manila envelope with the new ID under the front seat of the Suburban and drive out to my partner Benny's stash pad in Wellesley. Benny lives a few miles from my parents' home. I take the back roads, keeping a look out to make sure I am not being followed. These streets are as familiar to me as the scars on my body—many of those scars I got on these streets. My parents moved to a big house in the exclusive Cliff Estates section of Wellesley Hills when I was in first grade. In elementary school and junior high I had a paper route delivering the *Boston Herald* and the *Globe* to the stately homes in this bastion of white Anglo-Saxondom.

My senior year in high school there was one black family in this town, one black kid in Wellesley Senior High. He played halfback on the football team, I was the fullback. My best friend was a Jew from one of half a dozen Jewish families that moved into town but were not allowed to join Wellesley Country Club. His father owned a successful wool company. Judge W. Arthur Garrity, Jr., who ordered forced busing to desegregate Boston schools, lives in Wellesley Hills. Home to Wellesley College, Babson College, and Dana Hall School, Wellesley ranks first in the United States in percentage of adults who hold at least one college degree. Dumb people don't live here. Just elitists. Snobs. Closet racists.

I rebelled against all that. In the sixth grade at Brown Elementary School, I formed the first and probably the only gang the town has ever known—the Pink Rats, named after a gang of juvenile delinquents I saw in an episode of *Dragnet*. I was the kid parents warned their children to stay away from. At nineteen, I was hanging out in black jazz clubs in Boston and Beat coffeehouses in Cambridge selling nickel bags of commercial Mexican weed. Now the New England family of the hippie mafia is based here, supplying the nation with quality cannabis.

When I pull up in Benny's driveway and park, reach in the rear for my briefcase, I can't find it. I turn around in the seat and look on the floor. It's not there. My guts wrench. Gone. Vanished. *This can't be.* Panic. I'm stymied. *How?* Or better still: *Who?* The first thought that comes to mind is that DEA agents must have broken into the car and made off with the briefcase. I see Wolfshein's hand in this. It had to be him. The car appeared untouched back at the hotel parking garage. The doors were still locked, there were no signs of forced entry. It had to be agents. This was a professional job with a definite objective: *Get the briefcase.*

In that briefcase are my books—seriously incriminating financial records of major drug trafficking—and my address book with my contacts, all the shit I just cleaned out of my stash at the farm. *I am fucked.* This is a disaster. Illegally obtained for evidentiary purposes, true, but nevertheless the contents of that briefcase comprise a wealth of investigative intelligence.

Shit! How the fuck—?

Could this happen? They followed me to the hotel and while I was in the room with the Wizard, they broke into the car and stole my briefcase. That's the only explanation. Now I take it one step further. The agents will lie, say they seized the briefcase from the Toronado and use the contents against me. These guys are serious. It may be a game to me—and to them—but the consequences are real. People go to prison. People die. In 1980 they changed the law: it used to be no matter how much weed they busted you with, the maximum sentence the Feds gave out was five years. Then they upped it to fifteen. I feel like a fucking idiot. Worse than a fool. Why did I leave the briefcase in the car? Why didn't I take it into the hotel with me? I climb in back and check the stash under the seat. The money is still there. Thank God for that. Then I remember, as I was putting the money in the stash, the little voice within said: *Why not put your books and phone numbers in there as well?* But I didn't listen. I got lazy, sloppy. I figured I would need them to go over the numbers with Benny and never imagined Wolfshein would have the balls and the initiative to pull off something like this. My fuckup. Never underestimate the enemy.

* * *

THAT EVENING, VAL, my running partner and girlfriend, flies in from Aspen. When I pick her up at Logan Airport, she has more bad news. "Fucking Fred, your asshole friend," she says.

"What?"

"He drove Judy to the airport. On his way home, he fell asleep at the wheel driving his truck and ran head-on into another car. Killed the driver and a fourteen-year-old kid."

"Oh, Jesus, no."

"Yes!"

"Where is he?"

"He's okay. They took him to the hospital and let him go. The cops were there like immediately." She glares at me. "What're you doing with that guy anyway? You know he's a fucking Heat score."

All I can do is shake my head.

Val takes my face in her hands, looks me in the eye. "Listen, pal," she tells me. "You've got to get out of town. This isn't going away."

"What about you?"

"Me? Honey—I'm already gone."

And she is. She has been a fugitive for as long as I have known her. We had been doing business together for two years and been lovers for half that time before I knew her real name. Val is a founding member of the Brotherhood of Eternal Love, the original hippie mafia family based in Laguna Beach, California. The Brotherhood made their name importing fine black Afghani hash. Later they became the biggest manufacturers and distributors of Orange Sunshine LSD. Acid guru Timothy Leary was the Brotherhood's nominal godfather. After a massive bust in the mid-seventies, the Brotherhood scattered to the far corners of four continents. Dope-smuggling families took root all across North America. The Feds inadvertently created what became known as the hippie mafia. By this time the entire soft drug distribution network was controlled by half a dozen hippie mafia families. We were essentially nonviolent. Our motto was peace, love, and brotherhood—and, of course, money. No one carried weapons. If you didn't pay your bill, we just stopped doing business with you. We believed in karma: A good product delivered for a righteous price would only bring good fortune. All that began to change once the avalanche of Colombian blow buried the nation.

"Really, guy," Val says. "You think you can trust Fred?" And she answers her own question. "No way. You need to split. *Pronto*."

4

TOP OF THE WORLD

JIMMY CHAGRA WEARS a huge, gaudy, diamond-studded gold cross and gold chain around his neck. He's dressed all in black, black shirt open to mid-chest to expose the cross nestled in his hairy chest, handmade cowboy boots that probably cost ten grand, the de rigueur gold Rolex Presidential with a diamond-encrusted bezel. Gold and diamond rings and bracelets. He must be wearing a hundred grand worth of jewelry. He's a walking advertisement for the excesses of too much money made too fast. He might as well just hang a diamond-studded sign around his neck that says: DOPE DEALER.

He is with three other men when we meet at a restaurant on Boston's North Shore. Chagra introduces John and Gerry Grillo. The third man introduces himself.

"Hi. Mike Capuana." He offers me a limp handshake and a bland smile. "Rhymes with *marijuana*."

Capuana has an open, expressive, and soft, good-looking face. He's in his thirties, trim, not as ostentatious as Chagra but probably not as rich, either. He is a man on the make. Ambition lives in the quick of his movements.

The men are seated at a table in a rear room of the restaurant. The Grillo brothers don't say much. John is skinny, ferret-like, around the same age as Capuana. He exudes furtive malevolence. I make him for a killer, the kind of guy who would lurk in the bushes outside your home and shoot you in the back of the head as you unlocked your door. Gerry is older, better dressed, with minimal jewelry, and has a managerial air. Capuana is clearly in charge. Even Chagra, to a degree, defers to him, though this is Chagra's meeting. I'm wondering what these guys are doing here, not who they are. That's obvious.

As if he reads my thoughts, Capuana says, "We know about your deal at the airport." He gestures to Gerry Grillo. "Gerry is from Revere. The guy at the airport, Dominick, he's with Gerry." His voice takes on a more commanding tone. "You're not supposed to be doing nothing like that at Logan without Gerry's say so." And then he smiles. "Understand?"

Capuana is referring to my airfreight catch at Logan Airport. I understand the "we" does not refer just to the men at this table. Capuana is talking corporately. I had been wondering when I would be called to this meeting. "I just happened to mention to Jimmy that I needed to meet with you," Capuana continues. "Jimmy says he knows you. You handled something for him in Maine?" A question and a statement in one.

"Yes."

Jimmy leans into the conversation. "Red Beard is with Mike," he says. Red Beard is the guy Jimmy sent to Maine to work with my crew coordinating the thirty-ton off-load of the Panamanian freighter. "Where's the rest of the load, Richie?" Chagra asks. "We're short *ten tons*."

Now they are both looking at me as though I've got some explaining to do. I came to this meeting expecting to get paid. Chagra owes me somewhere in the neighborhood of $300,000. He and Capuana act like I'm holding out on them.

"Let me explain something to you," Capuana says, gesturing with his long, slim, and soft hands, hands that have never hefted a bale of marijuana. "Nothing happens between Rhode Island and Maine unless I okay it. I report directly to the Hill, in Providence."

He uses the commonly accepted euphemism for the rule of Raymond L. S. Patriarca, don of the New England Cosa Nostra family and a member of the ruling Mafia commission. "The days of the independent operator in your business—which is now my business"—Capuana says and pats himself on the chest— "are over. I have permission from Providence to organize the whole East Coast. Under our protection." He lets this sink in, still gazing at me with a bemused smile. "I was gonna tell you to get the fuck outta Logan, get outta New England, until I happened to mention your name to Jimmy. He tells me he knows you. He has a problem with the numbers on the thing you handled for him in Maine."

For years I have been hearing that the mob is looking to muscle their way into the lucrative wholesale end of the marijuana trade. I know sons of organized crime people in New York and New Jersey who used their fathers' connections to establish themselves as major players. The domestic distribution end of the business is controlled by three primary, loose-knit groups: the hippie mafia families that only deal pot, hash, and psychedelics, made up of mostly white, middle-class college kids who dropped out, turned on, and gathered small fortunes as they created the market—Val's and my people; the returning Vietnam vets, full-on action junkies with skills and guns, like Father Flaherty and Jimmy D; and, finally, children of the mob. The foreign import end of the business—my area of expertise—is a free-for-all with adventurers of all ages, nationalities, and stripes vying for territory. The Colombians, with their huge mother ships off-loading in our waters, have come to dominate the commercial marijuana market. Mexican cartels compete with tractor-trailer loads coming up from the Southwest. Cubans, Jamaicans, groups operating out of the Bahamas have turned South Florida into a dope smuggler's extravaganza. It is like Prohibition all over again. An avalanche of cocaine is changing the landscape. Extreme craziness, violence, and death have infected a way of life that was purported to be about peace, brotherhood, and money.

And now here is Mike Capuana-rhymes-with-marijuana smiling at me even as he threatens. My sense is that if I show the least bit of fear or intimidation, Capuana and Chagra will walk all over me. They will possess me. I will leave this meeting believing I owe them money instead of the other way around. The Grillo brothers are here so I get the message these guys are not fucking around. I am supposed to be scared—and I am, though I won't show it. There is a mean, aggressive, nasty streak in me, honed in reform school and street fights, that turns vicious when I feel threatened. I'm like a cornered animal, ready to throw the table over on Capuana and Chagra, spill food all over them, slap that crocodile smile off Capuana's fleshy face. Then grab Chagra by the chain around his neck and strangle him until he coughs up my money.

Instead, I lean in across the table and smile in Capuana's face.

"Listen, Mike, nice to meet you," I lie. "But my business is with Jimmy. I don't even know you. Jimmy hired me to get thirty tons of weed off a ship that would still be sitting out in the Atlantic, or probably busted by the Coast Guard by now if we hadn't stepped in and taken care of it. I did that for Jimmy. Not one bale was lost. Red Beard has all the numbers. There's around eight to ten tons of weed sitting in a barn in Maine that is no good—soaked in diesel fuel and bilge water. It's there for Jimmy or the Colombians or whoever to check it out and do whatever you want with it. I offered to let Red Beard see it, but he was too busy. I have another two tons I'm holding until I get paid. Or I'll take the weed instead of payment. But I did what I was hired to do, and now I need to get paid."

Capuana looks at Chagra, then he looks at Gerry Grillo, and he laughs. "I like this kid!" he says. "This kid's got balls!"

He flags the waiter and orders a bottle of wine. "The best bottle you got."

Then, to me, "You're okay, Richie. We're gonna do big things together. Get rich and famous. We'll send somebody up to check out the spoiled goods. As soon as we see what's what, Jimmy'll pay you. Or you'll keep the weed you got. Work that out with Jimmy. Right, Jimmy?"

"You're telling me eight fucking tons is no good?" Chagra says.

"That's what I'm telling you. At least eight."

"Fuck it," Capuana says. "Let the Colombians eat it. That's their problem."

Capuana wants to know if I can get some of the weed up to Montreal. He says he has people up there. Family. I say yeah, no problem, though all my instincts are telling me to get away from these guys as fast and as far as I can. Wine is served. Food. Gerry Grillo says he likes me too. He's impressed with the way we've wired Logan Airport. He wants to know if we can get heroin and cocaine in the same way.

"That's not my business," I tell him. "No junk. No coke."

"That's right," Capuana explains like he knows what he's talking about. "These guys just do the grass. They can move lots of grass. The other stuff, forget it. Too much Heat." He goes on to tell me he was doing a bid on a bank burglary beef when he met a New England dope dealer who clued him in on how much money there was to be made smuggling weed. For a while, Capuana and the Grillos were considering going into the business of ripping off the hippie pot dealers, who are known to be unarmed and easy prey. But Capuana reasoned he could make more money if he joined forces and got everyone working together—for him. "You understand what I'm saying, Rich?"

I glance at John Grillo, who looks bored, like he'd rather have gone with the more exciting rip-off plan.

"Let me explain how this works," Capuana continues. "You're gonna pay me a million dollars. For protection. And for permission to keep working. Then you're gonna give us half of everything you bring in through Logan."

My guts wrench. My pulse accelerates. The wine turns sour in my mouth. I'm trying to figure out how I'm going to leave this restaurant and get away from these guys without getting killed. "Protection from who?" I say. "You?"

The face smiles but the man is getting impatient. "Whoever. If you're with me, nobody's gonna bother you."

"Mike, in the first place, I don't have a million dollars—"

He holds up a hand. "You've got all that weed, Jimmy's weed. So you'll pay me out of that. You'll move some of it up to Canada for us. You'll work it off."

I shake my head. "Look, I appreciate the offer. But I'm going to pass. My deal at the airport, I give the Arabs a third for fronting the loads. I pay the airfreight guys—"

"Thirty grand," Gerry Grillo cuts in. "Peanuts."

"No. Not for what they do. They're happy with it. If I give you half, I'm losing money."

"That's not a good answer," Capuana says. The smile is gone.

I shrug. "It's the only answer I've got," I tell him and wait a moment before I add, "I'll speak to my *friend*. But I don't think we can do business."

Capuana hesitates, considering the way I said *friend*. He looks at Chagra, then at Gerry Grillo. To me he says, "Who're you with?"

"I'd rather not say."

"Listen, kid," he says, though we are around the same age. "This is not an offer. I don't know who the fuck you think you are, but if you don't want no trouble—"

"I don't want trouble. But you've got to understand my position. I can't do anything, Mike—I can't agree to anything until I speak to my friend. You know how that works. And you'll know who he is. But I'm not—I can't say anything until I clear it with him. Give me a number where I can reach you and you'll get a call."

I stand. John Grillo comes to attention. Capuana puts a hand on his arm. To Gerry Grillo, he says, "Give him the number at the store." But he's glaring at me. "I hope you know what the fuck you're talking about," he says.

I'm thinking: *So do I.*

Gerry writes a phone number on the back of a business card, hands it to me. "Just ask for me."

"My friend will call you," I say. And to Jimmy, "Thanks, Jimmy. See you later."

We don't shake hands. I walk away from the meeting feeling like a man who has just stepped into a minefield. As I get in the Suburban and start the engine, I fully expect to see John Grillo come running out of the restaurant with a gun in his hand. My hands are shaking, my mouth is dry, my stomach and bowels are in an uproar. *No, no, no*, I tell myself, they're not going to kill me, not now. Because if they do, they'd have no way of getting their weed back, and they'll have to answer to the Colombians and whoever I'm with. Yes, that's their move. The meeting was supposed to scare the shit out of me—and it worked. But fuck it, and fuck them. Fuck Mike Capuana-rhymes-with-marijuana. And John beady-eyed Grillo with his scrawny neck. I'll fuckin' strangle him too. And Jimmy Scumbag Chagra. Fucking crooks.

I'm an idiot to get mixed up with these people. I see myself stepping deeper into shit. And half loving it, half hating myself at the same time.

"HOW WAS YOUR meeting?" Val asks when I see her back at the hotel in Cambridge. I don't tell her, knowing what she'll say: "That's your karma, pal. For doing business with people like that." How was I to know Jimmy is mobbed-up? Of course, I had to know. I was introduced to him through a known wiseguy lawyer. Willful ignorance. This is just me playing games with myself, pushing myself into ever more dangerous situations, upping the stakes, looking to get myself killed. *Brilliant.* It's like that Neil Young song: *Why do I keep fuckin' up*? Must be because I like it, or I get something out of it. But what?

There is the sweet solace of sex. Drugs, sex, and rock and roll—works every time. Smoke a little herb, drink some wine, put on Eric Clapton or Stevie Winwood, and fuck until you fall asleep. Fucking is never as good as when you think you could be dead in the morning. Yes, pussy, Val's pussy in my face, and I feel like there is a safe place somewhere up in there for me if I could only crawl back inside and hide.

In the morning, I call my friend, arrange to meet with him at his golf club up near the Massachusetts-New Hampshire border. He's in his sixties. I call him Uncle George. Lebanese, though he was born here and has never even visited the mother country. He leaves that to his younger brother, who is tight with Amal, the militia wing of the Shi'a political movement in Lebanon. George is stocky, with a thick black mustache, fierce, bushy eyebrows, and penetrating, dark eyes.

"Who the fuck is this guy?" George says when we are alone, sitting in a sauna sweating our asses off. "He wants half? And a million up front? What is he, fucking nuts? Tell him to go fuck himself. Or I'll tell him."

"He says he's with Raymond."

George gives me a look. Shakes his head. After a moment he says, "We'll see about that. Let me make a call." He's old school, Uncle George, everything by the unwritten book, the code of criminal conduct. Coming up in the rackets, George did his own work. He put on the boots, the trench coat, and stood out in the cold with a piece waiting—then he pulled the trigger. He did what he was told to do, and he got respect. As a Lebanese, he could never be made, never be a wiseguy, but he always maintained he wouldn't have taken the button even if the Italians had offered it to him. "I don't need that kind of Heat," he told me. "I'm my own boss." And he prospered. He bought land. He went into real estate and narrowly averted getting swept up in the mob wars and turf disputes that still divide the Boston underworld. Through his brother's Amal connection, George cleared the way for our goods to leave Lebanon.

Now he lectures me about how to shower after the sauna. "Start with hot water," he says, "then make it gradually cooler, then cold. Cool off slowly so you don't catch cold."

That's the last thing I'm worried about. Still, George wants to be my mentor in all I do.

A DAY LATER I meet with George again, this time at the body shop we own in Lowell. He pulls up out front in his Caddy. I get in with him.

"You've got to do it," George says. "Pay the fucking guy the money. Give him what he wants."

"*What?*"

Then he turns on me. "You heard me! What the fuck're you, crazy? You stole from these people? *This guy is with Raymond!* You could get us both killed."

"Stole what? I stole nothing, not a fucking thing from no one." I go on to explain the off-load deal with Chagra, the spoiled product. Red Beard. A full accounting. "Nobody stole nothing."

"You better be telling me the truth," George says and gazes at me.

"What the fuck am I gonna do, lie to you? You know me better than that."

"This is bad," George says, as if I don't already know. "Very bad. You've got to make it right. It's out of my hands."

"Make it right? How? I don't have a million dollars. And if I give them half of our loads, there's nothing left for you and me."

"Look, you heard me. This guy has got permission from the Hill in Providence. He's very close to Raymond. There is *nothing I can do*."

"Well . . . then fuck it. It's over."

"What's that supposed to mean?" George snaps and glowers at me.

"It means . . . I'm out of here. Out of Logan. Out of Boston. Fuck these people. They don't want to pay me for off-loading their freighter, I'll keep the pot."

"You're crazy!" He shakes his head, wags a finger in my face. "No, no . . . you don't fuck these people! They'll find you wherever you go. And then they will kill you. Make no mistake about it."

"George, I did what Chagra hired me to do, that's all. I'm not giving them shit."

"Are you out of your fucking mind?"

"No. I just . . . I don't like getting fucked."

"You like getting killed?"

"They've got to find me to kill me."

After a moment, George says, "Maybe I can get you a pass on the million, because you're with me. But they're going to want a piece of everything you do from now on. That's just the way it is."

I can't even depend on Uncle George to help me out of this one. But I don't care. I tell George I'll deal with it myself. The more I think about it, the more I convince myself Capuana is full of shit. He and Chagra are trying to shake me down, and I'm not going for it. Stubborn Capricorn. Piss on them. George tells me that if I defy Capuana, I am pissing on Providence, and therefore he cannot protect me.

Two days later a load from Beirut arrives at Logan—135 kilos of primo blond Lebanese hash. My guy at the airport—not Gerry Grillo's guy, Dominick, who had to open his big mouth about our catch, but the guy I deal with directly, Kevin, an Irish guy from South Boston—he tells me they want the load out of there immediately. It must be picked up this very night before the customs inspectors come around with dope-sniffing dogs in the morning. "Understand?" Kevin says. "You gotta get it out now, Rich."

My first thought is that I'm being set up. Val drops me off at the airfreight terminal. Usually JD or Father Flaherty or one of the other drivers picks up the load. But this time I am doing it on my own. Out of necessity. The crates are marked ENGINE PARTS with JAL (Japanese Air Lines) stickers all over them, loaded into the rear of a panel truck parked at the loading docks. The hash was shipped from Beirut to Abu Dhabi, then transferred to JAL and relabeled ENGINE PARTS. I see my guy, Kevin, he gives me the keys, I hand him the envelope with thirty grand, and then I drive out without so much as a second look.

At my parents' home in Wellesley, I stash the hash in the Global Evangelism motor home parked in the driveway. The panel truck I leave at a prearranged spot in East Boston, near the airport. Put the keys in the ashtray and walk away, praying Capuana and his boys aren't waiting to drive by and clip me. I take a cab back to the hotel. But I am too antsy to stay there. Val and I drive out to Wellesley and spend the night in the motor home. We make love in air thick with the perfumed fragrance of fresh hashish.

I got the load out without giving Capuana so much as a gram. Now everybody is pissed at me. My local distributor, Benny, wants nothing to do with it. Uncle George doesn't even want his cut. "You're on your own," he tells me. My guy at the airport, Kevin, calls and leaves a message on my answering service. When I call him back, Dominick comes on the line. "Someone wants to talk to you," he says.

"Richie, you know who this is?" the guy asks.

"No . . . who?" I say. But I know.

"John. I met you with Mike the other night."

"Yeah."

"You think you're pretty fuckin' smart, don't you?"

"John, I got no beef with you or with Capuana."

"No? Listen, asshole. You know what I'm gonna do to you?"

"What're you going to do?"

"I'm gonna find you. And when I do, I'm gonna cut your balls off and shove 'em up your mother's cunt. Then I'm gonna kill you."

I have to hand it to John Grillo, it's a pretty vivid threat.

FOR THE FIRST time in over fifteen years in the dope business, I start to carry a gun, a .380 caliber automatic I buy at a gun shop in New Hampshire with one of the driver's licenses I got from the Wizard. I don't know what I'm going to do with the weapon, but it's there, either in my pocket or in my new briefcase. During my rational moments I know I'm living out some childhood fantasy life of crime. I see myself as a character in a Cagney gangster movie playing in my head. I fondle the gun. Go out in the woods and shoot at beer cans or to the dump and shoot at rats. As a kid at camp I was a pretty good shot, got all my marksmen badges with a .22 rifle. And at my friend Godfried's farm in Maine we used to target practice with his arsenal of handguns. But am I really going to shoot John Grillo or Mike Capuana or whomever they send to kill me, and leave them to die in the street? Do I have the balls to pull the trigger and kill another human being? Pick up a murder beef to add to whatever charges Wolfshein and the Feds have in store for me? I have my doubts . . .

Wolfshein . . . In all the excitement I almost forgot about him and the bust in Maine. *The stolen briefcase. Shit.* And I still have all that weed stashed in Maine to move. Plus the load of hash nobody wants to help me sell. Things are happening too fast. I begin to have vivid dreams about killing dark-haired men, fleshy-faced men with smirking smiles, and being consumed with how to dispose of the dead body. I'm in a house with a ton of weed in the basement and a chopped-up body in garbage bags outside in the rear of my car. Garbage bags full of weed, garbage bags full of body parts. I'm getting them mixed up. We call a pound of pot an elbow. Here, let me sell you an elbow. Or is it a torso? How much for a severed head? I'm shooting at these guys who are chasing me but my gun is like a toy, a cap gun. I'm really just a big kid beating them to death with my fists. But the blows are sluggish, slow motion, not really effective. Mike Capuana smiles back at me as I punch him in his round, moon face.

And still I'm not losing any sleep. I start to appreciate that I'm genuinely crazy, always have been. That's okay, I can deal with that so long as my behavior doesn't hurt anyone else—family, loved ones, girl-friends, friends, dogs. That is where my real fear lives. Grillo is indeed looking for me. George assures me Grillo has orders from Capuana to kill me. One night he finds me. Maybe he's been following me, I don't know. I'm with another guy, Jake, who is something of a badass himself, little Jewish guy like Meyer Lansky, an armed robber who did a bunch of time for manslaughter. Jake and his sister have been moving kilos of the new load of hash, sending it out to people in New Orleans, and they want more. We pull into a parking lot outside a busy club in Brookline where Jake's sister works as a cocktail waitress. I've got twenty-five grand on me, so I take a moment to put it in the stash. When I get out of the Suburban and we walk toward the club, I see

Grillo and another guy getting out of their car. Grillo follows us inside. I know it's him; this isn't a dream. I see him again at the bar, looking right at me. But I give him the slip in the crowded club. I grab Jake. His sister lets us out a rear door.

"What's wrong?" Jake asks.

"Someone I don't want to see."

"Fuck 'em. Let's go back and fuck 'em up."

"No. You don't want any part of these people."

After a few days of missed calls, I contact the man who turned me on to Kevin and the airport freight handlers in the first place. He's a successful Back Bay real estate broker with an expensive cocaine habit. Kevin has already clued him in on my problem with Capuana and the Grillo brothers. "Let me see what I can do," he says.

Meanwhile Val and I have to convert the hash into cash. The Lebanese want their end. Val and her partner, Judy, take seventy kilos in the Global Evangelism machine and drive it out to their people on the West Coast. My Canadian distributor and close friend, Rosie, in Toronto takes most of the rest of the load and turns it in a matter of days. I have a suitcase full of money, $130,000, to deliver to the Arabs, who await me at a hotel in Manhattan.

At Logan, I buy a ticket on the shuttle to LaGuardia and check the suitcase. As I am going through the security checkpoint, I place my new briefcase on the conveyer belt. At the moment the briefcase disappears into the X-ray machine, I remember: *Fuck*. The gun. *Oh, shit*. It's in the briefcase, the .380 automatic. *How can I be so stupid?*

I see by the look on the security guy's face when he spots the outline of the gun in my briefcase, he's as shocked as I am. I try to snatch the briefcase when it emerges from the other side of the X-ray machine and head back out of the terminal, saying something lame like, "I don't think I'll be going to New York after all." The security guy grabs the briefcase. We wrestle with it for a moment while his co-workers summon the state police. Massachusetts has a strict minimum mandatory five-year prison term for anyone caught with a gun. I am quickly locked up in a holding cell at the airport while my suitcase with all that cash goes on to New York without me.

This is one of those moments when I am forced to conclude that not only am I crazy, I am also careless. Not on top of my game. My briefcase has disappeared, probably sitting in an evidence locker at DEA headquarters. Wolfshein is planning his next move. The mob is trying to kill me. George has withdrawn his protection. The Lebs want their money. Wolfshein and the Feds and Capuana and the mob are tracking me. And here I sit in a holding cell at the airport charged with possession of a handgun. Carrying false ID in the name of Paul Quinlan of Austin, Texas, while my suitcase with a hundred and thirty grand travels off to New York by itself. It occurs to me that this is the second time I have been locked up in as many months—not a good trend.

The arresting state trooper lets me call my Boston-based criminal lawyer, Thomas Heffernon, a childhood friend who has risen to become one of the best trial lawyers in town, and who is now overseeing my defense in the Maine case. Hef, a big redhead with a basso profundo voice and Celtic verbal gift that can talk birds out of the trees, already beat one hashish importation case for me in the Eastern District of New York—the one Wolfshein mentioned, where the DEA stole the load and couldn't produce the evidence. Hef tells me to act agreeably and say nothing. He asks if he can speak with the arresting trooper. Whatever is said, I begin to get a glimpse of something out of the ordinary when the trooper tells me, "Your lawyer's on his way. We'll wait outside for him." And he leads me out of the terminal.

Hef comes directly in to the airport and gets me an immediate hearing in an East Boston court. "This gentleman, Mr. Quinlan, hails from the great state of Texas," Hef tells the presiding judge. "Out there, folks think nothing of carrying firearms. In fact, they consider it their God-given and Constitutional right as Americans to bear arms. He is not familiar with the Draconian statutes imposed in this fair state for what comes to a Texan as naturally as breathing clean air. This offense is an error of pure ignorance on the part of Mr. Quinlan. He is a law-abiding man and cannot be held to account for what he did not know. The trooper, however, was quite right in his interdiction of this matter. Even so, I ask the mercy of this Honorable Court on a true gentleman."

After a moment of reflection, the judge gives me a lecture on the laws of Massachusetts. He then imposes a fine, $200, confiscates the gun and releases me. Hef hands me my briefcase and gives me a hug. "Take care of yourself," he tells me. "You seem tense."

"It's been a rough couple of weeks."

"You're looking good in Portland," he says. "I don't believe they have enough to get an indictment. Unless, of course, someone flips."

I MAKE THE four o'clock shuttle to LaGuardia. When I arrive and go to the baggage claim area, I am amazed and gratified by what I see. There is my suitcase, still making its lonely way around the luggage conveyer six hours after it arrived, waiting for me to claim it. Overcoming a moment's hesitation, thinking that agents may have the place staked out and are just waiting to see who would claim the bag before they make their move, I grab the bag off the revolving belt and walk out of the terminal.

That evening, in Manhattan, I turn over a hundred grand to my Lebanese contact and tell him to start gathering together a big load.

"How much, Mr. Richard?"

"As much as you can get."

* * *

MY FRIEND, THE real estate broker, is in touch when I return to Boston. He tells me he has someone he wants me to meet, who might be able to help me with "my problem."

"Who?"

"You'll find out."

The meeting is set for the next afternoon at the broker's business on Newbury Street in Back Bay. When I walk in to a rear office, I am introduced to a man I immediately recognize as the legendary boss of the Irish mob, James "Whitey" Bulger.

"Hi, how ya' doin'?" Bulger greets me and we shake hands. "I understand you got a problem with Mickey Capuana."

He is wearing a lightweight black leather jacket, shades, jeans, and sneakers. The bright blond hair that gave him the nickname "Whitey" is thinning. When he takes off his sunglasses I see the famous icy blue eyes. Bulger is in his late forties, early fifties. Fit. Lean. Medium height. He's got the hard, contained look of a man who has done a lot of prison time. His younger brother, William Bulger, president of the Massachusetts State Senate, is one of the most powerful politicians in New England. Senator Bulger went to war with the Boston Brahmins, led by Judge Garrity, over forced busing in South Boston. "Don't worry about it," Bulger tells me when I explain what went down. "I'll straighten out Capuana."

A few days later I meet Bulger again, this time on his stomping grounds, at Castle Island in South Boston. He's leaning against his black Mercury Monterey when I pull up in the Suburban. "Let's walk," he says. He's wearing shades and a Red Sox baseball cap.

The peninsula of South Boston sticks out into the Atlantic like a left jab. It is a world apart from the rest of the city, almost entirely occupied by first- and second-generation Irish immigrants. As we walk around the island on the eastern tip of the point with a panoramic view of Boston Harbor, Bulger launches into a history lesson. He tells me that during the Revolutionary War, General George Washington placed his cannon on Dorchester Heights, high in the heart of Southie, and forced British troops to evacuate their garrison at Fort William and Mary—now the site of Fort Independence, a hulking, five-sided granite structure built in the 1800s. Castle Island was connected to the mainland in the 1930s by a man-made isthmus so streetcars could bring bathers to Pleasure Bay, known locally as the lagoon, a placid ocean pool skirted by white sandy beach.

"These fuckin' guineas," Bulger says and chuckles. "They think they run Boston. . . . Who ever heard of Mickey Capuana? He's a punk. He thinks he can walk in here and start shaking people down. No, that's not gonna happen. I'll shake him down, this fuckin' greaseball." He stops walking, looks at me.

"He's with Raymond. Big fuckin' deal. Raymond is in Providence. This is our town. Right, kid?" He takes off the shades and gazes at me with those shiny blue eyes.

"What do you want me to do?" I ask him.

"Just keep taking care of my guys at the airport," he says. "Maybe kick 'em up another ten, fifteen grand. It's a sweet little setup. My guys are happy. They got an extra five or ten grand a month to play with. If that fuckin' wop douche bag Dominick hadn't opened his mouth . . . But don't worry about him." He smiles, nods. "You're a good earner, kid. I checked you out. If there's anything else you need, let me know."

"What about Capuana?"

"I told you, I took care of it."

We start walking again. I'm wondering, *did he kill Capuana?*

"The contract is lifted," Bulger says and then, after a few moments, "I might need a favor from you." He goes on to tell me his people have a warehouse full of pot and may need some help moving it. I tell him I'll have my man come in and take a look.

"Good," he says. "Thank you."

I am impressed by how polite he is, reserved and respectful. Yet there is no question in my mind that he is a dangerous man. All the more so for his apparent intelligence. Walking around Castle Island, with the sun shining on Massachusetts Bay where my grandfather used to keep his sailboat moored, I feel like I have finally arrived— ascended to the pinnacle of the underworld. How appropriate that it all comes back to Southie.

My personal history with South Boston concerns the 175-acre island four miles offshore known as Thompson Island. One gets to Thompson Island by motor launch that leaves the mainland from

Kelly's Landing in Southie. I can see Thompson Island now from where Jimmy Bulger and I stand. In the 1800s, Thompson Island became home to the Boston Asylum for Indigent Boys, later named Thompson Academy. I was sent to Thompson Island in the eighth grade when I got kicked out of Wellesley Junior High. It was during my fledgling juvenile delinquent phase. Post Pink Rats. More like Marlon Brando in *The Wild One*. I wanted to be like the tough inner city kids I saw in *Blackboard Jungle*. Not some candy-ass rich kid from Wellesley Hills. I wore my hair like Elvis. Carried a switchblade knife. Wore a black leather motorcycle jacket. Hung out at one of the two places in Wellesley that had pinball machines—Ma's Lunch, run by a toothless, old, Italian lady who used to let us kids smoke cigarettes.

Early one day during a Phys Ed class at Wellesley Junior High, I was out on the pitcher's mound playing softball. But I had forgotten my sneakers. No sneakers, no softball—that was the rule. Mr. Wade, a student teacher from Springfield College—small guy, not much bigger than us eighth graders, a gymnast—ordered me off the pitcher's mound. I was a wiseass and Wade didn't like me. I refused to leave and Wade lost it. He came out onto the diamond, grabbed me, and tried to drag me from the playing field. We got into a knock-down, drag-out fistfight as Wade attempted to haul me up the hill to the principal's office. I got him in a headlock and punched him in the face. He broke free, grabbed a stone and tried to crown me with it. The girls' gym teacher was so freaked she herded all the girls into a bevy behind the backstop. I ran off. I ran all the way home, and I hid in the garage until my grandmother, Ba Ba, found me. I was expelled from Wellesley Junior High School. No other public or private school would take me, and as I was just thirteen at the time, Thompson Academy served as one wrong step away from a more serious reform school. The child psychologist my parents enlisted interviewed me and then signed some papers identifying me as a "person in need of supervision."

The day my parents delivered me to Kelly's Landing for the boat trip out to Thompson Island, it was freezing. I was terrified. Boarding that boat for the island, shivering, waving goodbye to my parents huddled on shore—when I saw the pained look on my mother's face, it broke my heart. I wanted to cry. But I couldn't show how I felt, not with half a dozen young toughs checking out the new kid. No, I had to suck it up, choke back any signs of weakness or emotion.

It was all about being tough. As a kid, I wanted to be tough more than I wanted to be smart or popular or good in school. I hated the idea of being thought of as a wimp, a sissy, or, worst of all, a coward. I was determined to be able to beat up anybody who messed with me—or at least give them a good fight. That year on Thompson Island I started lifting weights, I played football, and when the hormones kicked in I lost the baby fat and got strong. I was not the same kid when I returned to the placid, leaf-shaded streets of Wellesley Hills.

Now here I was standing with Jimmy Bulger, infamous Whitey, one of the toughest, most feared gangsters on the East Coast, accepted by him not as an equal but as someone who had something to offer. And he had just saved my life.

Top of the world, Ma . . . top of the world.

* * *

"WHY DIDN'T YOU tell me you was with Whitey?" Capuana wants to know when I am summoned into his presence once more, this time at Gerry Grillo's store in Revere. John Grillo is there, lurking in the corner. Gerry is answering the phone. I'm sitting with Capuana, having coffee.

"And George—" He calls him by name. "Listen, we can do business."

Capuana stops speaking; Gerry waves to him from the counter. He holds a phone with his hand over the mouthpiece. "It's Jimmy," Gerry says.

"Tell him—" Capuana starts to say.

"Take it," Gerry cuts him off. "It's important."

While Capuana goes to the phone, I sit there wishing I were anywhere but here. Men come and go, have hushed, short conversations with John or Gerry. Capuana takes the phone. I watch him. He blanches. "*What the fuck?*" he says and then huddles over the phone.

"They killed Jimmy's brother!" Capuana announces to the room when he hangs up. "They fuckin' whacked Lee Chagra!"

A tall, skinny guy comes in and whispers to Gerry.

"The Feds're outside," Gerry says.

"Fuck them!" says Capuana.

Our meeting is over. Capuana makes plans to fly out to El Paso, Texas, to see Jimmy Chagra and bury the oldest Chagra brother, Lee, a top-tier criminal defense attorney. Jimmy still has to send someone up to Maine to inspect the ruined tons of Colombian pot so we can settle up. But that can wait. My car is parked a few blocks from Grillo's store. I walk out, turn the corner.

And there he is: DEA Special Agent Bernard Wolfshein. I spot him sitting in an undercover car parked across the street. Wolfshein sees me, I'm sure of it; he may even have nodded. Or waved. I want to go to him and plead for protection. Just knowing he's there is oddly reassuring.

I turn away and keep walking.

5

GENERAL MARIJUANA

AT THE PLAZA Hotel I am known as Dr. Lowell. I pose as a psychiatrist to explain the eccentric guests coming and going from my rooms at all hours. Whenever I'm flush, I get a suite at the Plaza and spend lavishly. Room service spreads, magnums of champagne—it's the movable feast. Handing out hundred-dollar tips to hotel staff. Shopping sprees. Call girls—not for me, for the Arabs. Not that I'm too proud to pay for sex. I have a very good, very horny girlfriend in Val. She wouldn't take kindly to pros trespassing on her territory. Besides, it has never been just about fucking for me. I was never good at one-night stands with strangers. I'm into intimacy, a serial monogamist—almost. As in nearly every other aspect of my life at present, I seem to be pushing the boundaries, seeing just how far I can go, how many girlfriends I can maintain in the wreckage of my marriage.

The Arabs insist on female entertainment whenever they are in town waiting for me to appear from wherever I am with whatever they want—usually large amounts of money. And there is Dr. Kato, another phony doctor, Jamaican, from Philly, who owns shoe stores and sells lots of weed. Kato is a fiend when it comes to what he calls "laying pipe." He can employ the services of two or three girls on a given evening and still not be satisfied. It is sport for Dr. Kato, and he is an Olympian.

Kato is already checked in to the hotel when I arrive. He left a message to say he's asleep in his room resting up for the night's activities. My first meeting is in the Oyster Bar with Biff, a former magazine editor and bookie's bagman who has been working for me this past year primarily as a money courier, lately coordinating phone calls and meetings in the city. Biff has a big apartment on the Upper West Side, a wife and three daughters, and an overhead that was burying him when his bookie employer let him go. I met Biff through Norman Mailer; they've been friends for twenty years. Biff appeared in a couple of Mailer's underground films and worked on Mailer's outlandish mayoral campaign. When Mailer mentioned to me that Biff needed work, I shined him on. My experience with even semi-straight people who think they want to get into the dope business has convinced me that not everyone is cut out for a life of crime. Biff prevailed on me. Whenever we would meet at parties or Mailer events, Biff would remind me that he was available should I need help. I always need help. Given my predilection for stretching myself too thin, having someone based in New York City who could receive and deliver money became a matter of necessity. New York is key to the whole operation.

Biff is good at what he does. He looks perfect, mid-forties, balding, clean-shaven, perpetual tan, in decent shape physically, well dressed. He looks like a mid-level businessman and has the surface sophistication to talk his way in and out of most circumstances. We bought him some luggage, had the bags outfitted with money stashes. He had body-packs made to carry cash strapped to his midsection. Biff went out on the circuit, collecting money from my Canadian partner, Rosie, in Toronto and the Cannucks in Montreal and Quebec City, collecting money from my New York partners, or delivering money to them, picking up money from Val or Kato or Judy or Benny or whomever and usually delivering it to me wherever I happened to be or, lately, to the Lebanese. I kept him away from the product, left him out of the planning stages, the actual logistics of the various smuggling trips, kept him strictly as a money schlepper.

These past few weeks Biff has been seeing a lot of Mohammed, my main Lebanese connection, and Mohammed's oldest son, Nasif. He's been paying them off for the load we spirited out of Logan and getting them down-payment cash for the mega-ton shipment we are planning. Biff and Nasif meet and hang out in various cities around the world. Biff stays in touch with the Lebanese through Hammoud, a gruff New York City taxi driver who hails from the same village as Mohammed in southern Lebanon. Hammoud has been recruited as a driver, errand boy, and translator for Mohammed when he is in New York. Biff takes Mohammed and Nasif out to dinner, he gets them girls. He placates them when I am a day or two late getting to town. It was straight to Biff's apartment I went after I collected my cash-laden suitcase at LaGuardia. At one point he had over a half a million dollars in cash in a closet.

My partners and I are still in the early planning stages of what we anticipate will be the biggest hashish smuggle we have ever attempted. Biff is pleading with me for a bigger piece of the action. He's just returned from meeting with Nasif in Cyprus, delivering more down-payment money. "Nasif's going to call you tonight," Biff tells me when I join him at a corner table. He's wearing his hangdog expression, his sad puppy face: *Gee, why won't you let me in on what's really going down?* I've tried to impress on him and on other people who press me for information that what they don't know can't hurt them.

Biff is already a drink or two ahead of me when I order. "Listen, Richard, you've gotta admit, I'm the best you got," he goes on. "You got nobody better than me. I got balls . . . big balls. You gotta admit, I'm your guy. I'd go anywhere for you. Beirut. I went to Beirut, man. A Jew, right? In the middle of a fucking war. I wasn't afraid. C'mon, tell me . . . What's happening? What can I do to help? I need to make some real money. My life is . . ." He stops, shakes his head, it's too upsetting for him to go on.

I'm used to these self-pity meltdowns, heard it a dozen times when he's in his cups, and it irritates the shit out of me. "Have you heard from Val?" I ask.

He takes out his list of things to do, stares at it for a minute or two as though he can't read his own writing. "Yeah . . . She'll be in tomorrow morning. Taking the red eye . . . from ah . . . San Fran. Nasif'll call you tonight. I told you that. What else?"

"Doctor Kato. What did he give you?"

"Oh, yeah, Kato . . . I haven't seen him yet."

"Why not? He's supposed to have money."

This is what pisses me off. Biff wants more responsibility, a bigger stake in the action, and he can't even attend to the basics.

"Well, I ah . . . He just got here and—"

"No. He's been here all afternoon. I got a message from him. He was waiting to hear from you. He's upstairs, asleep. He's got money. You know how it is with Kato and money—anything can happen. You were supposed to pick up the fucking money. What happened?"

He changes the subject. "Norman wants to see you."

"I'm having dinner with him tomorrow night. What's wrong, Biff? You okay?" I already know the answer.

"I'm . . ." He shakes his head, looks like he's about to cry. "My life is over."

"What're you talking about?"

"I'm the best you got! The best. I got big balls. . . . You treat me like I'm a fucking kid."

Now I know he's loaded. He's into his maudlin, repetitive routine, singing the blues. Too far gone to trust with Kato's money. I feel like snapping at him: What the fuck do I need you for if you can't even take care of something as simple as picking up money from Dr. Kato so he doesn't blow it on coke and hookers? You're not the best I've got; Val is, and she fucks up. Everyone fucks up. Look at me. Busted in Maine on a fuckup. Busted in Boston on sheer stupidity. But that's not the point. The money goes to everyone's head. *Protect the money.* The lifestyle is insane. Most of the people you deal with are crazy. This is no nine-to-five gig with a weekly paycheck and benefits. This is *criminal activity*. There are the Bernie Wolfsheins and the Mike Capuanas and

Jimmy Chagras and the Whitey Bulgers of the world out there waiting to pounce when you slip up. The point is to keep your mouth shut and do what you've got to do or get out of the way before you cause even more problems.

"Go home and go to bed. I'll deal with Dr. Kato."

"No, no, I'll take care of it. . . . I'm good for you . . . the best you got . . . I can handle anything."

"Is everything all right at home?" Again, I already know the answer. Now I'm just trying to change the subject.

He shakes his head. He's got that stunned look on his face I know that comes after he's had too much to drink. And it doesn't take much. Three drinks and he is incoherent.

"She caught you fucking around—again?"

He shrugs. He is having trouble putting words into sentences. He blurts out something about his oldest daughter going off to college and he needs money for her tuition. Then there's the house in the Hamptons, the apartment on Riverside Drive. He shakes his head— *poor me*. He sees all that money we appear to be making, though I explain this is a cash business, a lot of that money is just passing through our hands.

"Take it easy, pal," I tell him. "You'll be fine."

What's unsettling about meeting with someone who is fucked up is that it reminds me how fucked up I am.

I'VE GOT ANOTHER meeting, and it is time for Biff to go home. I don't want him doing anything for me in the shape he's in. We walk out onto Fifty-eighth Street. A homeless-looking guy—filthy rags for clothes, and also drunk—staggers up and almost bumps into Biff.

"What the fuck do you want?" Biff barks at him. "Get away from me!"

It's the first intelligible statement he's made all night but not a good move. The homeless guy looks like a Vietnam vet: tattoos, crazy haircut, scars, and blood on his face. My sense of him is, drunk or not, he's nobody to mess with, and he's got a bottle in his hand. Biff turns his back on him, dismisses him. I hail a cab, step between them, and give the guy a twenty. Now he pushes up on me and spits on my shirt.

"Fuck you . . . keep your money," he says, but he holds on to the twenty and moves away less unsteadily. Biff misses the whole play.

"Fucking scumbag," Biff mutters.

"I shouldn't have to be picking up cash from Kato," I tell him, keeping one eye on the drunken homeless guy as he meanders along the sidewalk. Now I'm pissed, having been spat on and let it pass.

"I'll take care of it." Biff is about to cry. The cab pulls over. "I'm the best you got . . ."

"Look, this trip—the one we're putting together now—is going to be a serious payday for everybody. Just do your job, Biff. Keep your fucking mouth shut. Help us with this and I'll give you a bonus . . ." I search for a number. "Two hundred and fifty grand. But you've got to be there for me. No more fuckups. No more getting shitfaced and missing meetings."

"Who's fucked up? The best . . . the best you got," is all he can say.

"Go home. I'll call you tomorrow."

"Two hundred and fifty grand?" There is a glimmer of appreciation.

"But you've got to be on it, Biff. You can't be getting loaded and leaving a guy like Dr. Kato in a hotel room with a lot of cash. You know that. I don't need to tell you that."

"Who?"

"Never mind. Just go home."

We shake hands, I open the door to the taxi. He hugs me, kisses me. "Ah, man . . . bro . . . you're the best."

"We've got to make it happen first. There's a lot to do. And no guarantees."

The look on Biff's face as he sits in the rear of the cab is crestfallen but with the hint of a smile at the corners of his slack mouth. I know exactly what's working through the alcoholic haze in his brain: two hundred and fifty grand. He's already spending the money as the cab pulls away. The homeless guy is half a block down the street. I head back in the hotel to change my shirt. Just another evening with Dr. Lowell dealing with a couple of patients.

MY NEXT MEETING is with Sammy Silver. He picks me up in a rental. Sammy is young, rich, has a mansion on Todt Hill in Staten Island and a trucking company he owns and operates with his father in Jersey City. He hands me a fat joint of some hydroponic weed he's growing in a Brooklyn warehouse. "Fire it up, bro," he says and pulls out into traffic.

Sammy drives fast through the city streets. He's heading to a Japanese restaurant in the East Forties, one of his favorite haunts. Riding with him is like being in some virtual video game where you're fighting for every inch of road space as if it were enemy territory. Kamikaze pedestrians dart off curbs and dash across the streets. Huge potholes and bumps and trash in the street are all part of the obstacle course. The enemy knows no rules. They far outnumber us in their bright-yellow cars. They honk their horns and shout curses at Sammy in foreign tongues. He laughs and gives them the finger. He's a better driver than they are, has quicker reflexes even with all the THC in his bloodstream. He knows the streets and loves the game.

"Bro, check it out." Sammy nods toward the stairs up into the semi-private dining area reserved for big spenders.

We're sitting on the floor before a low table, sipping green tea, sampling from long, narrow plates of raw fish when Mick Jagger and David Bowie ascend the steps and take a table near ours. Sammy orders sake. He doesn't need to order food. The people in this restaurant know him well for his prodigious appetite for sushi. The owner gave him his nickname, Lord Toranaga, after a character in *Shogun*, the novel by James Clavell. Sammy drops thousands in this place each week and has the girth to prove it. With the weight he's put on, he's living up to his nickname, and his face has taken on an Asian cast.

"Those last slabs, those were *the kind*, bro. We need it all to be like that," Sammy says, referring to the recent load of Lebanese hash that we brought in through Logan Airport and almost had to give up to Mike Capuana. "The market is flooded with some dog-shit Leb. This has gotta all be primo, or we're never going to get our price."

I nod in agreement.

"When do you leave?" he asks.

"Good question. The war is bad. Americans're getting kidnapped every day. They're not giving visas except for emergencies."

"Is this gonna hold us up?"

"We'll see. I'm working on another way to get in, through Syria."

"Don't get kidnapped," Sammy says and rummages in the large leather shoulder bag he carries. He pulls out a US Customs manual and hands it to me. "Here's what they look for. I studied the whole profile. Our goods need to be paid for using a letter of credit from a legitimate, established company. No cash. That's a red flag. That trips the computer and causes Customs to give the shipment a secondary inspection. Plus what we're shipping needs to make sense from a business standpoint. Why would this company be importing these goods from this place at this time? Know what I mean? You don't want to be carrying coals to Newcastle."

"I understand."

It's not like we haven't done this before. Maybe never anything of this magnitude, but the details of the profile don't change. Still, Sammy is a stickler for the fine points of a scam, and I respect that in him.

"The goods need to be consigned to a known US import company with a well-established history," Sammy continues between mouthfuls of sushi. "Trucking company, bonded carriers, the warehouse—they all need to be bona fide businesses that will hold up if they run 'em through the computer. No fly-by-night bullshit companies set up for this one deal. That's a red flag. That'll also trip the computer. Okay?"

I nod and keep eating.

"Now, I got all that covered on our end. Bordo Foods, okay . . . my old man knows the guy there, and they need dates. They'll pay good money, and they'll provide the letter of credit. Our profile will be solid gold. *If* you can get the dates."

There is a war going on between Iran and Iraq. Because of the war, there is a demand that presents us with an opportunity: *dates*. First we must convince one of these huge food companies that we can get them Iraqi dates. "We'll get them," I tell him.

"You don't sound so sure. What does Mr. M. say?"

Mr. M. is Mohammed. "He says no problem. But that's what he always says."

"You gotta go over there yourself, bro."

"I know. I'm going."

"No, I mean to Iraq. You gotta check the dates yourself. Listen, there's what's called an infestation rate that you gotta check. Don't leave that to the Lebs. All these dates coming out of that part of the world, they have a certain amount of dead bugs in 'em. The people over there spray 'em and kill the bugs. But if there's too much dead bugs, the infestation rate's too high, then USDA will reject the dates. Understand? We can't let that happen. You follow me? If the dates get rejected, we're fucked. I'll get all the info from my old man. But you gotta be on the ground over there in Iraq and Beirut to check out everything every step of the way. You can't trust these fuckin' camel jockeys to do anything right."

He glances over at Bowie and Jagger's table. "Do you believe this shit? That's fuckin' Jagger and Bowie, bro. Icons. Nobody bothers them. New York City, I love this town. People leave you alone. Here's you and me, takin' care of business, planning the scam of a lifetime." He samples more sushi, sips sake. "And at the next table, rock legends."

After a moment, Sammy asks, "Are you comfortable meeting with the guy from Bordo?"

"Sure, whatever we need to do to make this work, I'll do it."

"Good. I'll have the old man set up a meeting. You're Richard Lowell for this, right, bro?"

I nod.

"From where? Where the fuck are you from anyway?" He laughs. "I'll have business cards made up," Sammy says. "Doctor Richard Lowell, Import/Export. From who-the-fuck-knows-where? When are you gonna settle down, bro?" He laughs again. "We need an address. I'll take care of that. Just be cool and act like you know what the fuck you're talking about." More laughter, louder this time. "Bro, this is so intense. We pull this off . . ." he gestures toward Bowie and Jagger—"we'll be as rich as those guys. Well, maybe not that rich. But cash, bro. Big stamp collections. Major cake. Tax free." He opens his heavy, lidded eyes wide and smiles. "I'll have the old man go along to the meeting with Bordo. Wear a suit. It's all about how you look. The profile. Let the old man do most of the talking. He'll tell you what to say."

Sammy polishes off more sushi, thinks, ruminates, masticates. He's one of what is known in the marijuana underground as the Kings of New York—five or six of the biggest wholesale dealers in the biggest market in the world. He rarely leaves the city except to go on vacation with his wife. He works every day, seven days a week. Long hours. Loves his work. Been doing it for years. Loves the product. He stays high, smokes only the best cannabis in the world. Over the past year he has invested a lot of money in his indoor growing operation. I visited once: a vast warehouse in Brooklyn full of expensive grow lights and hydroponic grow systems, fans, hundreds of graceful, green plants luxuriating in the artificial environment. He has three full-time workers under the tutelage of a guy Sammy calls the marijuana maven, the grow master, who has been profiled in *High Times* magazine wearing a mask and shades.

It's hard to say how much Sammy is worth. Unlike me, he keeps close tabs on his money. He's always got a few hundred grand in hundred-dollar bills available to invest if someone comes along with an importation trip that sounds like it might actually work. He doesn't buy planes and boats and trucks; he's a wholesale dealer as opposed to an importer. His biggest overhead expense, not counting the grow operation, is the several stash houses he maintains in Brooklyn, New Jersey, and Staten Island.

Sammy and I have pulled off a number of successful trips together—his money, my scam. He cashes out the product. We brought in a load of high altitude Jamaican weed known as Lamb's Bread. Sammy hooked me up with a friend of his who owns a hotel in Negril. My pilot, the one I call Jonathan Livingston Seagull, flew the load into the ranch in Texas and we delivered it to Sammy in New York. We do regular importations of connoisseur-quality Mexican sinsemilla from Guerrero and Oaxaca. The Mexican border is where it all began. We still work it on a nearly monthly basis during harvest season. Sammy has his own sources of commercial Colombian. The hashish from Lebanon we were bringing in through a catch at Kennedy Airport before that went bad. Then the Logan catch came into play. Sammy provides seed capital, becomes an investor as well as the wholesale distributor. We share a belief that if the product is good and the price is right and you don't cheat anyone along the way, good karma will hold sway and the trip will be a success.

"Now, here's the most important part," Sammy tells me, and he takes out a pen and notebook. "Packaging. We went over this."

"Ten times," I remind him.

"Cool. Let's do it again. Whatever you do, promise me you will not take the fuckin' rag heads' word for anything. Check everything ten times yourself. With your own eyes. Inspect the load before it goes and make sure it's packaged right. Okay? You promise?"

"I promise."

"Good. Good. Very good. I'm depending on you, Doc. *We're* depending on you. Our *lives* depend on you, bro. Our *freedom*. Our families. My old man's business. It all comes down to," he holds up a finger, looks over at Bowie and Jagger again, "proper packaging."

As we leave the restaurant, the owner embraces Sammy in a bear hug and they slap each other on the back. "Ah! Lord Toranaga! My emperor," the owner exclaims. "You eat well?"

"Very well. Always." Sammy pulls out a fat wad of bills and pays the tab. No plastic for General Marijuana.

THERE IS STILL no answer when I call Dr. Kato's room back at the Plaza. I'm pissed at Biff all over again for not picking up the money. One of the reasons Kato likes this hotel is that it's so big he can bring hookers up to his rooms without having to go past the front desk. We have most of the security staff on the tab. As long as we don't get too raucous, nobody's going to bother us. He could be in there laying pipe. He could be anywhere. I'm ready to call it a night. With Val arriving early in the morning, Nasif calling from the Middle East, I would just as soon watch some TV and pass out. But with Kato in the vicinity, that's not likely. He's a man who likes a drink, and it's still early. I try the Oyster Bar, the Oak Bar—no Kato. He's probably out prowling, trolling, looking for ladies of the night.

In the suite, the message light is blinking on the telephone. "Dr. Kato, room 944," his deep, melodious Islands lilt tells me what I already know isn't so. *Where is this guy?*

There is something about hotel rooms that causes me to feel lonely; it doesn't matter if it's a Motel 8 or a suite at the Plaza. I turn on the TV, pour a glass of champagne, and feel a twinge of guilt over all the money I'm spending—why? To what end? What is the purpose of all this? To make myself feel important? It doesn't work. Or to make me feel like I'm worth something? What am I trying to prove? That I'm better than the homeless guy who spit on me? Or that I am more of a man than my father who never could earn a living as well as he could play golf?

Enough of this crap. Who cares? I grab a towel from the bathroom, roll it up, and place it along the bottom of the door to keep the smell of pot smoke from seeping out into the hallway—not that anyone ever bothers Dr. Lowell—and take a few hits off the fat joint of hydroponic Sammy gave me. The brief encounter with the homeless guy left me feeling troubled. All at once, the THC trips the synapses in my brain: instant paranoia. That guy was a harbinger warning me of impending doom if I don't clean up my act. *There but for the grace of God go I.* When he spit on me, I felt as though I deserved it. I think about my parents, how they used to fight bitterly, almost always over money. Mother Mary spent too much; father Emery didn't make enough—whatever it was. Both were from good families who had seen better days, vanguards in the decline of the WASP. We went from the mansion in Wellesley's Cliff Estates, bought with help from my grandmother, to a duplex in one of the less desirable sections of town. In between, my father took a job as assistant golf pro at the Dorado Beach Hotel in Puerto Rico. He was a world-class golfer who was a decade ahead of the big purses on the professional tour. Judging by how he spent his days, he loved to play golf more than he loved his family. The one tried and true way I knew to get his attention was to get arrested. Is that what this is all about? Spending money like a sheik to convince myself that I am the man he isn't? Flirting with disaster to force my father to acknowledge me? *That's fucking pathetic.*

A surge of energy has me up and pacing, looking out the window. This suite is costing me upwards of a grand a day—I don't even know how much, don't care. New York City is the greatest city in the world, and I'm here planning the biggest trip of my smuggling career. *Stay focused. Keep your eye on the prize.* I haven't even told my parents about the arrest in Maine. Haven't told Sammy, either. It's like I'm not taking it seriously, like I don't even give a shit. Oh, but I do. That Jew Wolfshein worries me. I haven't told Mailer that I put up the farm as bond. Godfried knows. I'll tell Norman tomorrow night when I meet him for dinner.

The initial rush of paranoia recedes and delivers me to the other side. There is my mother, cheering me from the spectator's stands as I win the Massachusetts State Wrestling Championship in the 167-pound weight division my junior year of high school. She came to every wrestling match, every football game. She convinced me that I could do whatever I put my mind to, and those other kids, the ones whose parents wouldn't let them play with me, they were the ones leading me astray. Dear mother Mary, she spoiled me abundantly. Her mother, the indomitable Ethel Lowell Burnham, was my one constant adult influence. But she was frail and bitter in her later years. She lost a breast after an automobile accident and buried two husbands.

I'm deep in random contemplation, not even watching TV, way out on the pot train of thought going places I would never visit in my straight head. This is what I love about weed, and why I think everyone should smoke it at least once—well, maybe not everyone. Who am I to say what other people should or should not do with their minds? For this is a substance that alters the way the mind works. Good herb will take you places and give you insights you might otherwise run from and never face. I think of an evening I was visiting Godfried at his farm in Maine. He had a few guests there for the weekend: Dr. Hunter S. Thompson and Jann Wenner of *Rolling Stone*, a friend of Godfried's from Boston who is in the music business and his wife. Someone said something about wanting to get high. It wasn't Hunter, he was already ripped on acid. I was asked if I had a joint. Godfried smiled and said, "Of course he has a joint. Rick always has a joint."

I warned them the weed was powerful. It was Mexican lime-green-and-gold, lightly-seeded pot from high in the Sierra Madre del Sur near Acapulco. Really heady herb, the kind that instantly lights up your brain. No one heeded my warning. The wife of the guy in the music business got too high and had an anxiety attack. She became hysterical and began accusing her husband of cheating on her. It was true; the guy broke down and admitted he was having an affair with his assistant. All three of them had been living with this lie. The marriage would not survive the weekend.

A loud rapping on the door startles me out of my reverie. *Cops? Agents? Hotel dicks?* Relax. . . . It's Doctor Kato in a trench coat, carrying an umbrella in one hand and a paper bag in the other. He is wearing shoes but no pants. "Here, take this. I'm being chased," he says and hands me the paper bag as two wild hookers round a corner of the hallway in hot pursuit. Kato fends the girls off with the umbrella like a lion tamer wielding a prod. He's parrying like a sword fighter. Naked under the raincoat, his limp pipe drooping, Kato shouts, "Back! Back . . . you she wolves!" Then he whips a baggie of cocaine from the pocket of his trench coat and dangles it before their eyes like bait.

"Is this what you're after?" he bellows and laughs. He has a great laugh, deep unrestrained belly chortle. The girls double-team him. One grabs the umbrella and tugs on it, distracting Kato while her partner snatches the bag of cocaine. Now it's their turn to run with Kato giving chase.

Back in the room, I open the paper bag. Wads of small bills held together with rubber bands. Some figures scribbled on a scrap of paper. Counting money settles my spirit—or at least it gives me something to do. There is a little over forty grand in the bag. According to the figures on the slip of paper, Kato is not quite ten grand away from cashing out. That sounds right to me. What isn't right is that I'm sitting on that bag of money. "Fucking Biff," I mutter to myself and climb into bed.

When the phone rings well before dawn I am startled awake. *Who the fuck*? Kato? Is he in jail? Biff? Who else knows I'm here?

"Mr. Richard, how are you? This is Nasif," says a deep-accented voice from half a world away.

"Ah, Nasif . . . I'm fine." Relief. Short-lived, as I remember Biff told me Nasif would be calling.

"Sorry to call so early."

"Is everything all right?"

"Everything is fine. My father sends his regards. He wants to know when we will see you."

"Soon," I tell him. "I'm working on it. I may have to come another way. You understand?"

"Of course. We will make all the arrangements." He pauses, then says, "Your friend is here."

As this sinks in, I sit up in the bed. "My friend? *What* friend?"

"Pierre . . ."

I think for a moment. "I don't know any Pierre." But, of course I do.

"He told me—"

"Wait a minute. Blond hair? Clean-shaven? Maybe thirty, thirty-five? Big jaw and a goofy smile?"

Nasif seems confused. "Maybe . . . I don't know."

"Where's he from?"

"I think from Miami."

Then I know. Pierre my ass. It's that fucking Wizard. Then it dawns on me, it wasn't Wolfshein and his men who stole my briefcase. No! While I sat in the restaurant waiting for him, the Wizard broke into my car—expertly, I should add. He stole my briefcase. He got Mohammed's numbers and split for Beirut. *That motherfucker!* But at least it wasn't the DEA. I'm relieved and enraged at once. "What's he want?" I ask, though I know the answer.

"Merchandise. He said you recommended him."

"No, not true. Don't do anything with this guy. You hear me, Nasif? Stall him. Tell your father I did not recommend him. He stole my briefcase. That's how he got your number."

"I don't understand."

"Never mind. Just listen. I'll be there as soon as I can make travel arrangements. Whatever you do, don't agree to any business with this . . . Pierre. He's not my friend—he's a thief."

This fucking Wizard! I should have known.

I'm too worked up to go back to sleep. Val drags in at around seven in the morning. She drops her suitcase, strips, showers, and hops into bed.

* * *

THE ORIGINAL GENERAL Marijuana, Mailer, looks fit and jovial as he presides over a table at Nicola's Restaurant on the Upper East Side. His sixth wife, a tall, gorgeous, redhead; one of Mailer's teenage daughters, a college freshman; light heavyweight boxing champion José Torres; and Biff—forlorn, chagrinned Biff: they are all seated at the table with Mailer, me, and Val. As Anthony Quinn finishes his meal and gets up to leave the restaurant, he stops by our table to pay his respects to Mailer.

"Are you kidding me?" Val whispers. "Fucking *Zorba the Greek*."

Mailer is in good form, having delivered the manuscript of his long-awaited Egyptian novel *Ancient Evenings* to his publisher this afternoon. I pass him an envelope with a fat bag of weed under the table and his blue eyes light up. He leans over to me. "Hey, Rick . . . my man. Thanks. What do I owe you?"

"Nothing. Cheers."

While the waiter takes our orders, I look up from the menu and notice a man enter the restaurant. He looks around and then sits at the bar. I recognize him immediately. It's the blue-eyed DEA agent I helped when he was stranded at the side of the road leading up to Barn-swallow's pad. Before I even have time to absorb this, Wolfshein walks in, looks directly at me, and then joins blue-eyes as the bar.

Shit. I just handed Mailer two ounces of weed. I'm stunned with fear and guilt. I drew my Heat to Mailer, and now he is about to get popped holding enough pot to get him locked up in this crazy town. It'll be all over the papers tomorrow: Famous novelist arrested for possession of marijuana. *Fuck*. And now I'm worried about how long have these guys been tailing me. Are they on to Sammy, Dr. Kato? Were they listening to my call from Nasif last night at the Plaza and so hip to the Lebanese trip? I'm tempted to take Val by the arm and bolt from the restaurant.

"Can I take your order, sir?" the waiter asks me.

"Oh, yeah. I'll have—just a second."

I nudge Val's leg with my knee and nod toward the agents, who aren't even trying to hide that they are watching our gathering.

"The salmon, please. And another martini," I tell the waiter. Might as well go down with a good buzz on.

Val nods, excuses herself. I was only trying to clue her in, but she goes over to the bar, elbows her way between Wolfshein and blue-eyes, and in a moment engages them in animated conversation.

She looks a little like a young Ava Gardner tonight—the high cheekbones and oval-shaped face, dark olive complexion, large brown sloe eyes, thin dimpled chin, and her long auburn hair wound up in a French twist. She's elegant, has a kind of affluent hippie style all her own. She's wearing a dress, her skin deeply tanned from the Hawaiian sun. I can't help admiring her even as I wonder what the hell she could be talking about to these dope cops.

Soon Wolfshein and blue-eyes are laughing, Val has charmed them. She takes some money from her purse and lays it on the bar. The agents drink up, Wolfshein glances over at the table, smiles, and then all three of them walk outside. Mailer and the others at the table look at me perplexed. Did Rick's date just ditch him? How bizarre! Does she know those guys? I am as baffled as they are.

In a moment she is back. She sits down, smiles and says, "They didn't really want to be here." Later I ask her how she got rid of them. "I lied," she tells me. "Told them it was Norman's birthday and they were spoiling everything. The one guy, the dude with the glasses—"

"That's Wolfshein. The guy's all over me."

"He knew I was lying. He said Norman's birthday is in January."

"That's right. Aquarius. He knows way too much."

"Anyway, then I said I'd tell them what was going on if they let me buy them a drink and we could step outside. Outside I told them, 'You wanna know what's going on? Nothing. Not a damn thing illegal. We're just having dinner like normal people. Now please, leave us alone,' I said, 'or I'll make a really ugly scene and you'll be sorry.'"

TWO NIGHTS LATER, Mailer's home in Brooklyn Heights is broken into. Nothing is missing, but the bag of pot I slipped him under the table at Nicola's was removed from his dresser drawer and placed in the middle of the bed in the master bedroom. Norman sees this as a message. He tells me this while we stand on his balcony and look out at the huge monoliths that make up the Lower Manhattan skyline.

"The Feds are all over me," I say. "Those guys at the restaurant the other night, they're DEA agents." And I explain about the bust in Maine, putting the farm up as security for my bail. "I may have to jump, Norman. Get lost until things settle down."

Earlier in the day I received a disquieting call from Hef, my lawyer in Boston. He suspects that Fearless Fred Barnswallow is, in Hef's words, "off the reservation." Realizing the evidence against him was overwhelming, Fred had said he wanted to flee the country. We arranged for my nephew, Carlos, who has worked with me since he was a teenager, and the Captain, a former Delta Force member and part of an elite black-ops group known as Army Support Intelligence Activity, or ASIA, to sequester Freddy until we could get him some new ID, and then carry him off to Brazil and parts unknown. The Captain begged me to let him disappear Fred.

"This guy is a waste of clothing," the Captain told me. "No way he's going to hold up."

But I wouldn't hear of it. Murder was not part of what I signed on for—or so I believed. They got as far as South Florida. Val, using some of her Brotherhood contacts, got Fred new ID. The Captain left him and my nephew in a hotel in Pompano Beach and returned to his base at Fort Hood, Texas. After a few days waiting around for the boat to take Fred first to the Bahamas, from where he would catch a flight and continue on to Rio, Fred told my nephew he was going out to buy a pack of cigarettes and never returned. Now the lawyers believe he defected to the government's camp.

"Well, that place is pretty much yours," Mailer says, speaking of the farm in Maine. Over the years I bought out Godfried and Mailer, though his name remained on the deed. "By the way, how's Biff doing?" he asks after a moment. "He seemed a little subdued the other night, though he did say you had something big for him."

As usual, Biff's been talking too much. "He acts like some of the things I ask him to do are beneath him," I say. "And then, he can't do the simple stuff, yet he wants more of the bigger action. Where's that coming from?"

"He's a man whose talents never measured up to his ambitions," Mailer says, and I think he could be talking about me. "Listen, Rick. If it's not working out with him, fuck it. Let him go. You don't owe him, or me, anything. I was only trying to help him out."

"I know. He needs the money."

I feel for Biff. It can't have been easy being so close to Mailer these many years, seeing him triumph while Biff wilted in the long shadow Mailer cast. I saw how Biff eyed Mailer's new wife hungrily the other night, as if he were wondering why she was with Mailer and not with him. Norman goes on to tell me about a convict he's been corresponding with as part of research for a book he's begun work on about Gary Gilmore, a killer who demanded to be executed in Utah. "I think he's going to be getting out soon," he says of his convict correspondent, a guy named Jack Abbott. "Maybe you can use him."

"Please, Norman. No more referrals," I say with a smile, but I'm serious.

Mailer's brilliance sometimes blinds his judgment. Biff could well be his Fred Barnswallow. As Mailer tells me more about Abbott and the vivid letters he's been writing about prison violence that have been collected into a book titled *In the Belly of the Beast,* I'm thinking how curious it is that we are often better at recognizing other people's short-sightedness than our own.

"My advice, stay away from this guy," I tell Mailer. "He's probably half full of shit."

"No, Rick. His letters are extraordinary. He's given me insight into how prison life shapes a man that I might never have had."

"Fine. That doesn't mean you need to get close to him. I run into guys like this all the time. He's not operating from the same set of values."

"You may be right," Mailer admits. "That's one of the things I like about our friendship, we don't have to agree. But I've always believed that art is worth a little risk. In fact, I would go so far as to say, the more risk, the better the art."

I don't argue. I live for risk, hoping someday it might mature into depth of character and throttle my overbearing ego and pride.

"Look for the risk," Mailer writes in *Ancient Evenings*. "We must obey it every time. There is no credit to be drawn from the virtue of one's past."

Or, I would add, from the iniquity of one's past.

WHEN I LEAVE Mailer's home and walk out onto Columbia Heights, I see them: two men sitting in a parked car watching the front of the brownstone. Something turns me from the street and draws me out to the promenade. I stand on the parapet above the desolate Brooklyn docks. A crescent moon and single bright star hang in the sky above Manhattan. The East River slides ponderously into the sea.

Almost as though conjured from my mood, Wolfshein sidles up beside me. "Rich . . ." he says. "Beautiful night."

"Agent Wolfshein. Fancy meeting you here."

"You kidding? This is home for me . . . maybe not Brooklyn Heights. More like Crown Heights. But when they told me, 'Go to New York. See what Rich is up to,' I thought, 'Great, I'll get to visit my mother.'"

"Like a good son. Have you seen her?"

"Not yet," he says and smiles. He's wearing a staid blue suit, no tie, and with his horn-rimmed glasses and curly, salt-and-pepper hair he looks more like an accountant or a harried mid-level corporate executive than a pistol-packing federal drug agent. "Your girl there, she's funny. What's her name?"

I shake my head. "Who?"

"Your girlfriend. Val. I think that's what you call her, though it's probably not her real name."

"I don't know who you're talking about."

"Yeah, okay. Whatever." Wolfshein nods and pushes his glasses up over the bridge of his nose—a practiced gesture. "Have you ever heard of CENTAC?" he asks.

"No. What's that?"

"Well, let me just say, you have stumbled into it. Or maybe stumbled is not the right word. Waltzed may be more like it."

I love the way this guy talks, and his moves, every gesture suited to his routine.

"You know, I never was much of a believer in this whole hippie mafia peace, love, and brotherhood nonsense," he goes on. "Some of the men you're involved with—" He mentions Uncle George's real name. "These guys are not playing by the same set of rules as your people. I tried to tell you that, didn't I? During our little ride together. We talked about that."

For a fleeting moment I think he must have somehow bugged my conversation with Mailer. It is almost as though he is giving me back the same advice I gave Norman about Abbott, his convict correspondent. This guy, Wolfshein, is too much, I'm thinking. It's as though he has moved body and soul into my consciousness.

When I don't answer, Wolfshein shrugs, turns, and looks up at the balcony hanging from the front of Mailer's flat. "You and your buddy there, Norman, you're either kidding yourselves or you're full of crap—maybe some combination of the two. You think this is a harmless game of spy versus spy you're playing. Material for a novel." He pauses, looks at me full on, squints. Shakes his head slowly from side to side.

"You are going down, Rich. Bet on it. It's just a matter of time before we—maybe not me but whoever—are going to take you down. Hard. *And* your pal Mailer. His career will be ruined. All because of you and the business you are in. Then it will only be a matter of how much time you both wind up doing in prison. *If* you're lucky, okay? There are worse things that could happen." He nods, nudges his glasses back up his nose. "I think you know what I'm talking about."

After a moment I ask, "What would you have me do?"

"Well, you could quit. Give it all up. But that won't protect you from what you're already into—the case in Maine and whatever else may come down as . . . inevitably, people will begin to roll over and cooperate." He pauses, considers for a moment. "You've got a price to pay here, Rich. Listen to me." He looks around conspiratorially. "Where do you think what's his name is right now?" he asks, and then he mentions Fearless Fred's real name.

I look at him and make no answer.

"Never mind. That's not important," Wolfshein continues. "You know how much value he is to us on a scale of one-to-ten?" He makes a zero sign with his thumb and forefinger. "Less than zero. Except if he can provide us with enough information, perhaps, and testimony, again, perhaps, to indict and ultimately convict you. So you go away. Ten, fifteen years, whatever. Maybe we arrest your wife and your girl-friend there—Valerie, as she calls herself these days. People in Canada. People on the West Coast. Texas. Guys like Capuana and Chagra. You get what I'm talking about, Rich? This is a big conspiracy, okay? You know that. You helped put it together. They have a name for this. Call it RICO. Racketeering. Organized crime. Whatever. We're talking serious time. And Norman . . ." He breaks off, nods. "I think you know what I'm talkin' about."

Wolfshein holds up the zero with one hand and puts a finger from his other hand beside it. "Mailer on that scale is a ten," he says. "You want to help your friend so he can continue writing books and stay out of prison? You want to survive in this arena? *Learn to play the game.* There's a whole other level, a whole other dimension here is what I'm talking about." He pauses. "You know your friend there in Boston?"

"What friend?"

"Don't play stupid with me, please. We're off the record here, Rich. I'm talking to you as—what? An advisor?" He laughs. "As your *consigliore?* Trying to help you out before it's too late. Listen to me. I'm saying, the blond guy. Saved your ass, didn't he? You know who I mean."

"Even if I do, I don't know what you're talking about."

"I think you do. You're a smart guy. Stubborn . . . but smart. I want you to think about this, Rich. Give it some serious thought. The way things stand now, the Maine case could go away. No one would be the wiser. Your lawyers will get it thrown out and even they'll be patting themselves on the back."

Again he turns and glances up at Mailer's. "You're at a very interesting point in your career. It's like a fork in the road. It's up to you, Rich, which way you go. And I don't need to tell you, there are . . . a number of people whose futures are riding on the choice you make." He holds up a hand. "Don't decide anything now. I want you to think about this. You have time. Not much, but some. Think about it, and if you want to talk some more . . ." He hands me a business card. "That number." He points to a handwritten number. "That's my pager. Hit me on that number and I'll get right back to you." The knowing smile, a look of bemused yet keen understanding, like he's on the verge of explaining some deep, new concept. "CENTAC," he says. "Remember that word." He looks around, furtively this time, like a crook. "And don't say I didn't warn you. Because you're playing with the big boys now, Rich."

6

DON'T MESS WITH TEXAS

WHEN I ARRIVE at the airport in Austin, Herbert, the real estate agent who sold me the ranch in the Texas Hill Country town of San Saba, meets me at the arrivals terminal. I call him Herbert Humbert after the character in *Lolita* because he reminds me of a pedophile. Or maybe a flasher. Some guy who would pull out his johnson and wag it at school-girls. Herbert Humbert has sold me three ranches, all for cash, usually delivered in briefcases. He also sold me a florist shop in Austin—King's Florist: The Poinsettia King. I've been there twice, maybe three times. It's essentially a front to launder money.

He's originally from Massachusetts, old Herb, but he has taken to wearing cowboy boots and a cowboy hat since relocating to Texas. He's a slight, unhealthy-looking guy who chain-smokes Pall Malls, drives a big black Cadillac, and dresses in ill-fitting Western suits. Herb does business with me as Paul Quinlan, though I'm sure he suspects that is not my real name. I sense it in the way he says Paul and looks askance as if to say, "C'mon, who are we kidding here?" He's complicit up to his droopy earlobes in my flagrant washing of money and drug-fueled hubris. The first place he sold me was a fifteen hundred-acre spread—a postage stamp by Texas standards—in a Hill Country town called Goldthwaite, a lovely, little town. The land out there is spectacular with hills and ponds, a pecan orchard, and frontage on the Colorado

River. The house, though, was a wreck—no plumbing, no electricity. My ground crew and I slept in the Global Evangelism Television motor home or on bunks in the trashed ranch house like old-time desperados. Early one day, as I squatted for my morning constitutional behind a dilapidated old shed, I looked down and saw a fat diamondback rattler basking in the sun within bun-biting range.

While we waited for our trip to come in, I would take Karamazov for long walks around the property, pacing the boundary, living out my Jimmy Dean *Giant* fantasy. I sat in the early-morning light and meditated. We stocked the place with a few horses and some cattle for appearance's sake. A rattlesnake bit one of the horses, a paint named Zapata I bought from the Mexicans who worked for me. The horse's neck swelled up as though it had a giant goiter, and he staggered around like a drunk, but he recovered. One night, Jimmy D and I made a run into Brownsville to have a few drinks at a cowboy bar and use the pay phones. We were riding in an old pickup truck with a broken fuel gauge and ran out of gas on the way back to the ranch. I walked a half-mile down the farm road to the nearest house and rang the bell. It was about ten thirty in the evening. The door flew open and a totally nude young blond Texas honey stood there with her arms outstretched and exclaimed, "*Tadah!*" Once she realized I wasn't whom she was expecting, she blushed, went and grabbed a robe and apologized. "Not at all," I said. "I love being greeted that way."

Ah, yes—Texas. I couldn't imagine that happening back in Wellesley.

We landed loads in the field alongside the Colorado and the pecan grove using a Maule, a single-engine tail dragger aircraft. Four, five hundred pounds of weed per trip, specialty strains of cannabis sativa coming out of Guerrero, Oaxaca, and Michoacán: sinsemilla, *pelo rojo*, Acapulco Gold, foot-long *colas* we packaged in boxes like long-stem roses. I went to Mexico and purchased the weed, one of the pilots I work with flew down and picked up the load, JD and Father Flaherty transported it back east to market in the Global Evangelism Television machine, and Lord Toranaga sold it.

After half a dozen or so trips using the place in Goldthwaite, Herb sold it for me and we bought a bigger ranch with a livable home and good barns farther south, near San Antonio, outside a town called Blanco. The business ramped up. We began working the Mexican border with the Gulf Cartel, bringing in tractor trailers of commercial weed. A couple of different pilots would fly in the smaller loads of connoisseur product. One of the pilots, the guy I call Jonathan Livingston Seagull, is married to Avril, my wife Anaïs's younger sister. It was on a bet with the Seagull that I got back into the outlaw life full time after a halfhearted attempt to quit smuggling dope and go straight. The Mexican trip is where it all began back in the sixties, and it is still a steady source of income supporting my ludicrous grandiose lifestyle and out-of-control empire-building while Toranaga and I plot the Lebanese hashish mega-smuggle.

Lately Herb has been trying to interest me in a tract of commercial land along the northwest corridor near the corporate headquarters of Texas Instruments. We are on the way to dinner at one of his favorite joints, a Steak and Ale on Research Boulevard, the main drag out of Austin toward Lampasas and San Saba. When we drive past the property he wants me to buy and develop as a shopping mall, he slows his Caddy and nods. "There it is," he says. Before we get to the restaurant, Herb pulls in at an establishment known as The Safe Place where I visit my safe deposit box, clean it out, and extract a hundred grand for Herb.

"You can't go wrong on this, Paul," he tells me at dinner as he lights up another Pall Mall. "Even if you just hold it for a year or two and sell."

"Will you put that fucking thing out, please? At least until I finish my meal."

"Oh, yes, of course." He squashes the cigarette and gives me a flustered look. "Sorry." He knows I hate cigarette smoke, particularly when I'm trying to eat.

I'm sure the commercial tract is a good investment. Texas is booming, in particular Austin's northwest corridor. But with my looming legal entanglements, the last thing I need is to be buying more property. The hundred Gs I just gave him settles my bill on the florist shop. I'm thinking of liquidating everything and making myself scarce until . . . whatever. I am living absolutely in the moment, playing the hand, upping the stakes—something I can't explain to Herb. Still, my need to keep Herbert close and with his eye on the next big payday won't allow me to say no. "We need to sell the place in Blanco before we talk about buying anything else," I tell him.

"That shouldn't be a problem," he says and digs into his chicken-fried steak.

"I want to concentrate on the florist shop and the ranch in San Saba."

He nods, quick, jerky up-and-down moves with his narrow, balding head. "That's smart."

"I'm thinking of building some greenhouses out at the ranch and growing the plants and flowers we sell at the shop. Become my own supplier."

"I like that. That's good," Herb agrees.

Of course, I'm thinking of growing pot out there, if they ever legalize it. And jojoba. "You know about jojoba, Herb?"

"No, what is it?"

"Good stuff. The oil produced from the seed. And aloe vera. The future is in these natural products. Cosmetics. Oils and healing salves. Organic farming. That's my dream for the place in San Saba. Keep the whole horse-breeding business going. Raise some cattle. And use the shit to fertilize the fields. Develop that place into an organic farming enterprise." I'm waxing evangelical now. "Open organic produce stores right here in Austin. And be our own supplier."

"That sounds like a good plan, Paul."

"We'll even get you off those cancer sticks. And the chicken-fried steak," I chide him. "You know what that chicken-fried steak and all those cheeseburgers you eat are doing to you, Herb?"

He smiles, lowers his eyes, and looks away. "You've told me."

"Not only are you clogging your arteries—that's bad enough. But you're also lining the walls of your colon with dead animal fat. You know where that leads?" I take some perverse delight in lecturing this guy. "A clogged colon, Herb. And that leads to colon cancer. That's what they call literally coming to a bad end."

He chuckles, squirms in his seat as though feeling his colon backing up. He knows I enjoy teasing him, and that I'm trying to get him off the subject of buying more property. But Herb's tenacious, he says, "You could build your greenhouses right here on Research Boulevard. Be that much closer to the flower shop. These folks are ready to negotiate. I could make them an offer."

"Let me think about it."

We are having coffee and after-dinner drinks when Jonathan Livingston Seagull strolls in with his lopsided, forward-leaning gait. He too has taken to wearing cowboy boots and a black Stetson hat with a little gold marijuana leaf pinned to it. Before I left New York, I met with the Seagull and gave him the key to a stash house I'd rented in Dripping Springs midway between Austin and the ranch in Blanco. He had directions to the place and knew what to do once he got there: chill, look around, and find a suitable landing strip. We just bought a new, turbo-charged Aero Commander to haul 1,200 pounds of choice sinsemilla buds packed in big burlap bales out of Southern Mexico before the *federales* seize it.

"What should I tell these folks?" Herb asks as he lights another cigarette. We're standing in the parking lot outside the restaurant. I summon the will to say no.

"I can't do it, Herb. Not now. We need to put the place in Blanco on the market. Let me stay focused on what I've got going on and not get spread too thin."

"Gotcha," he says. "Okay, Paul. Thanks for the dinner."

"Fuckin' guy," I say as Herb walks off and gets in his Caddy. "He doesn't quit."

I look around the parking lot, nearly empty now going on eleven. The Seagull and I walk to the new Cadillac Eldorado we just bought.

"You want me to drive?" he asks.

"Yeah, you better. My head is spinning."

I fire up a joint, take a couple of hits, and roach it before getting in the car. Deep sigh of relief as I ease into the leather bucket seat. I seem to have shaken my Heat, left it back East. As I was preparing to leave New York, I went to elaborate lengths to make sure I wasn't followed. Playing out my *French Connection* fantasy, I took the subway to Port Authority, wandered around in the crowd, and then caught the bus to Newark where I flew out using a clean credit card. I want to believe that Wolfshein isn't aware of the Texas component to the operation and the Paul Quinlan identity—at least not yet, although he seems to know about everything else. I have a picture of the agent in my head, he's got that distracted Columbo look on his face as he wanders around in circles in his office muttering to himself like Elmer Fudd hunting for Bugs Bunny: *Which way did he go? Which way did he go?*

Hubris rears its ugly head. Why should I give a fuck? This is Texas, land of the outlaw. *Slap my mind.* The Heat has got not-so-Fearless Fred Barnswallow sequestered in their interrogation cage. Barnswallow may not know details, but he is aware we have something going on in Texas. I search my depleted memory banks to recall if I ever used the Quinlan ID in his presence. No . . . of course, he knows Val and her partner, Judy, but not their real names or where they currently live. Maria and the Colombians. *Shit,* I've got to call her and let her know Fred most likely flipped. The Captain, I'm sure, gave Fred no information. Maybe I should have let him terminate Freddy when we had the chance. If you are going to play this game, better play it all the way. It's like Wolfshein said, all that hippie-dippy peace, love, and brotherhood crap won't fly when you mix it up with real crooks and cops.

Soon a new concern occupies my mind: I am spending money at an alarming rate. If I don't get this load out of Guerrero and back to New York to market soon, I could come up short on the Lebanese trip, which I estimate will require somewhere in the neighborhood of half a million to finance. Toranaga would take up the slack, but I don't want to have to lean on him. Recently, I purchased a fifty-eight-foot power yacht I've never even seen that is berthed at a marina in Galveston. I tell myself it's an investment that we'll use to smuggle pot by sea from Jamaica and the east coast of Mexico into the Texas Gulf Coast. And the new Aero Commander cost a bundle, I don't even know how much; the florist shop; the money I'm spending out at the new ranch building an airstrip, an Olympic-size swimming pool, and more barns; horses, I bought a stud named Texas Gold for fifty grand; this car; a tractor . . . The list of properties, new toys, and projects goes on and on. To say nothing of the thousands I drop in restaurants and bars and hotels on a daily basis.

It's madness, I know, but I don't seem to be able to stop. The truth is, I am addicted to spending money. This compulsion to buy things must come from some deep-seated childhood insecurity, trauma caused by hearing my parents' fights over money—even though, by most standards, we were well off. And from growing up in the land of TV commercials, billboards, magazine ads, radio jingles drumming the notion that happiness in America means material things: cars, homes, clothes, jewelry, toys, and more crap we don't need. The sense I got as a child was that my father was a failure because there was never enough money to keep up with the neighbors and satisfy my mother's desires. We lived above our means. At a time when most American moms stayed at home with the kids, Mary went to work.

My grandmother, Ba Ba, moved into the third-floor apartment in the rambling Colonial house in the Cliff Estates and became my guardian. She would be at home, my only authoritarian presence, when I came in from school. I loved her but I feared her and resented her strict discipline. Even now, thinking of her, I miss her and wonder if I might have turned out differently if I had obeyed her. Before we moved to the big house in Wellesley, we lived in a housing development in neighboring Natick. I remember once when I couldn't have been much more than seven or eight, I was out front trying to cut the grass, struggling to push a hand mower. A couple of the local housewives passed by taking their babies for a stroll. When they saw me wrestling with the lawn mower, they laughed and said that was something my father should be doing. Wasn't I a little young to be trying to mow the lawn by myself? No one had told me to do it. I just thought I'd give it a try to impress my dad. Their laughter and comments hurt. I gave up and went inside to sulk. The old man was probably off playing a round of golf. A pattern was established: me trying to do what I thought the man of the house was supposed to do, be tough and strong. Do the man's work and provide and provide and over-provide, which amounts to spoiling. In Texas when we go shopping, we rent a U-Haul truck to bring all the stuff back to the ranch.

The road out of Austin is straight and deserted this time of night. Jonathan Livingston Seagull is uncommonly quiet. Something is on his mind. His boot is heavy on the pedal. The speedometer climbs past eighty, ninety, ninety-five. Small towns shuttered for the night flash past. The radio is on, low rock music on the Austin stations and country once we get out toward Lampasas. This is the land of Willie and Waylon. The dashboard glows red and green. Minimal amount of contraband in the car. Ten, twelve grand in cash. The profile solid once the Seagull removes his cowboy hat. As the rush subsides and my mind comes back from chasing down the THC runaway trains of thought, I'm pleasantly high and able to relax for the first time in weeks.

Short-lived. There is definitely something troubling the Seagull. It's not like him to be so still and meditative. "How'd you make out?" I ask him.

He loses it, suddenly chokes up, teary-eyed. The car swerves to avoid hitting a whitetail deer bounding across the road. "Whoa!" I shout. "Slow down! What the fuck's the matter with you?"

He's shaking his head. Slobbering. "I don't know . . . I don't know what to do."

Not another one. After Biff's meltdown, I don't know what to expect. I've never seen Jonathan show emotion like this before. He's one of those apparently supremely confident men who doesn't walk, he strides. Chest puffed out to diminish the girth of his waistline, arms swinging at his side, leaning into the next challenge. Always in control—or so he would have the world believe. Lives for the flash. He's maybe five or six years older than me, paunchy, with thick, dark hair and sharp, Semitic features. His beaklike nose in part contributed to the nickname. I'm sure it rankles that he's been reduced to working for me even if he's making more tax-free money than he ever did with a straight job.

"What's wrong?" I ask.

"It's all so fucked up."

"What?" My first thought is that he's been busted and ratted me out. A massive attack of fear and paranoia grips me. The Feds know everything. They got to Jonathan and he gave me up. "What the fuck is wrong? Tell me."

"That key you gave me, to the stash house . . ."

"Slow down. You're all over the road. You want me to drive?"

"Somehow . . . I followed your directions, but I got messed up and ended up at another house." He begins a story that at first I find hard to believe. "When I put the key in the lock, the door opened. Maybe it was unlocked, I don't know. Anyway . . . I went in. I figured it had to be the right place even though there were kid's toys around, and . . . things . . . stuff I couldn't . . . I didn't understand why it would be in a house you rented. I figured maybe you were doing it for show, so the neighbors wouldn't be suspicious. Anyway, I sat down and turned on the TV. Ate some leftovers in the fridge—which also seemed weird, meat, ribs, not the kind of food you usually eat. I thought maybe JD or Father Flaherty had been staying there. I was asleep on the sofa when the real owner came home from work."

I almost laugh. This is beginning to sound like something out of "Little Red Riding Hood": Who's been eating my food? Who's that sleeping on my couch?

"You're kidding."

"No, honest. I know—it's crazy. It gets . . . crazier. The owner, she's . . . ah . . ." He mumbles something about tits. ". . . great tits. Well, I . . ."

"Come on, out with it."

I'm enjoying the story until he blurts out, "I moved in with her."

"Hold it. Run that by me again."

"I moved in. I'm living with her."

"Get the fuck out of here!"

"She's divorced. Got two little kids. Wait'll you see her. She looks like a *Playboy* centerfold. Fucking incredible. A body like . . . you can't imagine. *Great tits*," he repeats as if that will somehow make it okay.

The woman comes home from work, she finds the Seagull perched on her sofa sound asleep, having chowed down on the leftovers in her fridge. Does she throw him out? Call the cops? No, once they both get over the initial shock, she invites him to stay for dinner. After putting the kids to bed, they end up fucking on the living room floor. And the next day, instead of moving into the stash house, he moves in with her.

This has got to be Texas.

All that would be fine if he weren't married. And to my wife's sister. After I hear the whole story, two thoughts immediately present themselves: Does his wife, Avril, know? And: Does the divorcée he is infatuated with know what business we are in?

"I found an airstrip," he tells me as if to mollify my growing apprehension.

"Does Avril know?"

The mention of his wife's name brings on more grief. But he prevaricates. "She took me to dinner at her golf club. And there I am eating, meeting her friends. I look out the window at this paved, forty-five-hundred-foot strip."

"Does *your wife* know?"

He starts to blather again. I know, he doesn't need to answer. He's a compulsive confessor. This would be bad enough even without the fact that Avril and my wife, Anaïs, own two homes and a business together in Toronto. They have been laundering millions of dollars in Canadian money and both have intimate knowledge of years of illegal activity. Anaïs and I split up when I proved incapable of giving up the outlaw life. We never had kids, which was a big part of our disconnect. She refused to get pregnant as long as I was still in the game. The love-making became a kind of unspoken negotiation: *You want to get righteously fucked, throw out the condoms and the diaphragm, you want to feel my cunt like a silken glove clutching your cock and massaging it all the way up the uterus into the seat of creation? You want little Rickys and little Rickettes bouncing on your knee? Ain't gonna happen, son, not in the visiting room at some godforsaken prison.*

Things came to a head after I nearly got busted and lost a load of pot in a disastrous smuggle. We were living on Cape Cod. I had successfully off-loaded three thousand pounds of Jamaican ganja from a private yacht and put it on the road in a rented box truck. The driver and his friend had detailed instructions and a hand-drawn map showing them the exact route to take from the off-load site to the stash house. Along the way they had a run-in with a local cop on patrol. It was never made clear to me exactly what happened. The driver ran a stop sign, panicked, and took off. They made a couple of wrong turns with the cop's cruiser in pursuit, lights flashing, siren wailing, the truck speeding up a street the driver had been told specifically *not* to use for the good reason that there is an arched stone underpass along that road, an old-time granite bridge that was a good six to ten inches too low for the truck to pass beneath. The roof of the truck hit the granite arch of the bridge and peeled back like the lid on a tin of sardines. Bales of pot ripped open and spewed buds all over the road. The truck hit with such force the guy riding shotgun was knocked unconscious when his head struck the windshield. The truck wrenched to a stop in the mouth of the bridge so abruptly the cop nearly crashed into the rear. His cruiser skidded to a stop as buds of ganja rained down on him from the hole ripped in the top of the box like ticker tape, blossoms of evidentiary manna from the great arbiter in the sky.

Lose your cool, lose your load. Leave your mind behind. Probable cause? *Why, yes, Your Honor. Contraband, vegetable matter suspected Schedule One controlled substance, i.e. marijuana, exploded from the rear of the truck when it hit the bridge. I immediately radioed for backup and proceeded to arrest the individual lying unconscious in the cab of the vehicle.*

The driver fled. He darted out the other side of the bridge, ran all the way to the stash house where I was waiting with my friend, the cousin of my childhood buddy from back in Pink Rats days, who had sold the first kilos I smuggled as a college kid. Trouble was, in his haste to beat feet, the driver left the map to the stash house, and the phone number with the notation, "Rick," in the truck. Everyone split. When the cops showed up, the stash house was empty. The guy who got caught in the crashed truck held his mud. We paid for an attorney, my friend Hef, who negotiated a plea down to two years; the guy was in a halfway house in six months. I lost most of my money and picked up some Heat. Anaïs insisted I quit the business. It became her mantra: "It's me or smuggling dope." We bought a three-family home in Provincetown, way out on the tip of Cape Cod. She was ready to settle down, get legally married and have a family. I could make a decent living as a carpenter, she reasoned, maybe start our own small construction company, and we would have income from renting the two apartments, save some dough and buy another place, fix it up, flip it. It sounded like a plan.

We were happy, broke but happy. I was borrowing money to finish work on the house. The lure of a fast score in a scam was never far from my mind. Glimmers of opportunity came my way, but I passed. I had a promise to keep. Then Jonathan and Avril came to visit one weekend. He kept riding me about being broke, paying for our dinner, flashing hundred dollar bills, offering to loan me money. I bet him that I could make more money in one month than he made in a year. I won the bet but broke my promise and lost my wife.

The Seagull and Avril have a young son and a supposedly viable marriage. If she's pissed off at him for taking up with the divorcée, we have problems that impact on more than just their relationship. Anaïs could go either way. She's loyal to her sister and says she is over me. Ours is essentially a business relationship now, which is odd given that she lobbied so hard to get me to quit. Last I heard she was seeing some straight guy. But the sisters have grown accustomed to the cash flow. They invested their money wisely. If it comes down to a matter of survival, the fact that Jonathan and I are both fucking other women will weigh heavily against us.

"Did you tell this woman why you were so happy to see they have an airstrip at her club?"

"No . . . of course I didn't." A lie, I'm sure. He goes on, "Just that, well, I—we—have a plane."

"We?"

"I mean me . . . my company. The plane is there now."

"The plane is at this woman's club?"

"Yes."

"What were you thinking?"

He's excited now, over the tears. "It's perfect! They think I'm this big land developer down here looking for deals."

"They? She's divorced, she has two young kids. You don't know shit about her husband. He could be a cop for all you know. And you're married and have a kid, and your wife knows a lot about what we do. How is this going to work?"

"Wait'll you see this place—it's just what we need," the Seagull says. "And her, you'll understand."

It's no use; there is no turning back. At a certain point these smuggles have a momentum all their own. Jonathan goes on to tell me he removed the rear seats from the plane. JD and Father Flaherty gathered a whole truck full of new appliances, electronics, a motor scooter, food and clothes, and cases of bottled water and soda to deliver to the Indians who live in the Mexican mountain village where the load is stored. The pot, all tight lime-green-and-gold seedless buds grown high in the mountains of Guerrero, is harvested, cured, and ready to go. The longer it sits in some adobe hut in Mexico, the more it costs, and the more we run the risk of losing it.

IT'S A BRIGHT moonlit night when Jonathan turns off the ranch road outside the county seat of San Saba, known locally as the birthplace of Tommy Lee Jones. I get out and swing open the gate. There is an engraved sign in the stone wall at the entrance to the driveway that reads *Tierra Alta*—High Country. The car rumbles across a cattle guard. I close the gate, get back in and we ride up the winding, mile-long limestone and caliche drive that mounts to the top of a gentle butte where the ranch house and barns sit above the surrounding landscape. When Herbert brought me out to show me Tierra Alta—6,000 acres bordering a real Texas-size spread of 40,000 acres owned by Clint Murchison, who also owns the Dallas Cowboys—I immediately fell in love with the place. My plan was to keep the ranch in Blanco for the smuggling business, move most of the horses and cattle and dogs and possessions here to Tierra Alta, and begin building the legal business.

Tonight the moon is so bright the limestone driveway glows like white gold. We drive past the airstrip, still under construction, past the acreage we are clearing to plant jojoba and aloe vera to realize my dream of legitimate respectability as a gentleman rancher and organic farmer. There is, of course, the matter of the case in Maine with Freddy spilling his guts, Wolfshein circling like a hungry wolf ready to lap up the entrails. Perhaps I can make a deal. He seemed to imply as much.

Fuck that. I'm an outlaw not a rat.

The perspective from the house, being high on the butte with a view of any encroaching armies of agents, appeals to my embattled sensibilities. I'm gonna fight this thing, I vow, fight it to the end. This is Texas, land of the Alamo. *Never say die.*

Jonathan pulls up in front of the house but doesn't shut off the engine.

"You coming in?" I ask him.

He shakes his head.

"Where're you going?"

"The house . . . in Dripping Springs—" he tries but I cut him off.

"Yeah, right—her house. Man, it's past midnight. That's a three-hour drive."

"Do you mind if I take the car?"

"What am I going to say—no? You're fucking crazy."

"I know," he says.

"That must be some good pussy, brother," I say and grab my bag. "You know what you've got to do. Weather permitting, day after tomorrow—we go. Be ready."

"I was born ready," he says, his bravado returning.

The dogs in the kennels out behind the house bark at my arrival. That's another enterprise I've embarked upon, breeding German shepherds. Jongo, the big male shepherd who lives in the house, is quiet, crouched inside, ready to rip my throat out if I am an intruder. When he knows it's me, he comes up and rubs his body against my legs, then lies down so I can scratch his chest. In the kitchen, I pour a glass of Patrón Silver on ice with a slice of lime and walk out back to sit by the pool and smoke my last doobie of the day.

I'm alone here tonight. The ranch foreman, Chet, who takes care of the animals, and his wife, Sherry, who pays the bills and keeps the books, live in town. I wish Val were waiting for me naked in the king-size bed, ready to fuck me to sleep instead of out on the road taking care of business. I worry about her when she's not with me—the girl likes to party. The moonlight is like pale, silvery daylight. From the patio behind the house I can see for miles in any direction—a big-sky view uncluttered by signs of modern civilization. Pyramid-shaped buttes glisten in the distance giving the sense one is living in ancient Mexico at the time of the Mayas and Quetzalcoatl or in Egypt in the age of the pharaohs. Not now, in the era of Reagan and the neon arches, DEA and CENTAC, whatever that is. It's curious how content I feel when I fully arrive in this part of our vast country. I'm here body and soul. It may be the one place I come to rest where I am not immediately ready to move on, not thinking about where I will go next, happy to be in this infinite moment. I could die here tonight, and they could take me out by the well and bury me behind the kennels where I could hear the dogs bark and feel the cool evening breeze, and my spirit would be at peace, no longer caught in the material world, trapped in this restless body.

My parents spent the year before I was born, just after World War II, in the East Texas town of Marshall. Being conceived in Texas explains why I feel more at home here than in Puritan New England. And it could also have something to do with the Mexican border and long coastline. As a kid growing up steeped in the TV lore of the Wild West, land of legendary renegades and rebels, men like Billy the Kid, Jesse James, Butch Cassidy, Wyatt Earp—who died on my birthday, January 13—I couldn't wait to get out of Wellesley. The first time I passed through the Lone Star State was after my freshman year at Arizona State University. I was on my way back East, hitchhiking across the country. I was a wrestler in high school, and Arizona State's Sun Devils had a highly competitive collegiate wrestling program. ASU offered me a wrestling scholarship. And there is where I strayed over the line.

That year, 1965, I shared a little bungalow off campus in Tempe with a pot-smoking radical leftie member of SDS, a graduate student I met while working out in the gym. When wrestling season ended, on weekends and over holidays, my roommate and I started going on excursions in his International pickup truck. At first we stayed in country, hiking and camping in the Grand Canyon and Saguaro National Park, hunting rabbits, getting high by the campfire at night. Later, after we had seen a fair share of Arizona wilderness, we took longer trips south of the border, to Ensenada, then down the Baja Peninsula and up into the mountains around the Sea of Cortez. As we headed back to Arizona after a week-long visit to Mexico over spring vacation, we got sidetracked drinking beers and shots of tequila in a cantina in the border town of Nogales.

"I'm not going anywhere with one of these girls unless she looks like Marilyn Monroe and only wants ten bucks," my roommate said, eyeing the flock of plump, young whores sitting around like wallflowers at a high school prom. Ten minutes later he disappeared with a chubby *puta* who looked nothing like Marilyn.

"You want a girl?" the bartender asked me.

"I want *mota*," I said. "Marijuana."

He called over his nine-year-old son, told him to hook me up. The kid brought me around the corner, down an alley to a place where they fixed flat tires. In a rear room a short, rumpled-looking guy named Pepe, who reminded me of a Mexican version of Humphrey Bogart, showed me a kilo brick of pressed commercial weed wrapped in brown paper. "I only want a couple of joints," I said.

Pepe shook his head. "I only sell kilos."

Out of curiosity I asked, "How much?"

He shrugged, wiped his greasy hands on his coveralls. "For you, one hundred dollars per kilo."

A hundred bucks a kilo. I had $300 on me. I did the math in my head. Commercial Mexican weed (the only kind of pot available in the mid-sixties) sold for $20 an ounce in Boston. Sixteen ounces in a pound, 2.2 pounds in a kilo. That's forty ounces per kilo times three. One hundred and twenty ounces at $20 each. I could gross over two grand on a $300 investment. On an entrepreneurial impulse, I bought the three kilos with no idea what I would do with them. Almost as if I were being directed by some external force—that which I have come to think of as the gods of cannabis—I asked to borrow a screwdriver from Pepe. I removed the panel from the passenger's side door of my roommate's truck and stashed the bricks.

In those days the border was as porous as skin. I figured if my roommate didn't know the weed was there, he wouldn't get nervous when we crossed back into the States. Turned out he was too wasted to drive. I was tense, my mouth dry, hands sweaty on the steering wheel right up until the moment the Customs guy at the US border crossing was beside the truck, asking how long we'd been in Mexico. I'd heard stories of pot prisoners serving life sentences for possession of a joint. I'm thinking they could execute me for three kilos. "Couple of days," I said. He looked over at my roommate, who was passed out, leaning against the door holding the hidden weed.

A clear, out-of-body calm took hold. It reminded me of how nervous I got before a wrestling match, then, as soon as I shook my opponent's hand and the match began, the fear was gone.

"Where're you headed?"

"Tempe . . . back to college."

"Have fun."

I wasn't sure if it was a question or an order. "Yeah, always," I said.

He nodded, waved us on, and I drove away.

What a rush!

America was wide open back then, still a gloriously free country. There were no security checkpoints and X-ray machines at the airports, no dope-sniffing dogs, no armed soldiers. Back in the bungalow, I packed the three kilos in my luggage and flew home to Boston. Deano, one of my childhood pals and a former underboss in the Pink Rats gang, had a cousin who sold ounces and helped me move most of the weed. I made $1,500 on that trip and was hooked.

Curious, I'm thinking, as I sit out by the pool and breathe in the Texas night, in a way I have the old man to blame for my becoming an outlaw. Little as I knew Emery as a kid growing up, I'm always impressed to see how much influence he had over me. He was a fine athlete, a graceful man skilled in the strokes of sports with balls. Tennis was his game until some malady of the lungs sent him to a dude ranch in the dry, hot air of Arizona. Those infrequent times he talked about

Arizona and the year he spent there, it was with a kind of nostalgia and reverence that stuck in my mind, for my father was not a man given to expressing sentiment. If the old man liked the Southwest, I figured I had to check it out. So when the Sun Devils beckoned, I answered the call.

Pot changed my life. After those first few hits in my '40 Ford Coupe out in the beer-drinking fields behind Babson Institute, and over the course of one academic year at Arizona State, I went from a crew-cut jock who believed his highest service to his country would be to join the Green Berets and kill Viet Cong to a long-haired, dope-smuggling, card-carrying member of Students for a Democratic Society. I quit ROTC in protest and became an early opponent of the war in Southeast Asia. I yearned for a cause, something to give meaning to my life. I was already disillusioned. Nothing ever quite brought me back from November 1963. I remember sitting in my girlfriend's home watching TV for hours on end after the first Kennedy assassination. Then Lee Harvey Oswald, the man who allegedly murdered our president, proclaimed for all to hear that he was just a patsy. We saw Jack Ruby live on TV as he walked into the basement of the Dallas police station surrounded by a gang of cops and shot Oswald dead. How could that happen? I sensed even then that we weren't seeing events in America as they really are, that there is no real law and order. There is just power and privilege controlled by a shadow government. The dream of America was forever corrupted. Then Bobby Kennedy got hit in Los Angeles by the Manchurian candidate, Sirhan Sirhan, who probably didn't fire the kill shot. And they murdered Martin Luther King in Memphis and hung it on some escaped con who didn't have the means or the motive. I began to see our government, or at least some aspects of what we think of as our government, as another criminal conspiracy. A gang, and treacherous in that many of these guys carry badges as well as guns. They wear the white hats, and they control the accepted history. They own TV.

In my reasoning, the marijuana underground stood in opposition to all that. Pot was the truth plant. Smoke it and the bullshit detectors were activated. *Hell no, we won't go. Question authority.* Forget the News, here's what's really going down. I would leave for Canada or go to jail before I would go to Vietnam and kill people who never called Muhammad Ali nigger. Not that I was afraid. I craved danger, I was ready and willing to go into battle. I just didn't want to go to war with a phantom enemy.

And now Bernie Wolfshein of the Drug Enforcement Administration, my enemy in the so-called War on Plants, has added a new equation to the calculus in my brain, tangled up in shades of gray: there are no black-and-white answers anymore. If I hear him right, he's saying at a certain level crooks morph into cops and vice versa. And it is okay. It is the American way.

Stars wheel overhead. The evening breeze picks up across the West Texas plains, and I am blown away. I take a deep hit and roach the joint, gaze up into the dizzying reaches of the cosmos. These wide-open skies will do it to me every time, make me feel so insignificant in the overall scheme of creation. None of this really matters. It is not real. Material life as I know it is all symbol, pointing to something other. The universe is so vast, so beyond my ken, stranger than I can think: How can I ever know my true purpose? Only if I follow my path wherever it leads me.

By the time classes finished at the end of my freshman year at ASU, I had done two more successful smuggles from Mexico, never more than three kilos at a time, and amassed a small bankroll, a little over five grand, which was a lot of money for a nineteen-year-old in 1965. I decided to drop out of college and embark upon the hippie highway in search of cannabis and satori. I could have bought a plane ticket home, but I yearned for the adventure of the open road. I had just finished reading Kerouac's *On the Road* and George Orwell's *Down and Out in Paris and London*. I began my journey hitching from Tempe to Wellesley with the idea that once I arrived there I would just keep going.

It took me three days to cross Texas. The road I followed dipped down through this part of the Hill Country, a few miles from where I am right now. I recall a warm night in May spent sleeping by the side of the road, a night not unlike tonight with billions of stars glittering in the skies over Texas. Those heavenly bodies felt as near and as much a part of me as the cells of my body. At times I would wake and sense myself lifted up above the planet, hovering in space and vibrating with energy.

Early in the morning as I was getting ready to head back out to the highway, just as the sun rose over the hills to the east, I was overcome with an intense sensation that I had been there before, in that exact spot, and that what I was living through at that precise moment had happened previously at some unknown time in the past, even though I knew it was impossible. It was all so familiar, the feeling so strong—of being in a timeless state, of having left my body and expanded into some new dimension. I fell to my knees in praise, overcome with reverence for all life. I placed my hands on the earth and gripped rocks and soil to assure myself I was alive in this time and space.

What I saw that morning was nothing like how I imagined Texas. In spring the land is carpeted with wildflowers with names like Indian Blanket, Mexican Hat, Texas Paintbrush. Brilliant splashes and pools of color thrown like paint on canvas-covered hills, vales, and swaths beside the highway. The land west of the geographic lesion known as the Balcones Fault bucks and heaves in buttes and razorback ridges with names like Devil's Backbone before it settles down onto the vast, open plains of West Texas. Wild oak, mesquite, and lofty pecan trees circle the lakes and stand at ease beside the rivers.

This is outlaw country; there is a tradition in these parts of living outside the law. In the later part of the nineteenth century, when there was no law west of St. Louis and supposedly no God west of Arkansas, the territories were known as Robber's Roost, a safe haven for remnants of the Missouri Border Raiders and Texas Freebooters. For me it would be the same—a place to hide out between runs across the border into

Mexico to gather booty; then to rest up and regroup while the spoils were distributed back east.

NOW IT IS all on the table, anted up then raised like so many stacks of poker chips. Fred is in bed with the Feds, I know it, knew it even before it happened. Had I listened to the still, small voice within I never would have brought him on board, never would have been on Barnswallow Hill that fateful snowy afternoon to play Good Samaritan, never would have picked up the Heat swirling around Fred's roost. True. But then I would not have had the pleasure of matching wits with Bernie Wolfshein. Nothing to do now but play the hand I dealt to myself.

I get up and wander into the garage. *What's this?* One whole bay is stacked high with wooden crates. I don't even want to imagine what is in them.

* * *

THE DAY OF the smuggle begins ominously. I'm at the ranch in Blanco, spent the night here last night. I get up before dawn, go into the bathroom to take a leak, and step on a scorpion. My leg aches all the way up to the thigh. Then one of the horses, a gelding that apparently didn't understand his balls had been cut off, tries to jump the fence to get at the mares and impales himself on a fence post. The Mexican ranch hands and I have to cut the fence post with a chain saw to get him off. When I remove the stump, his guts spill out onto the ground and he dies.

Meanwhile, Jonathan Seagull is making me crazy. He offered to drive into Austin last night to pick up my attorney, Hef, at the airport. Ordinarily, I would have gone, but I was busy coordinating the pickup in Mexico, waiting on calls at designated pay phones. Jonathan was supposed to check into a hotel and get a good night's rest so he could be up early and in the air on his way south of the border with the planeload of appliances, clothes, and other items for the Mexicans. Then get the plane loaded with pot and fuel and be back in Texas well before nightfall. But no, he takes his new lady friend and Hef out for dinner and drinks. Now he's hours behind schedule. He should have landed in Guerrero by this time, loaded up and refueled, and been on his way back. There is a storm front moving in from the north. I've been watching it all night. This morning it's over the Panhandle. I'm out in the paddock cleaning up, commiserating with the heartbroken young woman who takes care of the horses, assuring her it was not her fault the gelding died. We bring in a backhoe to dig a grave for the dead horse.

Then—out of the southern sky—come the deafening sounds of a turbo-charged twin-engine plane dive bombing the ranch, roaring overhead barely above tree level. Not once, not even twice. Three or four times. It's the Seagull, of course, in the Aero Commander, buzzing the ranch like a fighter pilot strafing an enemy compound. As if we don't hear him the first time. Or the second. The horses are spooked, prancing around the paddock. The Brahman bull is alarmed—no more so than me. JD drives over from the stash house and picks me up. He says he got some garbled communication from the Seagull fretting about the weather. JD has no tolerance for Jonathan. I feel like a fool for trusting so much of this operation to people who just don't seem to understand that what we do is illegal, and there is no room for fuckups. And yet fuckups abound. Right now I am the chief fuckup.

As we drive over the Devil's Backbone, down toward Startzville, I spot a DPS car—Department of Public Safety, Texas's version of state police—pulled into a scenic overlook. The trooper stands beside his car with a pair of binoculars trained on the landing strip where the Seagull touched down minutes ago. "Shit . . . there's the Heat."

"What do you want me to do?" JD asks.

"We should just leave this fucking idiot there. Let him talk his way out of the pile of shit he just dumped on our whole trip."

JD pulls over, starts to turn around. The cop gets in his car and takes off in the direction of the airstrip. But I can't do it, something in me will not allow me to abandon Jonathan or anyone else in the field. "We gotta go get him."

We arrive at the airstrip at his new girlfriend's golf club. Jonathan is still sitting in the Aero Commander cockpit. He can't get out. The rear of the plane is packed full of merchandise JD and Father Foley loaded in for the Mexicans, blocking the rear cabin door. I walk up to the plane. Jonathan opens the window. His face is flushed; he's sweating. "Get me out of here," he says.

The DPS car noses up onto the runway. JD sits in the driver's seat of a GMC suburban, which is registered to the ranch in San Saba. He looks at me, cocks his head in the direction of the DPS car. "See what you've done?" I say to Jonathan. "Brought the fucking Heat down on us. What is wrong with you?" It's all I can do to keep from punching him in the face.

"The weather . . . I never would have made it back—"

"You would've had plenty of time to get there and back if you'd left at five this morning like you were supposed to."

"He's leaving. Please . . . it's hot as hell in here."

The DPS cop makes a slow U-turn, eyeballs us, and drives off. I motion to JD. We unload a few of the appliances, make space for the Seagull to climb out of the plane. Then, for lack of anything better to do, we put everything back in the plane, lock it, and drive off. Less than a mile from the club, the DPS cop pulls us over. JD is driving, cool as always. The Seagull is in the backseat, drenched in sweat. I'm riding shotgun, dismayed by the turn of events.

"License and registration," the tall, sunglassed DPS trooper says. JD hands him his Maine driver's license. I get the registration out of the glove box.

"What's the problem, officer?" Jonathan pipes up from the backseat.

The cop leans down, looks in the car. "Out of the vehicle. All of you," he orders.

"Officer—"

"Shut up. Just do what he says," I tell him.

We stand by the side of the road. The cop gets in the car, rifles through the glove box, looks under the seats.

"Let me see some ID."

I give him my Paul Quinlan Texas driver's license. The Suburban registration. The Seagull gives him an Ontario driver's license. The cop takes all the papers and goes back to his car.

"There's nothing illegal in the plane," Seagull says.

"No shit," JD snaps.

My mind is crowded with distressing thoughts. We are on a head-on collision course with the Heat. We've blown the ranch in San Saba, no doubt the place in Blanco as well. The new plane is now burnt; the call numbers will be recorded on an aircraft hot sheet, and we'll get tossed every time we file a flight plan. Paul Quinlan, already nabbed carrying a concealed weapon in Massachusetts, will go down on some list of suspected dope smugglers along with JD and Jonathan in their real names.

"What the fuck were you trying to do, buzzing the ranch like that?" I ask as we wait for the trooper to return. "Every cop in the county had to hear you."

"To let you know I was turning back so—"

"We have a radio for that," JD says.

"I radioed."

"We heard you."

The cop is on his way back. "Just shut up. Please."

"What am I going to find if I get a warrant and go back and search that plane?" he asks.

"Nothing, officer . . . nothing illegal—" Seagull offers.

The cop nods. "Just a bunch of shit for the Mexicans, right?"

If I could kick the Seagull, I would. But he manages to keep his mouth shut.

"You think I don't know what's going on here?" The trooper looks at me, squints. "Buncha Yankees . . . and you, Paul, if that's your real name." He shakes his head. "What is this, the three stooges?" He hands JD all our IDs and the Suburban registration. "If I were you boys," he says, "I'd get the hell out of Texas. And stay out."

Good advice.

MY LEG STILL throbs from the scorpion sting when I limp in to meet with Hef at the bar in the Driskill Hotel in downtown Austin later that evening. "I almost needed your services today," I tell him, then recount the whole regrettable story of our brush with the DPS cop.

"I'm afraid that's the least of your problems, my friend," Hef says and orders more drinks. "I spoke to my contact in DEA the other day," he continues after we have been served. "Actually, played golf with him and his partner—of course, I let them win. Later, over drinks, I inquired about CENTAC." He shakes his head. "Not good. Not good at all. My DEA man said to me, 'How the fuck do you know about CENTAC?' Apparently your man Wolfshein has been talking out of school. It's allegedly highly classified. I would call it a task force, but it's more than that."

"You didn't say where or how you'd heard about it?"

"No, why would I? I told him another lawyer mentioned it to me. What CENTAC is, from what I can gather, is a unit within DEA that was formed to target a specific criminal organization suspected of being involved in RICO activity. You are aware of the RICO statute and what that means?"

"More or less," I say. "Racketeering. Organized crime." Which strikes me as absurd, given what my crew has been up to lately—more like *dis*organized crime.

"At any given time," says Hef, "there may be as many as fifty DEA agents around the world, as well as agents from IRS, Customs, FBI, state and local cops, and foreign police all assigned to gather intelligence and eventually dismantle the target group from the top down. And they do not disband the unit until they have accomplished their mission. If indeed your happy, little family has gained the dubious distinction of birthing its own CENTAC, or if you've been adopted like the proverbial redheaded stepchild by someone else's CENTAC, well, you might take that as a compliment in that it merits a certain prestige. It also means, however, that vast resources have been budgeted toward ensuring your downfall." Hef pauses, takes a swallow of his drink.

"Having said that, I can now also state with certainty that the individual in question—" he identifies Fred by his government name "—is cooperating with the government. The US Attorney's office in Portland is preparing an indictment as we speak. They may, however, seal the indictment and allow you to go about your business while CENTAC continues gathering intelligence for what would then become a superseding indictment, perhaps brought in another jurisdiction. They were actually quite surprised when they stumbled upon you in Maine."

"'Stumbled.' Wolfshein used the same word . . ."

"Stumbled, indeed, my friend. You stumbled." Hef holds up a finger. "But you have not yet fallen."

"How do I merit my own CENTAC?"

"Perhaps it's not your CENTAC. As I said, it could be the company you keep."

I press on. "And Wolfshein's veiled proposal, what do you make of that?"

"I can only speculate. I did float a hypothetical scenario for my DEA friends. What this agent may be offering—and if he's as highly placed as he appears to be, it would make sense—is an unholy alliance wherein you would be allowed to continue to go about your business unmolested, so to speak. Given a pass on your current difficulties. And then they would have you act as what is known in the trade as a CI—a confidential informant. As opposed to a CW—a cooperating witness—which is what your friend in Maine has become, someone whose only value is as a witness at the trial of others. As a CI, on the other hand, you would be expected to keep working while providing information on a completely discreet basis to whoever was designated as your handler. You become, in essence, a double agent. You would not be required to appear in court or wear a wire, nothing of the sort, until the CENTAC unit has accomplished its objective. Perhaps not even then. Some of these CIs stay active ten, twenty years, amass a fortune setting people up, and then move on. They get to keep their ill-gotten gains and disappear into some rat retirement program."

"It sounds intriguing. But a rat by any other name—"

"—is still a rat." Hef finishes the thought. "And you get to live out your life with a big bull's-eye on your back."

"The only thing I like about this is that it seems to argue against my being the target," I add.

"Yeah. I would venture that's the case," says my attorney. "But there are targets, and then there are targets within targets, so to speak. Even if you are not the only bull's-eye."

"And Mailer?"

Hef shrugs, sips his drink. "Collateral? To put more pressure on you? Or, simply prestige. The Feds love a big name like Norman's on the indictment even if they suspect he's not directly involved."

"He's not."

"I believe you. But you know how vague these conspiracy statutes are. As one of my clients put it, 'They could indict a ham sandwich.' You and Mailer own property together. He has accepted payments from you for that property knowing you have no legitimate source of income. That could be presented to a grand jury as money laundering and interpreted under the law as his having been a member of the conspiracy."

"They have no proof I paid him anything. That was all done in cash with no records. His name is still on the deed."

"Good. That's all very good. But you have to understand that once he or anyone else is implicated in the overall conspiracy, it becomes almost impossible for a jury to differentiate who is in fact culpable for exactly what. One gets painted with the broad strokes of the government's sweeping charges. And with a name like Mailer's, you know there are kudos to be claimed for taking him down. He becomes a bargaining chip."

"Fucking nasty."

"Indeed . . . it is. But then, you've always known that. You knew that going in."

"I learn it over again every day."

"That's good. Keep it that way," Hef says and orders more drinks. "Perhaps it's time for a change of plans.

"Just keep them coming," he tells the waiter and holds up his glass. "When you see the glass is nearly empty, bring another round."

We both sit mulling it over, drinking and thinking.

"What would you do?" I ask him.

"Ah, my good friend, dear Richard. Is there any question in your diseased mind?" Hef reaches across the small table between us, takes hold of my head and hugs me. We are laughing now.

"What would I do?" he says and raises his glass. "I believe one never really knows the answer to that question until one is faced with the predicament. But knowing you," he nods, grins, "I would never presume to advise you in such a matter. As your attorney, my only advice is—drink up! And when that drink is gone, have another! And when the alcohol has sufficiently dissolved your inhibitions, smoke some pot and let your megalomaniacal fantasies run wild. You have never been at a loss for coming up with a creative solution. And remember, life is short, my friend. In a situation like this, one must act expeditiously. He who hesitates is lost."

Driving back out to the ranch in San Saba later that night, I work it all out in my head. I still have a few things around here I need to clear up before I can even consider what to do next—though, in truth, I already know what I must do. The wild wide-open land itself speaks to me: *Just go, and keep on going. Never mind some puny, stupid, man-made laws. This is Texas, son, where a man can become the law unto himself.*

* * *

MY FRIEND JAKE from Boston flies down to Mexico with another forty grand for Adelberto, the village chief, his family, and the growers in Guerrero. The Mexicans are getting antsy; they need money. Jake stays in the village to watch over the load until we can devise another means to get it out. The Aero Commander is unloaded, all the stuff we bought for the Mexicans is stored in a barn at the Blanco ranch. Jonathan then flies the plane to Austin and parks it at the civilian side of the airport. After two days sitting on the tarmac, the plane shows signs of having been tampered with—a couple of small screws left on the floor by the avionics compartment when the agents were forced to beat a hasty retreat. Using a sweeper, we detect the GPS tracking device the Heat installed.

Now the Seagull is relegated to leading DPS, DEA, Customs, and whoever else is bothering to follow the Aero Commander on a wild goose chase around the state, down toward the border and then back up into Oklahoma, where he is finally halted and detained while the plane is thoroughly tossed by a team of narcotics agents. Meanwhile, at the strip on a neighboring ranch in San Saba—unbeknownst to the absent owner—we land the bulk of the load in two back-to-back trips using the Maule. Jake takes the remaining 300 pounds by land up to the Rio Grande and crosses it at Roma, Texas, with the help of the Mexicans who work at the ranch. JD buys a new truck and six-horse trailer. We transport the weed and the last of the horses from the Blanco ranch back east, deliver the pot to Lord Toranaga at a stash house in New Jersey, and the horses to the farm in Maine. We move all the cattle to San Saba. Herbert puts the place in Blanco on the market.

All this takes two weeks. And throughout there has been no sign of Wolfshein, DPS, or any other law enforcement agents. I'm betting on the time lag it takes for the various cop honchos to coordinate their intelligence and devise new marching orders to allow me occasion to get out of Dodge. I could feel a sense of accomplishment; at least I have not let the Mexicans down. Adelberto and the Indians in the mountains depend on cash from this business for their subsistence.

The San Antonio and Austin newspapers are filled with stories on the murder of Jimmy Chagra's older brother, Lee, the renowned criminal defense lawyer and high-stakes gambler who was shot to death in an apparent robbery at his El Paso office. In a late-night, pay-phone-to-pay-phone conversation with Capuana, he tells me to see what I can find out from my people in Texas. He says Jimmy Chagra is incensed, convinced the Feds had his brother Lee whacked. "The FBI surrounded his office right after the body was found. They were taking out boxes full of his files," Capuana says. He goes on to tell me the Chagra organization is in disarray, with Jimmy hunkered down at his Las Vegas mansion trying to figure out his next move. "Stumbled," Wolfshein said. He had been surveilling my meeting with Capuana in Boston. As I try to fit this piece into the government's investigative puzzle, I see how it is beginning to shape up into a CENTAC. Like Hef said, it may be the company I keep.

After I hang up with Capuana, I sit for another fifteen minutes waiting for a call from JD, who is back in Maine. Nothing like the sound of a lonely pay phone ringing in the night. More than anything else, this moment in time, this picture—as I sit in the Cadillac Eldorado listening to Willie Nelson sing "You Were Always on My Mind" on the radio, thinking of my wife and how I miss her, waiting for the pay phone to ring—this picture from my outlaw life strikes me as iconic. Inter me in a phone booth with a bag of quarters, and I will make my calls from the other side.

"It's fuckin' hot up here, boss," JD tells me. "And I don't mean the weather." He says cops and guys who are unmistakably federal dope agents have the farm, the airstrip, and the lodge under surveillance. The plane, the crashed DC-6, however, has disappeared. JD says he heard from the locals that some scrap metal dealers from Lewiston took it apart and carted it off in a tractor trailer. Good riddance. So much for Yogi's disco. I tell him to wait until things cool down and then go ahead and move the weight we have stashed from Chagra's freighter trip, as it appears that is the only way we'll get paid for the off-load. As for the spoiled tonnage, no clue what to do with that. JD gives me a number for Val.

"Call her. She's flipping out."

"How are you?" I ask when she answers.

"I'm okay," she says.

But I don't like the way she sounds: distant, groggy, evasive when I ask her whom she's with.

"Nobody. Just me. You need to call Maria. She's stressed," Val tells me and gives me the number of a restaurant in Miami. "She's there right now."

"Everything all right?"

"*No* . . . you?"

"Things are a little intense right now."

"*Hello* . . . what do you expect? This is fucked, Richard. Fred can hurt a lot of people."

"I know."

"When am I going to see you?" she asks.

"I don't know."

"Why do you have to—Oh, never mind."

I hear her crying quietly. "I have a couple more things to finish up, then I'm going home," she says, muffling her sobs. And she hangs up.

Maria, when I reach her, is no less concerned. "Are you certain, Ricardo?"

"Yes."

"This is bad . . . very bad. He knows my brother. And my uncle. They will not be happy."

I decide it would do no good to remind Maria that I warned her against giving Fred cocaine. That would be like reminding myself not to do business with people who are in the coke trade. The fallout is hitting everyone.

Then there are the crates in the garage: M-16s, Mac-10s, enough ammunition to supply a small army, all destined for Houston, where they will be shipped to Lebanon. The Captain appears at the ranch and tells me not to worry, so long as he is in the area and the weapons are in the garage, no agents of the law will trouble us.

"How can you be so sure?" I ask.

In a hushed conversation out by the pool, the Captain tells me this weapons venture is "authorized," whatever that means. He has arranged the shipment at the direction of his superiors. He is, he says, "untouchable."

He's a wiry, short guy, the Captain, a registered pharmacist, speaks several languages. He's a pilot and martial arts expert, Lebanese by birth. His father is Abu Ali, boss of the Bekaa Valley hashish growers. It was Abu Ali and Mohammed who arranged for me to meet the Captain a couple of years ago. He's stationed at Fort Hood, still on active duty, though he always dresses in civilian clothes and his military function seems to be confined to dealing weapons. He once told me that he was on Operation Eagle Claw, the failed attempt to rescue American hostages in Tehran. He claimed they deliberately sabotaged the effort to disgrace Jimmy Carter and assure the election of Ronald Reagan. There is a certain authority to everything the Captain says.

"I told you," the Captain says and heaves a deep sigh. "You should have let me get rid of that drug addict Fred when we had him out on the road. Now . . . it's not so simple."

Only one thing will soothe my frazzled nerves. I make a run into Austin to say good-bye to the women at the florist shop. Nifirg, the black girl who does the flower arrangements, and I have dinner, then she spends the night with me in a hotel. When I ask about her name, she says it is Grifin spelled backwards. "My father wanted a boy."

"Tell him I'm glad he had a girl."

"How long will you be away?" she asks after we make love.

"I don't know . . . could be a while."

"That's no fun. I'm gonna miss you."

"I'll miss you too."

Yes, it's this outlaw life. Always on the run. Never in one place long enough to really get to know someone. And she's fine, Nifirg. She likes to wrestle, likes to close her legs together in the missionary position. She likes to get up on her knees and stick her hard, round ass in my face. I love the smell of her body. She's a cyclist and a gymnast. Got six-pack abs and thighs that could break my ribs in a scissors hold. She loves it when I rub her feet. In the morning, as we sit having breakfast, Nifirg says, "You're a criminal, aren't you?"

"You could say that."

When I return to the ranch, Sherry, the ranch foreman's wife, is weirded out by the Captain. He has moved into the guest room with his pet giant python. He (the Captain, not the snake) sleeps on the floor, under his bed. None of that would bother Sherry. But the Captain invited a few of his military friends from Fort Hood over for a barbecue. He took one of the M-16s from the crates in the garage and shot a Brahman cow. Then he cut her open and ate her still quivering heart.

7

FLOWER OF BEKAA

THE MIDDLE EAST Airlines flight from Paris to Abu Dhabi makes a scheduled stop in Beirut. Once the plane taxis to the terminal, I glance out the window and see an official-looking Mercedes sedan idling on the tarmac. Little red, white, and green Cedars of Lebanon flags flutter from the front fenders. The flight attendant makes an announcement in Arabic, French, and English: "Please remain seated."

No one moves. The Mercedes approaches slowly. I figure there has to be some VIP or high level government minister on board they want to disembark first. Two men in military uniforms get out of the Mercedes, climb up the stairs into the plane. In a moment they are standing at the head of the aisle, where they confer briefly with the flight attendant. Now they are marching down the aisle toward me. When they stop at my seat I think, *Shit . . . I'm under arrest.*

"Mr. Paul Quinlan?" one of the men asks, using the alias I am traveling under.

"Yes."

"Come . . . please."

They don't touch me, they simply escort me from the plane. I am reminded of the first and only other time I was arrested in Beirut, which is how I met Mohammed in the first place. Late one evening, I checked into the Commodore Hotel after meeting with a hashish merchant in the Christian village of Zahale. I was holding a baseball-size sample chunk of blond Bekaa Valley hashish. As I was getting undressed for bed, there came a loud, imperious knocking at the door. I sensed it was the Heat before they identified themselves. Two plain-clothes inspectors from the drug squad showed me their IDs and said I was to go with them.

"Where?"

"To see the judge."

By then it was nearly midnight. We visited the judge at his home. He invited me in for Turkish coffee, cognac, and baklava. "I know you are a big hashish smuggler from America," the judge said when we were settled in his study.

"No," I protested. "Just a tourist. I smoke a little, that's all."

At the time, mid-seventies, we were doing small and midsize loads, a few kilos per trip using couriers with false-bottom suitcases, and a sailboat load of 400 kilos we landed on Long Island. Hardly a big hash-ish smuggler, though there were larger loads in the works. The judge nodded. The door opened, and in walked Mohammed. His bulky fig-ure loomed over the frail, older judge. Mohammed's ample jowls were blue with four o'clock shadow. He was dressed in a custom-made silk suit. He smiled a Cheshire cat grin and offered his meaty hand.

"From now on you will do business only with this man," said the judge. Mohammed and I smiled and nodded to each other. "He is chief of customs in Beirut. Nothing leaves Lebanon without this man's approval. Do you understand?"

I said I did. Mohammed proved to be an industrious, well-organized if obstinate partner. Over the next few years, as airfreight catches opened in New York, LA, and Boston, and with Uncle George's people facili-tating movement of the product within Lebanon, we increased the pay-load of our shipments from multiple kilos to multiple tons. Mohammed retired from his official position as chief of customs. Retaining his con-tacts, he devoted all his energies to helping me acquire ever-bigger loads of the best hashish available in Lebanon's Bekaa Valley. Supply was never the problem. Lebanon produces thousands of tons of hash each year. The challenge has always been finding ways to smuggle the hash out of Beirut and into North America without getting caught.

Mohammed is seated in the rear of the Mercedes sedan. He has that same sly smile on his face and looks even fatter and more prosperous from the years of our partnership. He knows I am pissed—tired, hungry, feeling betrayed. "Mr. Richard . . . welcome to Beirut," he greets me in his broken English. We kiss on both cheeks. Mohammed smells faintly of French cologne and Turkish coffee.

The Mercedes pulls up to the terminal. Men in military fatigues and armed with machine guns escort us inside. The place looks more like an army encampment than an airport. Heavily armed troops standing around outnumber the travelers. I have no visa for Lebanon. My ticket says I am booked through to Abu Dhabi, as is my luggage. None of that proves to be a problem. Mohammed speaks to the immigration officials at the airport, I show them my Paul Quinlan passport, they nod their approval and hand it back without the telltale stamps in the back pages that could be cause for concern when I return to America. We shake hands. A representative from the airlines who speaks English explains that my suitcase will be delivered to my residence after it has been removed from the plane. Mohammed gives them an address. He hands out *baksheesh*—bribes and tips. We walk out, get back into the Mercedes, and drive off.

"Nasif?" I ask after Mohammed's oldest son, who speaks fluent English and acts as our interpreter. I want to get right to the subject of the Wizard and suspect Mohammed has not brought Nasif along so he can delay the confrontation he knows is coming.

Mohammed nods. "Nasif later," he says. "No problem."

"Pierre—"

He cuts me off, waves a hand. "*Maalesh*. Never mind. No problem."

But it is a problem, and I want him to know it. So I brood. Mohammed has his worry beads in his fleshy hand. His thick, manicured fingers work the delicate beads, clicking them one against the

other, sounding like a random timepiece as he gazes out the window
and ignores me. The military men in front talk quietly to each other.
All around us is devastation. The drive along the airport road takes us
from a military base gagged with sandbags and occupied by troops into
a war zone of ever-shifting alliances. We pass the Shatila and Sabra ref-
ugee camps, teeming with displaced Palestinians. Ragged children play
in the rubble. The Hippodrome racetrack appears as yet unscathed, a
monument to better times. And then we enter the besieged heart of the
city. Wreckage and debris litter the streets. Bombed-out hulks of buildings, jagged steles of inscribed masonry, and pale heaps of concrete
stand like tombstones and burial mounds beside the pocked roadway.
Ragtag militias, heavily armed teenage boys with red-rimmed eyes and
vacant stares, man impromptu roadblocks. They gape at us as the sedan
slows and slides past. It troubles me to think that the weapons in the
crates the Captain stored in my garage at the ranch could end up in the
hands of these feckless boys.

Such is the curious confluence of the Drug War and wars of insur-
gence. Money from illegal drugs funds the purchase of weapons.
America buys the drugs; America manufactures and sells the arms.
The Captain is a walking embodiment of this paradox: an officer in the
United States armed forces ostensibly seeking to promote peace in the
world in the service of a nation dedicated to eradicating the produc-
tion and distribution of illegal drugs. Yet he acts as a go-between for
American matériel destined to and paid for by warlords who make
their money in the illegal drug trade. And he does it all with Uncle
Sam's sanction and blessing.

"War bad," Mohammed says. His jowls wag as he shakes his head.
"Beirut, no good," he remarks with sadness, seeing how I am fixated
on the destruction of this once magnificent city. The irony, however, is
that for our particular business war is good. There is virtually no law
enforcement in Lebanon, no central government with authority, and
no unified military forces capable of keeping order. No DEA, no FBI,
and certainly no IRS. CENTAC? Perhaps. The country is crawling

with CIA agents and military spooks of all cast—like the Captain—who are more likely to facilitate and have a hand in the dope business than to seek to bust me. Anarchy reigns. A good venue for a fugitive hash smuggler. Surrounded by chaos and death, with Western hostages being snatched off street corners like dustbins by the derelict armies of the jihad, I feel safer here than I do on the avenues of my homeland.

We arrive at a small apartment building on a narrow side street off rue Bachir al-Kassar in West Beirut. I stay in the car while our military escorts get out to check the street. Mohammed hands me a pair of Arafat-style sunglasses and a checkered *kaffiyeh* to wrap around my pale head. Saad, Mohammed's right-hand man, who serves as my body-guard and factotum while I am in Beirut, steps from the apartment building foyer carrying his ugly black Uzi. Mohammed and I enter, followed by Saad. The three of us take the elevator to the penthouse. Saad nods and disappears down the stairs. A short, compact man and former soldier, Saad speaks even less English than Mohammed.

The front room of the apartment makes me uneasy. It is walled with hand-carved mahogany panels inlaid with ivory depicting jungle scenes—tigers and exotic birds, intricate floral designs, elephants, monkeys, and giraffes. The shelves are cluttered with carved ivory figures. Two huge elephant tusks frame a miniature African village carved from ivory. It's like walking into an elephant's graveyard. I feel the ghosts of a herd of magnificent bull elephants haunting the room, and immediately I want to leave.

Mohammed leads me into a large living room with sliding-glass doors opening onto a wide, empty patio. He wags his finger at me, indicating the doors to the patio. "No good," he says, warning me away from the outside. The bedroom at the rear of the apartment is dark and cool. There are splayed gray gouges in the concrete walls from stray machine gun fire. Mohammed's other instruction besides avoiding the patio is not to flush soiled toilet tissue down the commode. The shit wads are to be deposited in the plastic bucket beside the toilet so as not to clog the septic system.

We return to the front rooms. Saad, his wife, and four daughters, ranging in ages from seven to sixteen, stand before a dining table laden with platters of food. The Saad family lives in the apartment below the penthouse, connected by a stairway reached through the kitchen. They will serve as my personal household staff during my stay and prepare copious amounts of delicious Lebanese dishes, providing a continuous feast as though fattening me up for the kill.

For the next couple of days I am a virtual prisoner in my penthouse suite. I have been traveling for days. My mind and body are numb, depleted by jetlag and tension, so I welcome this respite and embrace the solitude even as I worry that the Wizard is hatching his schemes while I rest. I lay in my bed in the dark bedroom meditating, listening to the sounds of war. It all seems so unreal, like a soundtrack playing over giant speakers outside the apartment walls: artillery rumbling like a distant storm, sometimes getting closer; the occasional loud crack and *rat-a-tat-tat* strafing racket of machine gun fire; sonic booms as Israeli fighter jets streak across the endless blue sky, flexing their supreme military muscle. In the morning I wake to the melodious chant of the muezzin from the minarets summoning the faithful to prayer. All throughout the day and into the evening, the Saad females wait on me as though I were a caliph.

Outside my precarious sanctum, Lebanon writhes in the death throes of civil war. Yasser Arafat's PLO occupies the land like an unwanted guest. Factions and tribes as old as this land kill, maim, slaughter, and plunder in a struggle that is at once impersonal and mindless and as near and heartfelt as blood vengeance. Bombs, mortars, and rockets strike indiscriminately. *You kill me and my whole family, or I wipe out your village and every member of your clan.* The Syrian army with their Soviet ally; the Army of God backed by Iran; America and her sister Israel: these forces stand behind the barricades, rooting, cheering, sniping, and jeering, lending their dubious support. Through it all, life and death in this caldron simmer and boil, and the hashish and heroin trade boom.

Officially, I am a fugitive from justice. When I failed to appear for a pretrial hearing in Maine, a warrant was issued for my arrest. With Fearful Fred ratting, there is no way I was going to beat that case. So I split, hid in the trunk of the Eldorado. The Captain drove the car down the long driveway and away from the ranch to a local airstrip. He flew me in his Piper Aztec to Love Field in Houston. There I caught an airport bus to Houston Intercontinental and fled the country on a flight to Mexico City. From Mexico I flew to London, spent a day traveling by train to Paris, and flew out on the Middle East Airlines flight to Abu Dhabi. One thing I am certain of: no one followed me.

I toss and turn in restless sleep. I have left everything and everyone behind—the farm in Maine, faithful Karamazov; the ranch in Texas with the horses and cattle and dogs; family, friends, employees, and loved ones; agents of the law, indictments, IRS investigations— to come to this ancient land beset by civil war, and to let it all ride on yet another toss of the dice. Mohammed and Nasif have been instructed to purchase as much of the highest-quality hashish as he and Abu Ali can gather together in one manageable load. All finest grade, nothing but the best—the mother lode. Tons and more tons. No more shilly-shallying with these airfreight shipments. No bucking the high seas in sailboats. A freighter load, brother. This will be the biggest shipment Toranaga and I have ever attempted—a trip to end all smuggles. The only thing that satisfies a degenerate gambler is to risk it all.

When Nasif finally shows up, late on my second full day in Beirut, he tells me what I already know. "The war is bad today," he says as though commenting on the weather. "Lots of metal in the air." He's tall, over six feet, heavy with thick thighs, though not as fat as his father. In his early twenties, he has a long, guileless, and chubby face. Nasif is charming, still boyish; he loves to laugh and joke around, and, unlike his father, he is seemingly incapable of duplicity. He tells me everything and often gets into trouble with the fat man. His abiding ambition is to go to college in America and chase long-legged, blond American girls. To that end I have been helping him apply to a number of universities. For now, his father's business—the business that is the mainstay for much of the economy of this country—occupies us both.

"What about Pierre?" I ask Nasif. "Did you tell your father how this thief got his name and number?"

"Of course. Don't worry. Everything is under control."

"Is he still here?"

"Yes. You will see him. Tomorrow night . . . if the fighting is not so bad."

"Where is he?"

"At the Summerland Hotel. His partner arrives today."

"Nasif. Listen to me. You and your father must not do anything with this man. Do you understand? I will not be part of any business that includes Pierre."

"Yes, of course, Mr. Richard. But he has money. Perhaps as much as $1 million. My father asks that you let him handle this business."

"I'm going to break this fucking creep's neck."

"No, no, please. You must promise me you won't do anything."

It's no good arguing with him. The possibility of getting cash out of the Wizard has clouded Mohammed's judgment, and Nasif is merely his messenger. After I give him and his father my word that I will be on my best behavior, and during a lull in the war, we meet for dinner at a restaurant owned by rogue CIA agent Frank Terpil.

When I enter with Nasif and Saad, the Wizard is already seated at the table with his moneyman, a cocaine importer from Miami. Mohammed is there with a couple of government or military types—Christians, from their uniforms—and more bodyguards. The party is already festive, everyone drinking Johnny Walker Black or arrack, and with that sense of conspiracy afoot—the hint of big black market money in the mood. Mohammed stands and embraces me, claps me on the back. He gestures to the Wizard, who gives me a snide smile but does not stand or offer his hand. It irks me that Mohammed has been entertaining these guys while I was isolated in my luxurious penthouse prison.

"I want to make one thing clear," I say to the men at the table after I've been seated and served a drink. "I—Nasif, please translate—I did not vouch for this man."

"Mr. Richard, not now," Nasif says. He refuses to translate.

Mohammed scowls at me.

"These men—" Nasif indicates the Falangist officers, "—are not connected to the business." That, I know, is not true. Everyone is connected to the business or they wouldn't be here. "These men come with Pierre," Nasif continues.

"We can work this out," the Wizard's partner says. "No worries."

He's Canadian. We met before in Miami when he and the Wizard bought several hundred kilos of hash. The Wizard gives me that smug smile that serves to piss me off all the more. After I have a few more drinks and am feeling rowdy, I say to him, "I never vouched for you. You stole my briefcase."

He shrugs, gives me a deprecating wave of his hand and dismisses me. "Yeah, so? You're greedy. You don't want to share the wealth."

"You're a fucking thief."

He sneers. "But a good one."

"I want my briefcase and everything that was in it returned."

He shakes his head. "Can't do it. I got rid of it."

I turn to Mohammed and the others at the table. *Suck it up, Stratton.* "If you trust this man, you're fools," I tell them. That does not go over well. More glares. But I'm brazen with alcohol and hashish.

Nasif kicks me under the table. "Not now!" he insists.

It's one of those moments when I seem to be outside myself, at once fascinated and appalled, watching the troublemaker stir shit up.

"No? Then when? I'm supposed to just go along with this? It's not right, Nasif. This guy is—"

The Wizard is suddenly in my face.

"Shut the fuck up," he hisses. "You're gonna blow this whole thing."

Threatened, I lose it. I haul off and smack him—an open-handed bitch-slap across his lantern-jawed face that knocks him over backwards and sends him sprawling. Glasses and bottles and plates tumble from the table and break on the tile floor. Half a dozen men jump up and reach for their weapons—including Saad, who is at my side. Someone grabs me from behind—Nasif. I am ushered out of the restaurant, put into a car with Nasif and Saad.

"You promised!" Nasif exclaims. "You could have been killed. Those men are with him. Do you know who they are?"

Saad is laughing, smiling. He gives me a hug.

"I don't care who they are. I'm telling you, Nasif, the guy is a crook. You can't trust him. If you and your father do business with him, he'll fuck you. Guaranteed."

"Listen to me. My father—we can't do anything without those men. They control the road from the Bekaa. They control the port. Pierre has done business with them before and has their trust. My father is going—" He breaks off, shakes his head. "I promised him you would not cause trouble."

"Pierre has *already* caused trouble. I'm ready to kill this fucking guy."

"But he has money! You must not upset this business. Pierre and his friend are bringing over *one million dollars cash*," Nasif scolds, like that should make all the difference. His eyes light up. "Maybe we'll take his money and *fuck* him."

He translates and Saad nods eagerly. I begin to wonder if the whole setup is not simply an elaborate ruse to rip off the Wizard, which does nothing to ease my concern about having anything to do with this business. One bad deed does not necessarily deserve another.

We wind up the night at a supper club in a casino where we are entertained by a host of beautiful, plumed-and-costumed women in an elaborate floor show. Tits, hips, legs, and asses, exotic females adorned in feathers and spangles strutting before me—such a spectacle will take my mind off just about anything. One would never know there is a war raging outside.

* * *

A FEW DAYS later Nasif tells me Pierre and his partner the Canadian coke dealer have gone to Colombia to score a large amount of cocaine. There is an emerging coke market among wealthy Beirutis. Mohammed likes to do a blast from time to time. Their plan is to smuggle coke from Colombia to Beirut and trade it for hash.

"We will make a lot of money." Nasif smiles, nods. "Yes?"

"We're already making a lot of money," I say. Wonderful, now they want to involve me in a cocaine transaction.

"So. We will make more!"

"No, not me. I told you how I feel about this guy. Whatever you do with him, count me out. I want nothing to do with the coke business and nothing to do with *any* business Pierre is part of. You must understand, this is personal, Nasif. The man stole from me. I can't let that go. I want nothing to do with this thieving, low-life piece of shit."

"Please," Nasif begs, "speak to my father."

WITH THE WIZARD out of the country, Mohammed at last appears ready to shift his attention to my business. It's like the Wizard was never here. Mohammed refuses to discuss him or the outcome of his visit. He picks me up at the apartment, and we fly to Baghdad, check in to a hotel. The next few days Mohammed spends visiting various date merchants while I make calls to New York to finalize the letter of credit from Bordo Foods. I see little of Mohammed, and when we are together we hardly talk as there is no one to translate.

There is tension between Mohammed and me carried over from Beirut. He seems to have shifted his trust from me to Pierre. Each day that the letter of credit is delayed, each time I try to impart that the dates must not exceed the specific infestation rate to assure they will pass inspection by the Department of Agriculture, that there cannot be too many dead bug carcasses or too much insecticide spray permeating the dates, and that Sammy in New York is demanding to have samples sent before he authorizes the letter of credit, with each new request Mohammed's patience is tried and his frustration mounts. He clicks his worry beads furiously. I don't know what Pierre and his partner promised him, but whatever it is has served to cause my cautions to appear at once trivial and burdensome.

Finally, the letter of credit is verified. Samples of the dates are sent to New York. Based on Mohammed's word that the dates in the shipment will meet USDA standards, Mohammed uses the letter of credit to purchase half a million kilos of soft brown pitted dates—the kind of dates used in cake mixes and prepared foods. Mohammed shows me several samples of dates wrapped in waxed paper. His mood improves. I have no way of judging if the dates will pass muster with USDA inspectors. It's not like I'm examining a sample of hashish. I look the dates over for dead bugs, chew on a handful. They seem fine to me. Sweet. Sticky. I nod my approval.

Mohammed smiles. I'm happy that he's happy. He's been upset with me for so long any little glimmer of joy in his murky dark eyes makes me feel better. I just want to get back to Lebanon and begin buying hashish. Iraq is at war with Iran, and though the fighting hasn't reached Baghdad, we are both concerned that the load of dates gets packaged and shipped to Beirut before anything happens to delay this trip further.

Mohammed stays behind in Iraq to see the dates on the road, transported overland by truck to a warehouse at the port of Beirut. I fly back to Lebanon. Nasif and Saad meet me at the airport and return me to my suite. That evening there is a small gathering in the penthouse. With his father still out of town, Nasif relaxes and parties. He invites a young lady who lives in the building to join us, and she brings a friend. The women are refined, educated. They speak fluent English and French, as well as Arabic. Beautiful and elegant young Lebanese ladies. It is a treat just to listen to them speak in their accented English. The woman who lives in the building, Laila, is married to a doctor, but she flirts openly with Nasif, who returns her affections. After a three-hour dinner, we repair to the living room for coffee and are entertained by the Saad daughters belly dancing to the enchanting Lebanese chanteuse, Fairuz. Soon the older women are up showing the girls how it is done. Artillery bombardment flashes behind the dark cityscape like lightning on the horizon. For a few hours I forget about the war and the hash business. Later, as the muezzin begin their timeless incantations, I drift off to sleep with a head full of images of dark-haired beauties and undulating belly buttons.

When Mohammed returns and learns his son is carrying on a dalliance with the doctor's wife, he chases Nasif around the dinner table with a fork. He's laughing, they are both laughing, but when he catches Nasif and stabs him in the ass with the fork it turns serious. Mohammed orders his son to quit the affair with Laila. The doctor is a respectable man even if he can't control his woman.

* * *

WEEKS PASS. MY suitcase never arrives from the airport; fortunately all I lost was my clothing and toiletries. I spend my days lounging around the penthouse in a long, embroidered robe, eating, smoking hashish from a three-foot, floor-standing *narghile*. The eldest Saad daughter lays the bowl of the hookah with hot coals. I sprinkle fine, resinous hash on the burning coals, suck hot smoke down the stem of the pipe and up through the cooling water to fill my lungs with fragrant essence of Muse. My mind wanders, all right brain now. Anything is possible . . . if I can just imagine it with sufficient intensity. I will survive. I will get through this and leave Beirut, escape with the goods. I will find some safe haven and become an exiled godfather of the hippie mafia—a Lucky Luciano of hashish. If this endless war would just cease long enough for me to get the load out before the whole Middle East descends into mindless fratricide, I'll be done. If we can get the load past US Customs and distribute it, get paid, if we can do all that without getting busted, I'll be a millionaire several times over. In cash. The scheme sustains me.

Mornings I drink sweet, rich Turkish coffee and eat fresh croissants with butter and jam. I read books and newspapers Nasif brings me. I watch TV, episodes of *Dallas* with JR yammering away in Arabic. I listen to Fairuz and to the war seething all around me. West Beirut is under attack by Christian Falangist forces to the east, on the other side of the Green Line dividing the city. Some days it is too bad even for Nasif and Mohammed to venture out. On those nights I eat alone, served by Saad's daughters. The evening meal begins in late afternoon with pistachio nuts, almonds, grapes, figs, and arrack. Then there is an array of *mezze*, dish after dish of pickled vegetables; tabbouleh, chopped-parsley salad with mint, tomato, and cracked bulgur wheat; hummus laced with garlic and glazed with a pool of olive oil; baba ghanouj, grilled eggplant with *tahina*, olive oil, lemon juice, and garlic puree; deep-fried falafel patties of spiced, ground chickpeas; *kibbeh*, stuffed fried lamb or *kibbeh nayyeh*, raw lamb eaten like steak tartare; *labneh*, strained yogurt eaten with pita bread; grape leaves stuffed with seasoned rice. Then comes the main course: fish, chicken, roasted lamb, dove. My veggie diet goes out the window. When in Rome . . . or Beirut. The meal goes on for hours. We drink arrak, local wines, and Johnnie Walker and withdraw to the living room for music, hash, more whiskey.

Such is the nature of this business: Hurry up and wait. Long spells of idleness and frustration interrupted with bursts of intense activity. During a lull in the fighting, Nasif takes me out shopping for a new wardrobe in the boutiques along Hamra Street. I'm not happy with how my waistline has expanded during my captivity. I must have gained fifteen pounds gorging on the delicious dishes prepared by Mrs. Saad. I feel fat and sluggish. We stop in a bunker-like long-distance phone center near the war's front line. An armed and boisterous crowd of PLO militiamen barges in and commandeers the phones. I can see why the Lebanese want these people out of their country. At last I get through to Toranaga in New York and Val in Maui. They both have one question for me: "Are you okay?"

Once it appears the most recent ceasefire may prevail for more than a few hours, Mohammed orders me to be ready to leave Beirut. The next day we set out on the road to Damascus, traveling in Mohammed's Mercedes. Nasif drives, I am in the rear; we leave the warmth of the coast and head up over the snow-clad Chuf Mountains into the Bekaa Valley. There is any number of roadblocks on the way, a checkpoint nearly every mile along the fifteen-mile stretch to Zahale on the western edge of the valley. The PLO checkpoints are adorned with the likeness of Yasser Arafat. Christian Falangist militia checkpoints are draped with patriotic banners and posters-size pictures of their dead martyrs and living leaders. The Druze hang their holy colors over their checkpoints in the Chuf. Maronite Christian gunmen nod their approval and wave our car through while the checkpoints manned by Shi'ia guardsmen display the glowering visage of Ayatollah Khomeini; at those stops we are questioned more thoroughly. The soldiers gaze at me like I am a prize. "American?" "No, Canadian." "Hashish?" They nod and wave us on. No one fucks with the hash trade. The American dollars from the drug trade fund the various militias.

We stop in the Christian village of Zahale for lunch, dining on shawarma and local wine. Mohammed and his family are Shi'ia Muslim, though only his wife is devout. They hail from a village in the south, near the border with Israel, now occupied by Israeli forces. I know all this; still it makes for conversation. When I question Nasif and Mohammed about the conflict that is tearing their country apart, Mohammed is resigned, accepting war as part of life. Nasif grew up in the midst of war. War has been the only constant the people of Lebanon have known since the French created the state in 1920, he tells me. In 1948, when the Israelis drove the Palestinians from their land and established the state of Israel, the seeds of the current conflict were planted. Mohammed says he is sympathetic to the Palestinians' plight, but he doesn't like them. He sees them as an unworthy foe: disorganized, rude, brutal, and yet feeble compared to the Israelis and their mighty ally, America. On only one point is he emphatic: the Syrians must be driven from Lebanon. As we descend into the Bekaa, it becomes apparent why Mohammed wants Syria out of his backyard. They threaten Lebanese hegemony over the drug trade. Syrian troops and Hezbollah Party of God militiamen and Iranian Revolutionary Guard dominate in the valley.

Entering the Bekaa is at once like driving into the cornfields of Iowa and traveling back in time. Vast expanses of emerald green stretch away from the highway in every direction. The ancient stone villages and towns, the old women in black burnooses inching along the roadway like beetles, speak of another time and place. The fields are not corn but the short, bushy, splay-fingered *al-Kayf*, cannabis plants of the *indica* variety arrayed in neat, orderly rows as far as the eye can see. A sea of green, millions of plants, mile upon mile of hashish fields quilted around Old Testament settlements.

We ride past the fields and up through the valley to the prehistoric village of Baalbek. Known to the ancients as Heliopolis, City of the Sun, Baalbek is the present-day commercial center of Lebanon's hashish industry—and a stronghold of Hezbollah. If the Bekaa is outlaw country, Baalbek is its El Paso, a frontier town where everyone, it seems, is armed, including young boys and old women. They carry Kalashnikovs, Mac-10s, handguns.

Mohammed's main man, the Captain's father, Abu Ali, meets us at a restaurant in the center of town. He carries a Glock nine millimeter in a holster at his side. Tall and lanky, with a round potbelly, Abu Ali wears a traditional checkered headdress and has a full, bushy black mustache. He speaks a little English and some French. We are friends, old friends. In many ways I am more at ease with Abu Ali than I am with Mohammed and Nasif. He is a farmer, a man of the earth, has a hashish plantation of his own, many hectares of healthy plants, and he serves as an agent for some of the biggest growers in the region, so he understands my love for the plant and never questions my demands for quality control. Mohammed, the middleman, the businessman, the facilitator, is impatient with my insistence upon the best goods and all about maximizing profit. Abu Ali shares my belief that the better the quality of the hashish, the better the energy of the business, the easier the money follows. And, like Sammy, Abu Ali is a stickler for detail.

As they talk, both Mohammed and Abu Ali have their worry beads out. The soft clicking of the beads is hardly audible over the noise of the restaurant. But I can tell by the way their fingers work the beads— black obsidian in Mohammed's hand and white coral with amber spacer beads in Abu Ali's—thumb and forefinger drawing the beads along the string apace with the conversation, they are not discussing family or politics. This is business.

The restaurant is crowded. I am the only *ifrangy* in the place. Everyone seems to know why I am here. The men who stop at our table to greet Abu Ali and Mohammed eye me knowingly. This town and most of its residents subsist on the dope trade. An estimated 10,000 tons of hashish are produced and shipped worldwide from this valley yearly. Not to mention the expanding heroin production—a growth industry. Turkish opium is refined in labs in the valley. Opium poppies sprout on the hills and mountainsides in the northern reaches of the Bekaa. A lush swath of land half the size of Rhode Island, this valley is one of the major drug-producing regions in the world.

Outside, after a two-hour meal of *mezze*, local delicacies, and much heated discussion between Abu Ali and Mohammed, none of which I understand and which Nasif refuses to translate, saying only "business," the worry beads go back into their pockets, and Nasif tells me it has been decided. I shall remain here in Baalbek as a guest of Abu Ali. I am to stay until I am satisfied with the quality of the goods and I sign off on the labels stamped on the sacks. Once I have worked out all the details for the preparation of merchandise, about which I am a constant source of irritation to Mohammed, and when the load is ready to be transported from the Bekaa to the port, then and only then will I be returned to Beirut.

Nasif goes on to tell me that he and Mohammed must get back to Beirut immediately to receive the shipment of dates and "prepare everything," or they would stay as well. But he assures me they will return for me "in a couple of days . . . as long it takes until everything is ready," a Lebanese oxymoron.

Mohammed nods, shakes my hand, kisses me on both cheeks. "No problem," he says.

"Besides," Nasif adds with a smile, "here is more peaceful."

I haven't planned on this. I brought nothing with me but the clothes I'm wearing. I have a momentary twinge of concern that I am being left here as some sort of hostage until whatever it is that seems to be at odds between Mohammed and Abu Ali is resolved. No doubt it has to do with money. But it makes no sense to protest. After all, I am here to do business, not to lounge around an apartment in Beirut getting fat. Nor do I give any indication that I am surprised or alarmed. Recall the smuggler's motto: Go with the flow.

Mohammed climbs in the Mercedes, Nasif gets behind the wheel, and they drive down the dusty road out of town. Abu Ali and I stand in the street and look at each other. "Mr. Richard," he says, "come. You are my guest." And he walks me over to his Land Rover.

Abu Ali and his extended family live in a stately, old French Colonial villa on the outskirts of Baalbek. We turn up a tree-lined dirt road and come to the home and outbuildings set well back from the highway in the middle of a clearing surrounded by cypress and cedar trees, palms and fruit orchards. Fields of hashish plants blanket the foothills gently sloping away from the villa. The air is fragrant with cannabis pollen and jasmine. When we pull up in the Land Rover in front of the house, cousins and uncles, sons and grandsons sit on stone benches or stand around a charcoal grill drinking coffee or tea. There are no women in sight.

All the men are armed, even the teenage boys have automatic weapons. I know some of the older men, who greet me with waves of the hand, slight bows of their covered heads. They wear traditional *jibbah* gowns and full headdresses or checkered keffiyehs. The younger boys, dressed in jeans and bright, polyester T-shirts, speak fluent English. They immediately want to know what I have brought them from America. I am embarrassed to admit I am empty-handed—close to a sin in this culture. Abu Ali explains that this is an unplanned visit. I tell them, please understand: Next time I will bring lots of gifts, jeans and T-shirts and sneakers and whatever else they want. Cassette tapes, they say. Rock and roll. Beatles and Rolling Stones. Jimi Hendrix. The Doors. "No problem," I say. The answer to everything.

Abu Ali shows me to my quarters. We stand in the late-afternoon sun and soft-scented breeze washing in through large open French doors leading to a balcony where I can breathe fresh air without fear of being shot at by snipers. He hands me a chunk of fresh hashish. I tell him of my most recent visit with his son, the Captain. He nods solemnly. The weapons the Captain shipped from Texas arrived safely, he says, and were delivered to the militia of Amal, the Shi'ia Movement of the Disinherited. But we must not speak of this, Abu Ali insists. It must not be known that America is providing weapons to the Shi'ia militia—for a price, of course. Or that I have anything to do with this business. Amal opposes the PLO and is allied with Syria. Here, in Lebanon, Abu Ali reminds me, and particularly in the Bekaa, there are many factions. It is complicated. One can hardly keep up with the political upheavals, assassinations, massacres, and fickle, short-lived alliances. Everyone, however, respects the business of hashish—except the Israelis. But I must not worry. There are no Israelis in the Bekaa. He gives me a wistful smile. "Not yet . . ."

"I'm not worried," I tell him. "How can I be worried? I am your guest."

Abu Ali nods and shrugs his broad shoulders. "Yes. My home is your home."

I know there is something more he wants to tell me—and that he will—when he feels the time is right.

Khalid, one of Abu Ali's many nephews, is assigned to serve as my companion, driver, guide, interpreter, bodyguard, and all-around gofer. He's a sweet kid, tall and in good shape, nineteen, on the verge of turning twenty. We celebrate his birthday while I am in residence at the villa. Khalid takes his Kalashnikov and Browning 9mm handgun on a drive into town to buy me some bare necessities. He tells me his father, mother, brothers, and sisters all live in Detroit while he travels back and forth. He has lived for years in the States and speaks perfect American English seasoned with the latest teenage slang. Though he does not come out and say so, it is clear he is involved in some aspect of the family business beyond simply acting as an armed errand boy for his uncle. He smokes hashish, as do several of the men who gather each day around the charcoal fire in the villa courtyard. He plays soccer when not busy driving me around. Khalid's real interest, however, besides cars, guns, and rock and roll, is the female of the species, young women or girls, something we see very little of at the villa, usually only at meals when they appear to serve the males.

The time-honored quest for top-grade hashish occupies most days of my idyll in the valley of Baal. Nasif was right about one thing: It is far more peaceful here in this fortified camp than in the war zone of Beirut. He was way wrong, however, in his estimate of how long it would take for us to gather and prepare the merchandise. Most days, after a light breakfast of coffee and fresh baked bread, Khalid drives me to various hashish plantations where I meet with Abu Ali and the local growers to inspect samples of their harvest. If we like what we see, a price is negotiated and bales of bulk hashish plants are trucked to a processing plant out behind Abu Ali's villa. There masked young boys and a few teenage girls beat the female plants on screens, after which they squeeze and sift the buds to a fine golden dust collected in stainless steel bins placed beneath the screens. The loose hash is scooped into white canvas sacks, heated in steam chambers and pressed into

500-gram slabs. Resins seep through and stain the sacks amber. The whole place reeks of fresh hash plants and pollen. Even with the masks over their mouths and noses, the kids are stoned on fumes by the end of a few hours working in the processing plant.

I tell Abu Ali that North America has been flooded with some huge loads of low-grade Lebanese hash, depressing the market. He nods knowingly, says it is the Christian Falangists, especially the family of Bachir Gemayel, who are responsible for these inferior shipments. Abu Ali claims the American government and Israeli military work hand-in-hand with the Falange to facilitate the big loads. They do not understand or care about the product and are only interested in maintaining Israel's dominance of the region, which, Abu Ali laments, is turning the entire Arab world against America.

We agree that for our shipment we will purchase only Number One, top commercial quality, or Zahara, zero, above the best, and Double Zahara, dealer's choice—the sticky resinous nodules shaken and gathered from freshly harvested female plants. We must collect and prepare as many tons of the best quality that can be found in the entire valley; anything less, I tell Abu Ali, my partners and I will have a hard time selling in America. He nods solemnly and gives me a concerned look.

"What is it?" I ask him.

He shrugs and says, "We shall see . . . *Inshallah* . . . God willing."

It takes weeks and drags on to over a month and a half and still we have only managed to acquire a little over two tons of Number One and a few hundred kilos of Zahara. I have designed the stamp to be affixed to the canvas sacks identifying the product as Flower of Bekaa, written in Arabic and English, with a picture of a rose—homage to my close friend and partner, Rosie, also known as Flower, the hippie godfather of Toronto.

Finally, about the fifth or sixth time I notice the mistrustful looks I'm getting from some of the plantation owners, and try to decipher the meaning of their guttural objections, I decide to confront Abu Ali.

Something is definitely wrong. There is an undisclosed friction between Abu Ali and Mohammed. Mohammed hasn't been back since he and Nasif left me here, and he has only called two or three times. The dates aren't getting any fresher sitting in a warehouse at the port. Sammy and his people in New York are getting frantic, and the stress has begun to affect me. I am not allowed to make calls from the Bekaa. Abu Ali claims that the CIA monitors all calls to America. I managed to get messages to Sammy via Nasif relayed through Biff that everything is moving forward, however slowly. Biff replied that Sammy warns the date deal will collapse if there is not a delivery soon. Meanwhile conditions in Beirut worsen by the hour.

Khalid drives me to meet Abu Ali at the "lab."

"What lab?" I ask him.

He shrugs. "Abu Ali's lab." He gives me a look like I should know what he's talking about and not ask any more questions. We pull up to a cluster of semi-industrial looking buildings about fifteen kilometers outside of town. Brand-new Allis Chalmers tractors and British Leyland harvester-combines are parked in a big, metal shed. Half a dozen other vehicles are parked outside the main, two-story building—cars and trucks, Abu Ali's Land Rover, a new Mercedes sedan—pulled up randomly as though the drivers all arrived at once and left their vehicles in a hurry. The walkway leading up to the building is lined with a hedgerow of stumpy hash plants. We enter a foyer, walk up a flight of stairs and into a large, open room on the second floor. From the moment I enter the building, I catch the strong odor of chemicals.

Ten men—mostly in traditional Arab dress with billowy white trousers or khaki work pants—are seated on low stools or pillows around a large, brass tray table. All wear headdresses except one, a short, compact, and perfectly groomed young man dressed like a well-heeled European businessman in a Brioni suit and pale blue shirt with no tie. As soon as I walk in and see the men, I understand this is the Arab version of a sit-down. And it occurs to me what Khalid meant by the lab. We are in an opium processing plant, a junk factory. The entire ground floor of the building is used for refining heroin from raw opium. These guys are all in the heroin business—including Abu Ali.

A few of the men I recognize as hash plantation owners Abu Ali and I have been meeting with over the past several weeks. Khalid introduces the guy in the suit as his cousin, Tamer. "Just in from the States. Tamer drove up from Beirut this morning," Khalid tells me.

"Hey, Rich," Tamer says and we shake hands. "I heard a lot about you."

Abu Ali motions me to a seat next to him with Tamer directly across the table on Abu Ali's other side.

"What's the problem, Abu Ali?" I ask after a few minutes of small talk as we sit sipping tea or Turkish coffee with the acrid smell of fresh heroin wafting up from the lab below. I look around at the other men, addressing them. "Why are these men not willing to fill our order?"

Abu Ali nods, speaks to Tamer. "He says you are right," Tamer explains after an exchange in Arabic with Abu Ali and a couple of the other growers adding their comments. "There is a problem. This is why Abu Ali has asked you here—to discuss this business with these men. It's not that they are unwilling to give you what you want. They also want to do business. But first they want to know when they will be paid for the last shipment."

I am stunned. "What last shipment? Does he mean the airfreight load? That was paid in full seven months ago." I speak directly to Abu Ali. "I paid everything right away. That business was finished in less than one month."

Abu Ali sips his coffee, shakes his head, replies to Tamer. I am already beginning to suspect what "last shipment" they are talking about and it is roiling my insides. Tamer translates. "He says, not the shipment from last summer. He means the goods from two months ago, the three-and-a-half tons of Number One. For that, they have received nothing."

Oh, fuck, no. Now I get it. Some part of me knew all along, going back to the first day I arrived in Baalbek, sensing the tension between Mohammed and Abu Ali— once again that conniving Wizard got over on me. Not only did Mohammed do business with him, but Abu Ali and the other growers are holding me responsible for the shipment.

"That was not my shipment," I tell them, struggling to appear calm. "I have nothing to do with that business."

My heart is pounding, my mouth dry. It's all clear to me now. Mohammed and the Wizard put together a load and shipped it to the States using my name as pledge for payment. Abu Ali and the other growers believe I owe them somewhere in the neighborhood of $2 million for something I wanted no part of, a trip I warned Mohammed was doomed. There is more discussion among the men. Clucking of tongues and clicking of worry beads. Heads shake. Shoulders shrug. Coffee is sipped. Meanwhile downstairs, heroin cooks. *What the fuck am I doing here?*

I speak directly to Tamer now. "Explain to them. This is wrong, Tamer. With all respect, I told Mohammed, I said it at a table with several others present—Nasif was there, Saad was there; they know the whole story. That guy is a fucking thief!"

"What guy?" Tamer asks.

"Pierre, the guy Mohammed made that business with. I was not part of it." I go on to tell him how Pierre suckered me, got Mohammed's name and number, and used my name without my knowing. I tell him about the night in the restaurant when I slapped Pierre. And that when Nasif told me about their proposed scam, how Pierre was going to send cocaine to Beirut in exchange for hashish, I insisted I was not part of that deal. I made it clear to Mohammed and Nasif I did not vouch for Pierre and I refused to be held accountable for goods consigned to him. "Ask Abu Ali: Does he really think I would be here trying to put together another load if I had not paid for the last one? He knows me better than that. How many years have we been doing business? Have I ever cheated him?"

As Tamer translates, Abu Ali nods, speaks to some of the other growers. Then he begins a long explanation of where it all stands. "He says he believes you. He trusts you. That is why you are here,"

Tamer explains. "Abu Ali knew there was something wrong the day you arrived with Mohammed, because Mohammed refused to discuss the other business with you present. But Mohammed assured Abu Ali that while you are here, while you make this new business, everything would be taken care of from the last shipment before you receive your goods. And still no money has arrived. These other men," he indicates the growers, "they do not want to extend any more credit. Not until they are paid. There are buyers in Beirut and here in the valley willing to pay cash. These are not rich men. Their families depend on the money from the goods."

So I am a fucking hostage.

"I understand," I say, speaking directly to Abu Ali. "I wish you had told me this sooner. It's been almost two months. My partners and I have invested a lot of money in this business. We have over a million pounds of dates sitting in a warehouse in Beirut. I would not have wasted everyone's time if I had known about this problem."

Tamer says, "Abu Ali was told the money was coming. Or the cocaine. And that it would be sold and then they would get paid."

"I know nothing about any of that," I say, feeling the utter lack of standing for my position. The Wizard—and Mohammed—used my name. No matter what I say, these men hold me responsible. Tamer nods. A long discussion in Arabic ensues, with several of the growers expressing their opinions. I'm thinking about the quarter of a million dollars, maybe as much as three hundred grand we have already invested in this trip, most of it went to Mohammed as down payment for the new load, and at least another forty or fifty grand in expenses. And the letter of credit, all the shit we had to go through to get that. The half-million kilos of dates in a warehouse at the port. Bordo Foods expecting to receive the dates in exchange for the money pledged using their bank's letter of credit. And me here in Baalbek, a guest in Abu Ali's home, yes, but also a hostage of a sort, being held in lieu of $2 million owed by some slick fucker whose real name I don't even know, a master of false identification, a thief—"but a good one."

I have a little over $200 in my pocket and no way to leave here, no way to get out of Lebanon even if they were to agree to let me go. I don't want to show these men any sign of panic or fear as an indication that I am not being truthful. I must make them believe I had no part of the deal. Yet at the same time I can't call Mohammed a liar.

"This is all a misunderstanding," I tell Tamer. "But we can fix it. Abu Ali knows in the past I have always paid for my goods. Let's make this shipment. Then, when I get back to America, I give my word I will do everything possible to find out what happened to the other shipment, whether it arrived safely and got into the country and was sold. And I will see that these men get paid."

Tamer translates. More questions and further discussion. "Do you know where Pierre lives? Or his partner?" he asks. "They are the ones responsible for the last shipment?"

"Yes, that's right. Pierre and whatever the other guy's name is. They live in Miami and Boston, I think. I'm not sure. But I will find out."

Will I? Can I find them? I have no idea. Probably not. The Wizard is an expert at disappearing. But at this point I'm willing to say I'll do just about anything to put this trip back together and get out of Lebanon alive and with my goods.

"He is your friend . . . ?" Tamer says, more a question than a statement.

"No. I don't really know him. I bought some phony ID from him. I told Mohammed and Nasif. He stole my briefcase, Tamer. He's no friend."

"Mr. M. told them he is your friend."

"I figured as much. But that's not the case."

Tamer nods, translates. One of the men shouts something and they all laugh. Then more serious conversation. The men look at me as if I can provide them with an answer. "Has Mohammed heard anything from him?" I ask. "Do we even know if the load made it into the States?"

No one knows the answer to that. More conversation, some angry, heated words. It is obvious some of the growers as well as Abu Ali have lost patience with Mohammed. Aside, Tamer asks me if I know Abu Ali's son, the Captain.

"I know him well. He stays at my ranch in Texas."

Tamer and Abu Ali have a short conversation between themselves. "He can find anyone," Tamer says, smiling now. "He's a badass . . . crazy motherfucker." Tamer and Abu Ali confer once again. "You know, it's not so much the money," Tamer goes on, speaking quietly to me. "Of course that hurts. But we can always make more money. These guys just hate getting fucked. It's their pride, their dignity. Something must be done. It doesn't matter how long it takes. This is how we are. We must have revenge."

Abu Ali and the others come up with a solution. They urge me to take ten kilos of "the other, the white" to make up for the money lost on the load they sent to the Wizard's people in Miami. Somehow I knew this was coming. Why else hold the meeting in a junk lab? "What am I going to do with ten kilos of heroin?" I say. "Even if I agree to take it, I wouldn't know where to sell it. Heroin is not my business. Hashish is my business."

"I will sell it for you," says Tamer. "My people will pick it up in New York or Jersey and cash it out in a couple of days. I'll get the money back to Abu Ali, and he pays these men. You never have to touch the stuff."

I pretend to give this plan some consideration. I said to myself I would do anything to get this trip back on track. Should I take the junk? They certainly make it sound easy. What the fuck? Why not? Meanwhile, everything inside me is shouting, *No! No, no . . . don't do it. You may be a criminal, Stratton, an outlaw your entire adult life. And, yes, there is money in that white powder. Big money. Certainly it is easier to smuggle than pot or hash.*

I have heard and listened to all of the arguments for getting into the heroin business. Including the most reasonable argument of all:

you can get just as much time if you get caught smuggling pot or hash as you can if you are caught smuggling junk. Cannabis and its byproduct hashish are Schedule One narcotics, according to the government, in the same category as heroin. The government makes no distinction between these two illegal substances. So why should I?

But I stopped adhering to the edicts of my government a long time ago. Just because those fools don't know the difference between junk and pot, I do. You don't put pot in a needle and stick it in your arm. You don't get strung out on pot any more than you get strung out on coffee or Pepsi. You don't die from smoking it, no matter how much you smoke. It won't turn you into a desperate junkie willing to sell out friends, family, yourself, everything you believe in to get that next fix. But it is all illegal, all criminal. Finally, for me, it all comes down to one consideration: If I make this move, if I agree to let them put ten kilos of heroin in with my load and turn it over to Tamer, how will I feel about that? How will I feel about myself?

I can't go there. I'll be a hypocrite, a phony, a liar to myself. All my life, since I was old enough to know what it meant, I railed against hypocrites. The teachers, the cops, the politicians, the suburban parents where I grew up who smoked cigarettes and told us kids it was wrong, many of them booze hounds, adulterers. Priests and Cub Scout leaders diddling little boys. The many liars, bigots, cheats. And cowards. Without the guts to stand up for what they profess to believe. Now I'm going to become one of them? Different perhaps but still the same. No. Do what you say and say what you do. Be who you believe you are.

Going against my principles is what got me in trouble in the first place.

I get up from the table, choose my words carefully. "Tamer, tell Abu Ali and these men I respect them. I understand their position and I sympathize with them. Nobody likes to get ripped off. But I must respectfully decline to handle *the other, the white*. Because, first of all, it is not my business. But more important to me, in a word, I do not want the karma that comes with it."

Tamer smiles. Khalid also smirks. Karma? Fucking hippie. Is there even a word for karma in Arabic? It's from Sanskrit, but there must be a comparable concept in Islam.

I bow slightly. Abu Ali stands. We embrace, kiss. The heroin cooking downstairs smells . . . good! I almost change my mind.

Fuck it, take the junk! Who cares? It's an ugly, cutthroat world. People are savages. There is no afterlife. It's all just shit anyway. If people want to kill themselves, destroy their lives sticking needles in their arms, so what? That's their business. How is it any worse than gorging yourself on junk food and dying of a heart attack? It doesn't matter how you die—or how you live. Nobody gets out of here alive.

No, no, no . . . go home. Empty-handed if need be. It does matter. We answer to a higher power, even if only within ourselves. Life is not all just shit. It means something. Or, at the very least, we invest it with meaning if we follow what we believe. Don't break weak, Stratton. *Be a fucking man.*

Khalid stands with me, and we start from the room.

"Just a minute, Rich," Tamer calls to me.

I look back half expecting him to pull a gun and say: *You are taking the junk or you leave here as a corpse.* Tamer speaks to Abu Ali, and then he walks outside with Khalid and me. "Go on," he says to Khalid. "I'll take him."

"Where?" Khalid asks.

"Meet us in town."

Where indeed? I don't even know where I'm going. Back to Abu Ali's villa? Back to Beirut? I have no money. Mohammed is going to shit when he hears about this. Somehow, this fat, greedy prick will convince himself this is all my fault and I am wrong for not taking the heroin, wrong for letting the Wizard steal my briefcase, wrong for allowing him to rip them off even if I had no part in it. There is some kind of twisted Levantine logic at work here, I know it is how Mohammed's mind works. How am I supposed to explain this to Sammy? He's going to go nuts. I neglected to tell him about the stolen briefcase, didn't want to admit it and worry him. I'm wondering if maybe the Arabs will allow me to take the couple of tons we have already prepared and try to salvage this trip. Certainly it won't be the payday we anticipated.

There is an infallible reasoning to living in the moment, I tell myself. It is the smuggler's creed: You are not out until the game is over. Anything can happen. The past is finished. Life goes on. It is all about the next twenty minutes. Where do I go from here? Wherever these next few steps take me. Because you never know what lies around the next corner. Death or deliverance.

Tamer walks me to his car, the new Mercedes. And we drive off. "You hungry?" he asks.

"I could eat." That's one thing about me: I can always eat. Nothing interferes with my appetite. And drink. Booze is my friend. Shuts up the worrywart living in the left side of my head. And fuck. Never too scared or too depressed to eat, drink, and fuck.

We dine at a restaurant in Baalbek. "Let me see what I can do," Tamer says as we eat.

"This is not negotiable, Tamer."

"I understand. You made that clear. Bad karma." He smiles. "How much hash do you want?"

"As much as I can get. As long as it's good. All Number One or Zahara. I can't sell commercial. The market is flooded with—"

"I know all about it," Tamer says. "You have a secure way to get it in the country?"

"Yes. Very secure."

He nods knowingly. "So they tell me. You never lost a load. How long will it take you to sell it?"

"If it's good, the money will start to flow within a week or two after we take delivery in the States. We'll cash out in a couple of months."

Tamer nods. "I will speak to them. They need the money."

"I'm not taking the junk."

"You said that. I respect what you say. Every man must have something he will not do . . . a line he will not cross."

"What's yours?" I ask.

Tamer smiles. Nice teeth, I'm thinking. He's a junk dealer but I like the guy.

"Good question," he says. "I guess . . . I don't fuck my friends."

KHALID WAITS FOR us outside the restaurant. Before returning to the villa, I ask him to take me to the temple complex of Bacchus and Jupiter, the fantastic ruins rising up like a dream landscape from the hill in the middle of town. Khalid has no interest in fallen temples, he leaves me to wander alone among the ruins. He stays by the car to watch the gaggle of tourists, mostly Beirutis, some young women with exposed heads who have come to Baalbek in small buses, and who pay to ride the tired, leathery camels tethered in the parking lot.

The war has all but eviscerated Lebanon's foreign tourist industry. The ruins are empty. I have visited this site on previous trips to Baalbek, perhaps even in other lifetimes. I'm drawn here as if by some unseen force, utterly fascinated by this enigmatic, sacred place and how and why it came to be one of the wonders of the ancient world—an obscure religious center well inland, difficult to get to, and with no political or trading significance. The temples at Baalbek were known as a place of oracular divination, a place where kings and conquerors, mystics and magicians came seeking elucidation of the present and a vision for the future. If it worked for them, perhaps it would work for me.

It is late afternoon, the golden hour. I sit on one of the massive slabs of cut stone and face the setting sun. The light is refracted through the columns. Time stands still. I let my mind go, enter the infinite, let the mystery captured in the stones take me higher even than my beloved *al-Kayf*—though, truth be told, when you smoke as much as I do you never really come down. There is a fundamental truth cast in these stones, an understanding of the meaning of life I must fathom to free my mind from the petty cares and woes of mere time-captured existence. Who cares about this hash trip? Why am I always obsessing about getting over on the Man? So what if I'm facing a shitload of time back in the States? There is no such thing as time. And who cares if the cops and judges are a bunch of assholes and hypocrites? What's that got to do with who I am? The government may be in the hands of a gang of conspirators—nothing new there. None of that matters; it is not important. Mere details. There is a secret locked in the giant rose granite columns rising from a foundation of limestone megaliths. Understand the truth fixed forever in the temples and platforms and sculptures harkening back thousands of years before Jesus Christ walked the earth, and this truth was foreseen and will still be here long after I am gone, long after Bernie Wolfshein and DEA, CENTAC, the American government, and these stupid, asinine laws cease to exist and are forgotten, these stones will still be here.

The place is a riddle in stone, compelling and humbling. There is no known explanation for how the original temple came into being, no written history left by the people who quarried and placed the gigantic foundation stones that lie beneath the Temple of Jupiter and the Great Court at the base of the temple. Long before the Phoenicians arrived here and built their temple to the god Baal, and thousands of years before the Romans conquered the lands of the Old Testament and built their temple of Jupiter on the same spot, some tribe of prehistoric, highly evolved artisans and engineers managed to cut, transport, and lift and precisely arrange unwieldy, colossal blocks of stone weighing hundreds of tons. They labored to build a temple to honor a god before all others. And then they disappeared without a trace.

Except for their mighty works, the stones. One stone, known as the Stone of the Pregnant Woman—the single largest piece of cut stone in the world—still lies partially buried and attached at the limestone quarry a quarter of a mile from the temple complex. It's as though the mysterious masons dropped their tools and fled before they could finish the job. To quarry, transport, and lift these stones is a feat that is beyond the engineering abilities of any recognized ancient or contemporary builders. It daunts me to contemplate how mere humans were able to cleave and shape and move and elevate these stones. But the greater mystery is what inspired them, what faith in what gods or almighty God motivated them and gave them superhuman strength?

Beside this mystery, who I am and what meaning my life has seems inconsequential. Or perhaps not. The oracle that dwells in these stones whispers that my existence is part of something vast and unknowable but worthy of reverence. Then it comes to me. I understand why this place is here and why I am here to hear the oracle. If nothing is random, then I have a part in all this. The beings who cut and fashioned these mammoth stones understood that there is purpose and meaning to life.

They lived and I exist to honor creation and worship the Creator.

8

CITY OF DEATH

ANOTHER THREE WEEKS slip into eternity. The weather is beautiful, spring in the Bekaa, the air ever fragrant, and the skies have an iridescent blue untainted by the smear of pollution. Early in the morning I meditate, exercise on the balcony, and breathe deeply the scented air. I walk around the grounds surrounding Abu Ali's villa complex, and I sit with the men in the courtyard and drink thick, sweet coffee. I scratch my balls in the loose pants and smoke bowls of hashish and talk world events.

Here I am in the thick of a conflict affecting the entire planet, yet it is the world outside the valley that seems to quake and tremble while I rest unmolested. I have only tenuous, secondhand contact with America. There is an American-made antiaircraft gun set up on a rear patio. "For the CIA planes," Khalid tells me. Everyone is convinced that Israel, backed by America, is preparing to invade Lebanon. The hush, the lull, the quietude may only be a prelude to the chaos still to come. We visit the hash plantations. The growers are more trusting now and gradually the load is coming together. Tamer left, returned to the States. Abu Ali assures me that, "Everything will be ready." Tamer personally guaranteed payment for the shipment. Why, I'm not sure. Nor do I know what he expects to get in return. This is vaguely troubling.

It's an odd time for me. I feel a nagging sense of guilt, for it was my carelessness that allowed the Wizard to penetrate our network and rip these people off. Why was I even carrying a briefcase? Who do I think I am? Some straight businessman selling insurance like my old man? No, I'm an outlaw, a criminal in their eyes. And criminals must be careful. *Trust no one. Watch your back. Protect your sources.*

I like the people of the valley—the growers, the kids and the old men, the girls and the women—and I hate to let them down. They are close to the earth and kind, generous, giving, like the land. I'm homesick, lonely, horny; and yet enjoying the irresponsibility of being completely unable to alter my circumstances. It's like being in jail. I am, in a sense, still a hostage, a prisoner of this business. For the time being the outcome of this enterprise is totally beyond my control. This is strangely liberating. I never would have chosen to be here all this time, never would have chosen to go through this test; and yet I feel I have learned some indelible truth—from the oracle that dwells in the stones of the ancient ruins, from the people of this ancient land. If I can just remember to let go, let whatever happens happen, and trust God, because it's not about what happens to me. It's all about how I respond to what happens.

I could have become angry and shouted at Abu Ali and the men at the sit-down; I could have cursed them and stormed out of the room. But I kept my peace. I could have agreed to take the heroin and become a merchant of death. But I held to my beliefs. I showed respect, and Tamer saw that. Tamer believed, based on what he saw, that he could trust me. Now, and through to the end of this, I have got to remind myself constantly to maintain my integrity and trust in my values.

I sleep well here in the valley, and I have vivid dreams. One morning I have a transcendent nocturnal emission, a wet dream that is in its own self-centered way better than any lovemaking experience I have ever had with a real woman. It is as though for once the fucking and the ideal fantasy of what sex could be merge and leave me utterly satisfied with no sense of guilt or entanglement. I am riding around with my dream girl in the old 1940 Ford convertible coupe. She's some combination of every woman I have ever loved. Anaïs, my wife, eclipses the others; she is, after all, the love of my life. But I also see glimpses of Laila, the enticing wife of Saad's neighbor. There is a proud Arab poise to my dream woman's carriage that only relaxes when she lies down and spreads her thighs. She has the hips of my high school love, Colleen. Val is in the contours of her rump. I could find a toe or finger to point to them all. We make leisurely love in a meadow by a stream under a huge weeping willow. The light coming through the tree's leaves is magical green. Entering her takes me to the center of the earth and out to the far reaches of the cosmos. The orgasm is timeless. My only letdown comes when I wake to find that I am alone, and the dream-woman has dissolved in a wet spot on the sheets.

* * *

NOW THE TRUCKS are idling in the courtyard—big, camouflage-green Syrian Army flatbeds with canvas back covers. Their engines turn over with a sluggish rhythmic rotation like the panting of beasts. There are two trucks and a jeep and a military personnel carrier. The trucks are loaded with 15,000 pounds, seven and a half tons, all Number One, Zahara, and Double Zahara—redolent in resin-stained white canvas sacks, graded and stamped with the Flower of Bekaa seal, packed in thick burlap duffel bags. There are also fifty gallons of honey oil included in the load, sticky, amber-colored essence of cannabis resin worth twenty thousand a gallon. A $15 million shipment wholesale, worth upwards of fifty million in the marketplace. My end alone is five million. All that remains is to get the hash safely from the Bekaa to Beirut, pack it with the dates, put the whole shipment in containers loaded on a freighter headed for New Jersey. Then I can go home.

Home? Wherever that is. I'm a fugitive, I have no home. That is the nature of being a fugitive: one has no place to call home. I live in the wind. Abu Ali's villa outside Baalbek is my home—for now. The penthouse apartment in West Beirut is my home—for the immediate future. The farm in Maine, put up to secure my bond, is subject to forfeiture by the government. The ranch in Texas is under the cloud of an IRS investigation. Besides, I can't go there, I'll be arrested. Where I go from here will be decided when the time comes. In the meantime: Play it by ear, travel light and leave no trail, be ready to drop everything and split at a moment's notice. Run . . . and keep on running.

The trucks are ready, the small convoy is under way before dawn. The Syrian army is transporting our load. How cool is that? I ride ahead with Abu Ali in his Land Rover. He assures me that there is nothing to worry about, everyone along the road from Baalbek to Beirut at the two dozen plus checkpoints has been greased with *baksheesh*. Fifty thousand dollars worth. Money, in fact, is Abu Ali's only concern—though, he admits, in Lebanon in these chaotic times, one never knows. Some new militia or some faction of an established militia or a renegade crew could materialize and try to shake us down. Abu Ali says he is broke. He needs money. He won't go into it with me, not now. That is something we must discuss with Mohammed once the shipment is safely delivered to the port.

We keep the convoy in view. Abu Ali tells me that nearly everyone understands contraband is being transported. The smell alone gives it away. I could smell hash fifteen feet from the trucks. He says no one will question the shipment because it appears to be done with the sanction and blessing of the powers that be, such as they are at any given moment. If there is a problem, he says, he will drive back to the checkpoint and straighten it out. But there will not be a problem, he assures me. We have Syrian soldiers on the trucks guarding our load. Nobody messes with the Syrian army. We are official. Hashish is the lifeblood of Lebanon. Still, I am nervous for the entire trip. There is a lot riding in those trucks. Anything can happen. We could be hit with a bomb or a rocket. This is like a military excursion in the middle of a land where there are no clearly drawn battle lines. My stomach tightens at the approach of each new roadblock.

Abu Ali and I separate from the convoy on the outskirts of the city, before we reach the Green Line. The load is entrusted to some bearded, machine gun-toting men dressed in military fatigues, who will escort the trucks to the port in East Beirut, unload the cargo, and stay to guard the warehouse. By noon, Abu Ali and I are at the penthouse apartment waiting for Mohammed and Nasif. I take a cold shower. This is like coming home for me: my books, my music, my new ward-robe, the family Saad, even the haunted elephant's graveyard and the gouges in the bedroom walls give me comfort. Much as I loved the beauty and tranquility of the Bekaa, I felt as though I were in a state of suspended animation. Now it's back to real life.

And I sense—by virtue of the fact that the load is at the port, ready to be hidden among the dates and then shipped to New Jersey—there has been a definite shift in the power dynamic of this endeavor. To some degree, I am calling the shots now. Soon the Arabs will need me more than I need them. Mohammed is cool to me when he and Nasif and Saad arrive at the penthouse. They go immediately into an intense conference with Abu Ali. I surmise by how agitated Mohammed is that there has been no word from America, no money and no delivery of multi-kilos of cocaine from Colombia. The worry beads are out and clicking furiously. Mohammed defends his position vociferously. He shrugs, scowls, his jowls turn a purple shade of blue. I sit there com-prehending only the tenor of what is being said. I hear Tamer's name mentioned more than once.

Money. It all comes down to money. Abu Ali wants money. He has put up money out of his own pocket to pay to have the load brought down from the Bekaa. Mohammed wants money. He must grease a dozen or two dozen palms to get the load safely aboard a ship and headed for port in the United States. They both look at me.

Then suddenly the mood shifts as food and alcohol are served. Everyone is more or less happy. Relieved. It really feels like we are under way. We have the load, and it is good. All good and even very good. Abu Ali drinks only tea. He chain-smokes Marlboros even while eating. The meal is sumptuous, as always. I learn that Mrs. Saad and Abu Ali are related, first cousins. The war, everyone agrees, has reached the point where something decisive must happen soon or Beirut will be destroyed and Lebanon will not survive as a sovereign state. Beirutis with the means are fleeing the city in droves. It is no better in the countryside, particularly in the south. Uprooted, impoverished refugees are flocking to the city and squatting in abandoned homes and buildings, camping in the parks. Israel's formidable army is rallying at the southern frontier. There is the sense everywhere one turns that life in Beirut is bought and paid for moment to moment. One's honor, value, integrity, self-worth are like pennies tossed in the street to groveling urchins. They mean nothing but a hope to survive.

The meal goes on for hours. Abu Ali leaves with handshakes and kisses. Then the imbroglio simmering all afternoon boils over into the front room. By this time I am several glasses of Johnny Walker past caring what Mohammed thinks of me. Besides, I know, beneath all his bluster and recriminations he understands he created this mess.

Why, he asks through his firstborn, did I tell Abu Ali that I had nothing to do with the business with Pierre?

"Because it's the truth," I say. "And your father knows it. You know it! Don't even try this shit with me, Nasif. Why did your father, why did you allow him to make this business? After what I told you? I told you months ago when you called me in New York that this guy was a thief. And after what happened in the restaurant? It makes no sense."

"Mister Richard, you must understand. It was my father's decision. I cannot go against my father."

"So ask him: Why did he make this business when I told him not to do it?"

Mohammed erupts, he yells at me as Nasif translates. *It is none of my business!* he shouts in Arabic.

"Then why am I being held responsible?"

Nasif translates. *Because you are American, Pierre is American. He used your name. It is assumed you are partners.*

"No fucking way I am taking responsibility for that load, Nasif. I told you not to do anything with this man. Of course he was going to rip you off. What did you expect?"

I'm yelling now, which serves to quiet Mohammed. There is a time to hold your peace; there is a time to yell.

Mohammed answers and Nasif translates. "He had money." Two hundred and fifty grand, Nasif tells me, not the million plus he bragged about. And a promise to send cocaine from Colombia, which has not materialized. "And never will," I say.

Glum silence. Mohammed is still seething, but he seems at last to have grasped the concept that this is his problem and not my responsibility. Do I have Pierre's phone number or an address in America? they ask for the tenth time. Nasif confirms there has been no contact with him since the load left Beirut. The number he gave them turned out to be an answering service. He has not responded to repeated messages.

"It's not my problem," I insist.

"Help us find him."

I shrug. "I'll do what I can. For now, let's make this business a success. Then we'll worry about Pierre."

But Mohammed is not ready to move on. His dark, heavy-jowled face flushes mauve, and his anger flares once more. *Perhaps if I hadn't insulted Pierre and humiliated the man by slapping him across the face, he would have honored his end of the business*, Mohammed sputters. *Perhaps he ripped them off because he wishes to humiliate me as I humiliated him*, he accuses me through his number-one son and storms out of the room.

Nasif shakes his head, smiles. "See you later," he says. "He'll calm down. It's all good now, yes, Mr. Richard?"

"Yes, Nasif. We have a good load. That's what matters."

Nasif follows his father out through the elephant boneyard.

* * *

RELATIONS BETWEEN MOHAMMED and me remain tense. Try as we both do to put the Wizard incident behind us, with his sophistic logic, Mohammed still holds me responsible because: I know Pierre. I allowed him to steal my briefcase. I never should have had Mohammed's numbers where someone could get them. Whatever the reasoning, he insists I owe it to them to do everything I can to help them locate Pierre when I get back to the States and make him pay. Or at least have him killed.

And he touches that guilty nerve. Again, through Nasif, Mohammed broaches the subject of allowing them to include ten kilos of heroin in with the load of hashish and use the profits to repay Abu Ali and the other growers for the stolen hash. I explain I have already rejected this proposal. They just won't let it go. Murder. Heroin trafficking. Kidnapping. Take your pick. Days pass. Another week goes by. My refusal to take the junk remains adamant. I begin to worry they may just hide ten kilos of heroin in with the dates and hash without my knowing.

Finally Mohammed reveals what he has been angling toward all along: more money. "Fifty thousand," Nasif tells me.

I lie. "I don't have fifty thousand."

"My father says you must call New York and have Biff bring fifty thousand or we cannot make this business."

Anticipating this, knowing it was coming all along, I have been in touch with Val, told her to reach out for Sammy, Rosie in Toronto, dig into the money stash, do whatever she has to do and find as much cash as she can. I was worried Mohammed would demand more like two hundred fifty thousand. I'm relieved it is only another fifty. That will bring our initial investment up to around three hundred grand plus expenses. Not a bad investment for a potential multimillion dollar payday. Still, these guys are Lebanese, they won't respect me if I don't haggle and play out the hand.

"There's no way I can get another fifty thousand. It could take weeks. Tell him to forget it."

Mohammed broods as Nasif translates. "Fifty thousand by next week or he says he will sell the load to the Dutch."

I shake my head. "He can't do that. It's my load. Besides, it would take the Dutch six years to sell that much hash."

"Not so long. They have American buyers, British . . ."

Now I am the one getting angry. "What about the money we already have invested? Is your father going to pay me back?" I stand and walk toward the balcony. "I'm finished, Nasif! I'm going back to New York. No more business! And tell your father, he can worry about paying Abu Ali and the others for the load Pierre stole."

Nasif jumps up and cuts me off before I step out onto the balcony. "Don't go out there!" he exclaims. "It's too dangerous! The snipers! Please, Mr. Richard, another fifty thousand and you will be rich. We want to make this business with you. But we must move quickly, before the war is too bad and they close the port."

This gets to me. The mounting chaos and threat of an Israeli invasion are real. "Fifty thousand," I say and go back inside, embrace and kiss father and son. "Not a penny more."

Mohammed shakes his head, chuckles. "Ah, Mr. Richard . . ." and says something in Arabic.

Nasif laughs and translates. "He says, now you are really Lebanese."

"Swamp Yankee," I say.

"What is this?"

"Never mind. Take me to the telephone office."

TWO DAYS LATER Val arrives on a flight from Zurich. She picked up money from Rosie in Toronto, seventy-five grand Canadian. Deeply tanned from weeks of lounging on the beach in Maui, she looks like she could be Moroccan, with big, gold hoop earrings and dark shades. She's traveling on a Canadian passport. Mohammed whisks her through

immigration with no Lebanese stamps in her brief. I offered to have
Nasif meet her in Cyprus and pick up the money. Or have Biff bring
it. But she wanted to come, said she needed to see me. Sometimes I
think she is as attracted to life on the edge as I am. "I'm so horny," she
whispers when we are in the back of Mohammed's Mercedes on the
way to the apartment. "I can't wait to fuck you."

That's encouraging. I give fifty thousand to Mohammed and hold
on to twenty-five in case we have to make a hasty escape. The airport
closes two days after Val arrives. The Falange are bombarding the Palestinians. The Syrians are massing troops and antiquated Soviet weap-
onry in the lower Bekaa, rattling their sabers at the Israelis. The Druze
and the Maronites are battling it out in the Chuf. I can't keep track of
who is on which side in this war anymore. The United Nations troops
seem utterly impotent. Everyone fears an Israeli invasion. It is not safe
for us to leave the apartment.

At first Val is fine with the enforced confinement. She fits right in
with the Saad women, she wants to learn how to prepare the Lebanese
dishes, she talks to the girls about life in America, and they are teaching
her to belly dance. There is something vaguely Middle Eastern about
Val to begin with—the olive skin, the Semitic nose and high cheekbones—and temperamentally, though she would never admit it, she's
like some nomadic Bedouin. Her ancestry is vague. Probably Eastern
European on her father's side. Her mother is half Sicilian, half Irish,
and all crazy, been in and out of institutions for the insane. Val is a
California girl. Dresses like a rich gypsy. Long skirts. Demure blouses.
String bikini underwear. She knows how to make herself and those
around her feel comfortable and could be accepted almost anywhere.
She has spent time in Afghanistan, India, Nepal, Mexico, Colombia.
She has the worldly aplomb of an experienced smuggler. And not yet
thirty, she loves to fuck.

Still, I feel fear quivering in her thighs as she lies beneath me or
sits on my face and throws her head back and moans to the rumbling
of far-off artillery fire. She flinches when the rockets land closer. As

bombs hit nearby and the neighborhood trembles, she clings to my side and buries her face under my arm. I look at her sleeping fitfully in the morning light after a night of desperate love. Our future feels as hopeless as the Palestinians.

"Why did you come?" I ask.

"I don't know. I felt sad. I was beginning to think I would never see you again."

"You happy now?"

"If I'm with you, I'm happy," she says, yet I don't feel it. "I want to have your baby," she announces.

"Really?"

"Yeah. Really. Knock me up. Send me home preggers," she says. And then, "I bought a house . . . in Maui. You're gonna love it. It's on the side of the volcano with a beautiful view. It's so quiet there, the nearest neighbor is half a mile away. I wanna fill it with kids and good food we grow in our own garden. You're gonna be happy there."

"How long do you think it would be before the Feds found me?"

"People have been living over there on the lam for years. Including me. The property is in a company name. No connection to me. Or you. No way they'll find you there."

It's something to think about. "C'mon," she says and reaches for my cock. "Come inside me."

* * *

AS THE DAYS turn into weeks we are both feeling the strain of this bizarre, luxurious captivity. Val's birthday comes and goes with muted celebration, and all you can eat and drink. We make love sometimes two, three times a day. Val looks at me, I look back at her, she cocks her head toward the bedroom with the gray gouges in the concrete walls, winks a big brown eye. If she's not knocked up now, she never will be. Insane as it may be to think of bringing a child into the world at present, two fugitive parents both facing prison sentences, there is something about the idea that seems right to me. An affirmation of life. And the sex is so good, so real and chancy. We have all the time in the exploding, ever-expanding universe. There is no such thing as death. I am already dead. I can smother my face in her sex and hide from the world crumbling outside.

Mohammed and Nasif come to the apartment late each afternoon for the endless evening meal. "When?" I ask them.

"Soon, Mr. Richard. Soon. Everything is being prepared."

Same answer, different day. The Holiday Inn has been reduced to a blown-out shell and massive rubble heap. The streets of what was once known as the Paris of the Middle East are a battleground stinking of death and something alive—fear.

Val and I get it on and lie in each other's arms sweating. "I want to go home," she says.

"So do I."

We discuss other ways to get her out of the country. By car to Damascus. Or to Israel. Mohammed has connections in the south that can assure her safe passage. Plans are made, but then Val balks. Part of her does not want to leave. She says it's the most time we've had together since we've known each other. She wants me to go with her, as if she fears separation will make me, or her, more vulnerable. Or maybe she's waiting to feel new life stir in her womb.

AT LAST THE day arrives. "Everything is ready," Mohammed assures me. He urges me to remain in the relative safety of the penthouse and take his word that he and his men have followed the precise, detailed instructions I gave them for preparing the shipment. But my word, and my New York partners' freedom, as well as fifteen million dollars worth of hashish, are on the line. Years of working with Arabs, Mexicans, Jamaicans, Colombians has convinced me they just don't understand the lengths to which North American law-enforcement agents are willing to go in order to bust our loads and lock us up.

"This is serious business," I remind him. "People go to prison."
Maybe not in Lebanon, not if you are the former chief of customs.

My Yankee WASP work ethic demands dependability and attention to detail. In more than fifteen years in this business I have never
lost a load due to sloppiness. My suspicious side nags that Mohammed
doesn't want me to inspect the shipment because he's gone ahead and
hidden the ten kilos of junk in with the dates and hash—not that there
is any way I could find it in half a million kilos of dates and seven and
a half tons of hash. Reason argues Mohammed wouldn't risk hiding
the junk in the load knowing that once the shipment has landed in the
States I'll have total control and he would have no way of recovering
the heroin. Except, of course, if he—or Tamer—has someone put a
gun to my head and demand I turn it over.

Saad checks the street and signals to me. I step from the dim ves-
tibule of the building, slip on my Arafat shades, pull the checkered
kaffiyeh close around my American face and duck into the rear of the
waiting Mercedes. Crouched on the floor for the dash across the Green
Line, I hear sirens, mortar fire, loud explosions of bombs and rockets
over the racing Mercedes engine and humming of tires. On the carpet
near my face is a dried, rust-colored stain that looks like blood. The car
has been shot up since our trip to the Bekaa. Nasif drives. Saad, clutching his Uzi, rides shotgun.

"You okay back there, Mr. Richard?" Nasif calls.

"Yeah."

Nasif and Saad rant on in Arabic; they laugh and shout curses at
the snipers on the rooftops. Nasif prides himself on being able to out-
maneuver the shooters poised along the verdant no-man's land sep-
arating East from West Beirut. Yet bullet holes pock the trunk and
rear quarter of the Mercedes. Once we cross the Green Line into East
Beirut, we are out of immediate danger of sniper fire. I sit up in the
rear seat but keep the kaffiyeh wrapped around my head. Here in the
Christian section of the city, the war is not as intense. It is a short ride
along the Rue Charles Helou to the seaport district.

The warehouse is under guard by the four bearded Uzi-toting heavies in green fatigues who escorted the load to the port. Half a dozen orange sea/land containers are stacked on the dock beside the warehouse; a seventh is backed up to a loading platform. Nasif pulls up out front, and I am quickly hustled inside. As soon as I walk through the warehouse door, I am met with the spicy perfumed odor of premium-grade hashish mixed with the syrupy sweet smell of dates. Hundreds of brown waxed cardboard cartons labeled *khistawi* dates in English and Arabic are piled along the rear wall. The rest of the load has already been packed into the containers on the dock, waiting to be hoisted aboard a Greek freighter due to arrive in Beirut in a few days. As Mohammed told me, everything is ready. Or so it appears. *Check the boxes yourself, Doc. Make sure they do it right*, I hear Sammy admonish me. *Leave nothing to chance. Trust no one. Believe only what you see with your own eyes.* Fifteen million dollars—or fifteen years in prison—hang in the balance.

It will take all seven sea/land containers full of cartons packed with dates and hashish to conceal the contraband. Four of the containers will hold just dates; the other three are to be packed with dates and hash. The cardboard cartons containing the hash are wrapped with red plastic strapping to distinguish them from the boxes with only dates, which have green, blue, or yellow strapping. The hash is packed into sealed tin boxes. According to instructions I gave Mohammed, the tin boxes full of fragrant hashish are supposed to be packed into the cardboard cartons, then covered top and bottom with a thick layer of dates within those boxes. I walk to the rear of the warehouse and take down a box with red straps. It doesn't feel right—too hard.

I snip the plastic bands and tear open the carton. Inside is a sealed tin box and no dates. I look at Mohammed. "Where are the dates?"

"In the other cartons," Nasif answers, "as you wanted."

I shake my head. I'm beginning to feel dizzy; I can't believe what I'm seeing. After I waited weeks to get this load packed and shipped, they fucked it up. Is it stupidity, do the instructions get lost in translation, or are they just plain perverse, testing me to see if I am serious? I take down another red-strapped carton and rip it open. Again, they simply shoved the tin box with the hashish inside the cardboard box without packing it in layers of dates on the bottom and top as they have been told many, many times. I even drew them pictures to show how it must be done. But no, they ignored my repeated directions. As it is, if a US Customs agent were to choose to open one of the red-strapped boxes, the load is busted.

"No good," I say, fighting to control my anger. "You've got to unload all these containers. Repack the cartons. And cover the tin boxes of hash with dates. Thick layers of dates! On the bottom and the top. The way I showed you *fifty fucking times!*"

As Nasif translates, I see Mohammed starting to turn purple with rage. Did he think I wouldn't check the load? That I would just let it go and trust in Allah to get it past Customs? "But Mr. Richard, that will take days. Maybe more than one week," Nasif protests. "We'll miss the ship. It could be weeks before we can arrange new transport. And the war—"

"You tell your father I'm sick of this shit! It doesn't matter how long it takes. I told you how I wanted the cartons packed. You—he—ignored my instructions! We can't send it like this!" I'm yelling now. The dudes with the Uzis are getting tense. "It's got to be done right," I say, "or I'll take every one of these fucking boxes and throw them into the sea!"

There is a lengthy discussion in Arabic between father, son, and one of the men guarding the warehouse. They give me a look that says, *Forget about it, pal. The shipment's going the way it is.* As the former chief of Lebanese Customs, Mohammed just can't understand that, unlike in Beirut, US Customs is not totally corrupt. To break the impasse and let them know I'm serious, I grab one of the cartons I opened, take it out onto the dock, and heave it into the murky Mediterranean. "Every fucking one!" I yell and head back inside. "I'll go back with nothing. I don't give a fuck. *I don't want to go to prison.* Can't you understand that?"

Finally, Mohammed relents. The men fish the box of hash from the sea and laugh at me. Crazy American! I feel my grandmother's spirit swelling with pride. He may be a dope smuggler, but at least he's a conscientious dope smuggler. After all, hadn't some of our forebears made their fortune smuggling opium and God knows what else? It is a Yankee outlaw tradition to thumb one's nose at the government and break the laws that are perceived as wrongheaded. Henry David Thoreau taught me that in his essay "Civil Disobedience." Governments and their picayune laws are for the uninformed masses, the sheep. Every great fortune is founded on a crime, Balzac said. As a native New Englander, I was brought up with the rumors that Joe Kennedy made his family's fortune smuggling booze during Prohibition—and his son went on to become president. The laws against cannabis are a cruel joke. It is only a matter of time before pot prohibition is repealed. In the interim, fortunes will be made. I paid my dues. No reason I should not be a marijuana millionaire.

BACK IN OUR penthouse prison one afternoon as we lay in bed, Val announces she is going stir crazy. "I've got to get out of this place," she tells me. "I don't care how fucked-up it is out there." She shows me an ad in the English-language newspaper. *The Shining*, starring Jack Nicholson, is playing at a movie theater on Hamra Street. "Take me to the movies. Or I'll walk."

We go to a matinee. On Hamra Street, as we walk from the car to the theater, a man walking behind us pulls a gun and opens fire on a group of men standing on the other side of the street, then he runs off. Val ducks behind me. "*Sheesh!* What was that?"

"Drug dealers," Nasif says.

The movie is in English with Arabic subtitles. The audience loves it. So does Val. She is happy, at least for a couple of hours. After the show we go to dinner at Frank Terpil's restaurant and drink whiskey and champagne. "I want to go home," Val says, clutching my hand beneath the table. "I mean *home* home. Enough of this place already."

"Soon, baby. Soon."

"Soon . . . You sound like Mohammed."

"Another week, maybe ten days."

Nasif has arranged a car and driver to take us back to the apartment. We are both a little loaded, feeling mellow. Val rests her head on my shoulder and closes her eyes. She grips my arm and nuzzles up to me. "I love you, daddy," she says.

When we turn down our street, I see swirling red-and-blue lights. Ambulances and emergency vehicles are pulled up outside the apartment building. The neighborhood has been struck by heavy rocket fire. Dazed, I get out of the car and look up at a gaping black hole in the sky where our bedroom was. Half of the top three floors of our building are blown away. Rescue workers search through the rubble for a family who lives on the floor beneath us.

"Saad . . . Saad!" I call to one of the rescue workers. He shrugs. I tell our driver to ask for Saad and his family. No one knows anything. I look around at the faces of the people gathered in the street but recognize no one.

Val is in the backseat of the car, sobbing. "No . . . no, no more. Please, I want to go home. Now."

We spend the night at the Commodore Hotel. Val cries, begs me to leave the country with her. "You know I can't go, baby. Not until the load is safely on its way to New York. We've come this far. I can't quit now."

"You're crazy! You're not thinking straight. These people are all insane. They won't stop until everyone is dead."

"I'll be okay."

"Richard, honey, listen to me. All that money won't do you any good if you're dead."

The next day Nasif arranges for Val to be driven by car across the border to Israel, where she catches an El Al flight from Tel Aviv to JFK. Nasif says eight people who lived in the building were killed or badly injured. Laila and her husband, the doctor, are among the casualties, Nasif tells me with the resignation of a man who is accustomed to announcing death. The Saad family, however, is safe, staying at another apartment building owned by Mohammed. "It is bad, Richard. You must leave soon."

"Of course," I say and manage a smile. "I wasn't planning on staying."

Once I get word Val is on a plane heading back to the States, I reach a point beyond fear. Nothing matters to me now except getting the hash secured on board a ship headed for New Jersey. It is demented, I know, but I value my life less than the load. Call it stubbornness, but what I fear most is failure. Going back with nothing but my dick in my hand. Humiliation. Then for the rest of my life I'm going to look in the mirror and say, *Stratton, you ain't shit. You let a half-assed war punk you out.*

I stay at the Commodore with the foreign press corps. Drink in the evening at the downstairs bar with the intrepid barstool journalists who rarely leave the hotel and get their reports from wire machines clattering away in the lobby. I foster the fantasy that I am some kind of spook who meets nightly with a fat man straight out of *Casablanca*. The war still seems oddly unreal, an offstage tragedy for audiences who will never understand, as I never will, what it is all about, why so many people must die.

At last Mohammed shows up with the bill of lading. Our freighter carrying the load of dates and hash is one of the last ships to leave harbor before Israeli gunboats blockade the port.

In the morning, I flee east. Back to the Bekaa, where I am certainly not safe. Syrian and Iranian warriors encamped here are preparing for war. The Israelis are encroaching from the south. Americans have a price tag on their head. I keep traveling east into Syria, to Damascus, where I mail the shipping documents to Sammy in New York and board a plane for Dubai. From Dubai I fly to New Delhi, India to rest for a few days—stranger in a strange land, the only real peace I know. On to Hong Kong and a long flight to Honolulu. Then a short hop to Maui, where Val waits for me in a house by the sea on the slopes of a volcano.

9

A DATE WITH TEN MILLION DATES

THE GREEK FREIGHTER carrying our goods is at sea headed for the port of New Jersey. Using a clean set of phony ID, I fly from Hawaii to New York. There I check in to a suite in the funky Hotel Chelsea to wait for my ship to come in. Creature of habit, I stay at the Chelsea when I am waiting for a load. Once the goods have landed and the cash starts to flow, I will move to a suite at the Plaza and resume my pose as Doctor Lowell, the eccentric shrink who hands out money and free psychiatric advice like the Magic Christian.

Pre-load, what I like about the Chelsea is that cops or Feds will not go unnoticed here. The staff knows me and of my aversion to agents of the law. There is no need for false pretenses. Freaks, artists, writers, musicians, dope fiends, and dope dealers live in suites and rooms at the Chelsea. The place has history. Dylan Thomas was staying here when he drank himself to death in 1953. Sid Vicious killed his old lady at the Chelsea in 1978—the same year I was busted while staying here. The beat poet Gregory Corso wanders the halls talking to himself. I fit in. The desk clerk will tip me if anyone comes around asking questions. The Chelsea is a good-luck place for me, and I am as superstitious as a medicine man.

No one knows my real name. I have three sets of false ID and have to remind myself each morning who I am today. I make no calls from the room. To stay in touch with my people, I use a pay phone at the rear of El Quijote, the garish Spanish restaurant adjoining the hotel. I come and go, drink tequila at the bar, make my calls, waiting for word the load has landed. In the room I smoke joints and watch old episodes of *Get Smart*. Listen to music, Bob Dylan's "Sad-Eyed Lady of the Lowlands," which he wrote while staying at the Chelsea. At night I drift off to sleep with visions of dark freighters crewed by mustachioed Greeks steaming across the sea.

An article of faith in the dope smuggling business is *shit happens*. On an earlier scam—the infamous '78 hash trip Wolfshein alluded to during that uncomfortable drive in Maine—I waited in this same hotel for a ton and a half of Lebanese hash coming in by airfreight to Kennedy airport. The load was disguised as a shipment of jet engine parts being returned to the US manufacturer for retooling. Every day I would meet with my Lebanese contact—Nervous Nick, I called him— for a progress report. Nick's nervousness was contagious. We met at a coffee shop on Third Avenue in Murray Hill. Nick couldn't sit still. He kept glancing over his shoulder. Wouldn't look me in the eye. I assured myself that Nick was too nervous to be an undercover fed or a rip-off artist setting me up for a robbery. He was skinny, with a perpetual three-day growth—a rank amateur in his early thirties who admitted he'd never done anything like this before. His family owned a Lebanese restaurant in Brooklyn. Relatives from Montreal recruited him. He agreed to step in to ease some personal financial pressures.

"I will die if this business fails," he told me.

From the start I suspected there was something amiss with this trip. It had been put together by the Canadians: a Lebanese crew working out of Montreal; my partner, Rosie, who was in jail at the time; and his former partner, Michael, who warned me there might be a weak link somewhere between Beirut and New York. That was why they asked me to receive the load: they knew I would take the risk. Without risk there is no chance for the unexpected, no hope for true adventure and, perhaps, enlightenment. One has to ride out there on the wave of chance to grow.

So I met with Nick, and I waited at the Chelsea between meetings. Each day hash dealers came to my rooms to smoke dope and check on the status of the load. One day, Brendan, a Toronto smuggler who would pick up a heroin habit and die a junkie's death in Bangkok, showed up with a slab of fresh Lebanese hash that I knew, from the stamp on the sack, came from the load I was expecting.

The load was in. How could this be? Someone had received the goods before me. *But who?* When I met Nick that afternoon, he was more nervous than ever. He said what Brendan showed me had to be samples or part of a similar load, because the first 500 kilos of the ton and a half we were expecting had now landed and cleared customs and was ready to be picked up at the airport.

Things were going from weird to weirder. I called Toronto to see what Michael knew. He never returned my call. Rosie was still in the slammer; no way to confer with him. I called Jimmy D. He drove down from the farm in Maine. We drank in the bar at El Quijote. "What do you want me to do, Kemosabe?" he asked after I told him of my reservations.

"What do you want to do?"

"You know me, chief," he said. "I'm a grunt. I follow orders."

"I'm not ordering you to do this. We could be walking into a trap."

This guy had hardcore nerves forged in the jungles and rice paddies of Vietnam. There was a part of him that didn't give a fuck. Those are the most dangerous kind of outlaws—the ones who figure whatever comes their way they'll handle it, or die trying. JD changed the subject. He told me he was fucking the wife of the guy who lives in the farm next to our place a half mile down the road. They were rich hippies. She was a trust fund kid. Her old man was a musician. They were good friends with Anaïs, my estranged wife.

"Does her old man know?"

He nodded. Jimmy D reminded me of Kris Kristofferson, long hair, close-cropped beard, long and lean, a twinkle in his eye, and a face etched with experience. "Yeah. He moved out. He's cool with it."

"So, does this mean that you want to bow out?"

He belted back another shot of tequila and waved to the bartender to refill his glass. "Hell, no," he said. "What gave you that idea?"

We agreed to exercise all caution even as we skirted out on the edge of peril. The next day, I dropped JD off down the road from the airfreight terminal at JFK. He walked in to pick up the loaded truck containing the first 1,500 pounds of hash in the rear in two large crates. I stayed behind the wheel in a rental car parked along the access road leading to the airfreight terminal. There were two men with me: the guy who owned the farm in Orange County where we would stash the load—another ex-Marine, Vietnam vet—and Peter, a former editor at a publishing company, who became enamored of the outlaw life reading articles in *High Times* magazine and quit his straight job to join our ranks.

After a ten-minute wait, we saw JD drive out of the fenced-in terminal yard and onto the access road. We watched as not one but several vehicles—some beat-up looking junkers, other muscle cars, a big white Lincoln Continental, all bristling with antennae and peopled with bearded, long-haired thugs who could only be undercover narcotics agents—drove out in tandem behind our truck. We had Heat. Serious Federal Heat, of that there was no doubt. Peter, the editor turned would-be outlaw, was ready to flee. Drive off and let JD take the fall alone. There is always some guy who wants to run. I offered to let him walk, but he calmed down and actually got more excited and less afraid as we took off in pursuit of the followers.

Once we were out on the highway, headed northwest from the city, I pulled up alongside JD in the loaded truck. Peter, riding shotgun, signaled to JD; he pointed behind him to alert him that he was being followed. JD grinned his toothless grin and jerked his thumb to the rear of the truck, indicating he had the crates. "No . . . you're hot!" Peter yelled, and we sped on ahead.

Traffic was heavy. I didn't want the DEA agents to notice us and connect us with the truck. Soon we were driving into hilly country and onto back roads. The new plan was to get far enough in front of JD and the truck, with the parade of DEA cars following, then drop off the guy who owned the farm, leave him by the side of the road where we knew JD would be traveling. JD would see him and stop to pick him up.

The weather turned stormy, dark clouds and then rain the farther we got from the city. This, we would learn later, worked to our advantage, as DEA had a surveillance plane in the air following the truck, guiding the chase cars, and the weather forced the pilot to turn back. Once the truck JD was driving reached the winding back roads and hills of Orange County, the DEA could no longer pick up the signal from the tracking device planted in the crates. JD lost the followers long enough to pick up the guy we left standing on the road and continue on without being seen.

They drove into an apple orchard and dumped the crates. JD found the DEA's tracking device and ripped it out, smashed it, killing the signal. He left the guy who owned the farm to guard the crates, came back and picked me up near the village of Warwick, New York. I got in the truck with JD. Peter drove off in the rental car to pick up the guy in the orchard and secure the load.

"Are you serious?" JD said. "Did we really just steal a load of hash from the DEA?"

"No. They stole it from us," I said. "We stole it back."

As we drove around the corner into a parking lot, DEA, local, and state cop cars swooped in from all sides and converged on the truck.

We were surrounded. "Come out with your hands up!" one of the agents called to us over a bullhorn.

I turned to JD. "Here we go," I said. "Just like on TV. Tell 'em you've got nothing to say. You want to call your lawyer."

We got out, hands in the air.

"Go around to the back of the truck!" the agent ordered.

We did as we were told. At least twenty agents and cops all with guns trained on us stood at the ready. They made us stand with our backs to them and our hands on the rear of the truck.

"Open the left door!" came the order over the bullhorn.

I opened the door. Nothing inside but empty space.

"Open the right door!" There was a trace of panic in the agent's amplified voice. But that was nothing compared to the freak-out when the agents discovered they had arrested an empty truck. They couldn't believe it. They threw us down on the parking lot, shoved our faces in the pavement, and stuck their guns to our heads.

"*Where's the fucking load?*"

They were ready to wail on us right there, but there were too many witnesses. Civilians had come out of the shops to watch the excitement. I had a face full of blacktop, grit in my mouth—but I was smiling. One of the agents screamed at another agent, a techie working the controls on their tracking device. "You better get a fucking signal! You better locate that fucking equipment!"

No signal. No crates. No contraband. No evidence. We were taken into custody, held incommunicado at a state police barracks for ten hours while the frantic agents scoured the area trying to find their crates. They beat JD, I heard them slapping him around and kicking him in the next room. They never laid a hand on me. I gave them a phony name, but a Royal Canadian Mounted Police narcotics agent, who was coordinating the operation for the Mounties, recognized me and told the DEA agent-in-charge that I was a principal, not merely a grunt.

"Asshole Number One," was how the agent-in-charge referred to me. He was a stocky little guy, a martial artist. He called JD, "Asshole Number Two." I listened to him on the phone talking with headquarters in the city, trying to explain to his supervisor how the truck was empty when they busted us, how they still had not been able to locate the crates, the load of hash or their tracking device, and after he hung up, I said, "I guess that makes you Asshole Number Three."

He pulled me aside and told me the Mafia was going to kill me. So I better tell them who owned the load. "Why would the Mafia want to kill me?" I asked.

"For losing their fucking load, asshole!"

"Then I guess it must be the Mafia's load."

"Listen," he said, playing the good cop role. "You know what we were doing while we waited for you to pick up that truck?"

"No, what did you do?"

"We sat around smoking joints and snorting coke. This is all a big game," he instructed me. "If you're smart, you'll start playing both sides. Otherwise, you're the loser." Then he gave me some free legal advice. "Here's what's gonna happen when this goes to trial," he said. "We're gonna get up there and tell our lies. Then you're gonna get up there and tell your lies. It's just a matter of whose lies the jury believes. Guess what. Juries always believe the cops' lies."

Two black agents in the white Lincoln Continental drove JD and me into the city to DEA headquarters. They wanted to know, off the record, how much JD was going to get paid for driving the truck. JD asked me, "Should I tell 'em?"

"What truck?" I said.

"C'mon, man," the agent driving said. "It won't leave this car."

"Promise you won't take it as some kind of admission of guilt," I said.

"Man, what're you talking about? There was nothing in the truck when we busted you."

"So why are we being arrested?" I asked.

"It's just a formality," the driver said, and we all laughed.

"If I was driving that truck, and I'm not admitting I was," JD told them. "And if there was hash in that truck, and I'm not saying there was, but, you know, if there was hash in it, I wouldn't do it for less than thirty grand."

"Damn, man, we're in the wrong business," the agent said to his partner.

Maybe not, as it turned out. But they were with the wrong crew. When they stopped to get gas, I joked that we should start yelling to the gas station attendant that we were being kidnapped, two white guys in handcuffs in the back of a Lincoln driven by two black guys; there had to be some mistake. At the old DEA headquarters on Fifty-seventh Street, we were booked, fingerprinted, had our mug shots taken, and were asked again if we had anything to say. Finally, we were given an opportunity to make a phone call. I called my lawyer and close friend, Hef.

Late that night we were removed downtown and locked up in the Metropolitan Correctional Center, MCC, the federal holding facility next to the courthouse in Foley Square. There we spent a tense week-end. What did the cops have? Nothing. An empty truck. Yet the TV news played it as a multimillion dollar drug bust with two suspects in custody. Before court Monday morning, they took us to meet the assistant United States attorney who would be handling the case. Her name was Rhonda something, an attractive young black woman. When JD and I were brought to her office, she asked if we wanted to make a statement, perhaps cooperate with the government. We looked at each other and broke into song. "Help me Rhonda, help, help me Rhonda." She smiled and threw us out of her office.

In court, Hef told the magistrate, "These men are not criminals. They are men of the earth, farmers from Maine." The magistrate released us on our own recognizance pending the outcome of a grand jury investigation. Some weeks later we were back in court for a hearing. "Wait a minute," the judge said to Rhonda. "You're telling me DEA agents put the hashish on the truck. But when these men were arrested driving the truck, there was no hashish."

"That's correct, Your Honor. It was a controlled delivery."

He shook his head. "You're not answering my question. Was there hashish? And, if so, where is the hashish?"

"Well, actually, the agents removed the hashish and replaced it with sand," Rhonda explained.

"Let me repeat my question: Where is the hashish? These men are charged with possession with intent to distribute hashish. Defense counsel has made a motion to have the government produce the evidence. I need to know where the hashish is, how much hashish there is, and how and in what circumstance these defendants were in possession of it."

Rhonda and the agent who had called me Asshole Number One had a quick, hushed conference. "Ah, I will have to get back to you on that, Your Honor," Rhonda told the Court.

At that point, Hef produced evidence that the hashish had actually been distributed on the streets of New York. He showed the judge some empty sacks I got from my friend Brendan. "Judge, these are wrappings from the hashish my clients are alleged to have possessed. I submit to you that the hashish in question was never in their possession. It remained in the possession of federal agents, who somehow lost or . . . misplaced it."

We had learned from a corrupt DEA source that the agents sold the load. Months later I read a Jack Anderson column in the *Washington Post* that told how rogue DEA agents had stolen the load, turned it over to their snitches, then tried to arrest the guys the load was intended for—us. Our crates contained mostly sand with a cover layer of hashish, about 200 kilos, which barely covered my expenses.

The judge dismissed the case. "These are men of the earth," he told Rhonda, referring to JD and me, recalling Hef's words. "Farmers. Let your agents go out and arrest the real criminals who are infesting the streets of New York City with heroin."

"We'll meet again," Asshole Number Three said to me as we left the courtroom.

* * *

BETWEEN DRINKS, AT my pay phone in the rear of El Quijote, I get the call.

"Bro, we got a problem." It's Sammy Silver, whose father owns both the New Jersey trucking company that is to pick up the containers at the docks and the bonded warehouse in Jersey City where the containers are to be delivered. "Meet me at our spot under the West Side Highway in an hour."

My stomach is in knots. *Fuck*. Now what? *What the fuck?* After all I've gone through to bring in this load—no, please don't tell me it's busted.

It is Thursday night when I meet Sammy to hear about our problem. He tells me that even though everything had been done following his explicit instructions, for some reason Customs flagged the load of dates. They called Sammy's father at the trucking company and told him that they had sealed the containers and were going to escort them from the port to the warehouse, where they would conduct a thorough secondary inspection.

"*Shit* . . . why?" I ask.

"I don't know, bro. Could be because the load was shipped out of Lebanon. It's known as a source country for narcotics. Not dates."

True, although because of the First Persian Gulf War, beginning in 1980, lots of goods from the Middle East were being transshipped through Beirut.

"Maybe they were tipped off," Sammy muses aloud.

"By who?" I say. "No one knows about this trip except me, you, and the Lebs—and they're not about to rat out their own load."

"Val?"

"Please. Be serious."

"What about Biff?"

"He knows nothing."

"So maybe Customs ran dogs around the containers and they picked up the scent," Sammy speculates.

"Not possible. Not the way it was packaged. And if that were the case, they'd hold the shipment at the docks and wait for us to pick it up, then bust us."

"I don't know, bro. It's fuckin' crazy. But we *can't* pick up that load."

I'm stunned. "What d'you mean we can't pick it up?"

"We gotta just . . . we gotta leave it at the docks."

"How can we do that? If we refuse to pick it up, they'll know we know it's hot."

"But they won't know who to bust," he argues. "They won't have any evidence. We can say we don't want to touch it if they think there's contraband in it. Put it back on them. Whatever . . . I can't let my old man take a fall. He'll lose the business."

"Brother, if this load goes down, we're out of business."

I want to discuss it with Sammy's father. To refuse to pick up the containers seems to me like a clear admission of complicity. To pick up the containers and play out the hand seems to me the only reasonable, albeit a risky, plan. The bold way is the best way. Just act like nothing is wrong and we know what we're doing: picking up a load of dates consigned to a major food importation company. Business as usual and as planned.

We drive across the river to meet Leo, Sammy's old man. At a diner in Paramus, we sit in the car in the parking lot and debate what to do. Leo is in favor of picking up the containers. He's a tough old Brooklyn Jew, a former boxer who doesn't believe in giving up without a fight. He agrees that to refuse to pick up the containers is as good as admitting we know they contain controlled substances. "There's too much at stake here," Leo says. "We've worked too hard to let it go."

"Fifteen million dollars worth of goods," I remind them.

"Yeah. And we're looking at fifteen years in the joint if they bust us," Sammy says.

"That's the nature of the business," I say. "We wouldn't be making this kind of money if it were legal."

Leo and I look at each other. "What do you want to do?" he asks.

"I say we go for it."

I go over the details again. Of the seven containers, three contain hash and dates; four contain only dates. "These are the numbers on the four containers that have only dates." I write the figures on a slip of paper and give them to Leo. "Why don't you call Customs, tell them you're backed up, you can't pick up the shipment until tomorrow afternoon or first thing Monday. We show up late Friday afternoon. Weekend's coming. The agents are thinking about going home for the weekend."

Leo is nodding. So far he likes it.

"Then, first we pick up two or three of the clean containers with only dates. Let Customs escort those and inspect them at the warehouse. Maybe . . . you never know, maybe we'll be able to finesse it. It's risky. But I don't see what other chance we have."

Leo agrees. He says he doesn't think Customs has been tipped off; he feels it's a routine secondary inspection because of all the heroin coming out of Lebanon. So we have a plan. A hairy plan but still it's something. I go back to the Hotel Chelsea to wait. Now the waiting becomes ten times as intense. Sammy and I have four hundred grand invested in this trip. All that work, the months of risking my life in Lebanon putting the shipment together. Going to Baghdad to buy the dates. Shipping them overland to Beirut. The upheaval with Mohammed, Abu Ali, and that thieving Wizard. Holed up for weeks and then months in the Bekaa and Beirut. Nearly getting blown up in the war. No, I can't just walk away.

And if we make it, if we get the load in and sell it all without getting busted, I'm all done. That's it. Retirement time. I'll have enough money to stash in some offshore bank accounts and live on the interest, spend the rest of life in the wind. Or at least until they legalize this plant and give amnesty to all former pot smugglers.

All day Friday at the Chelsea, I pace. I'm so nervous I can't sit still. I watch the news. No reports of massive loads of hash busted in New Jersey. I try to read but I can't concentrate. I go out and walk the streets. Not even the lovely New York ladies in their skimpy summer outfits can distract me from my date with ten million dates. *Stratton*, I tell myself, *you're a fucking lunatic. It's way past time you quit this insanity. Just let me get this load in, dear Lord, let this one through and I swear I'll give it all up and*—what? What would I do? How could I ever get the same rush I get from doing this?

I call Biff and tell him to meet me. We go for a walk in the park beside Riverside Drive. "You wanted to get more involved. This is it. We're going to need your help."

He blanches. "Me? What can I do?"

"I don't know. I don't know what any of us can do. But we need you to be here in case . . . whatever happens. This is what it all comes down to: hanging in, trying to figure out what to do," I tell him. "Let's see how big those balls of yours really are."

He stammers, looks down at the ground, breaks weak. "I . . . I can't. Listen, I have a family. I'm . . . I have to go away. I'm going out to Amagansett for the weekend."

FRIDAY EVENING SAMMY is out front of the hotel in a rental car.

"You're not going to believe this," he says when I get in and we drive off toward the Holland Tunnel.

"Try me."

But I can't believe it. I have to see it with my own eyes—and smell it with my nose. When I walk into the warehouse in Jersey City, I can smell hashish. Yes, unmistakable—at least to me—fresh hash, mixed with the smell of the dates, but hashish nevertheless. It's the same smell that greeted me when I walked into the warehouse at the port in Beirut—an odor as thick as perfume on a cheap French whore. How can this be? It's like a dream. I'm having an out-of-body experience, walking into this thick aroma of contraband.

And there are the cartons! The ones with red plastic strapping. The ones containing hashish that we agreed *not* to pick up. But there they are, sitting out on the loading dock. And there is one of the containers we agreed we would *not* pick up. But here it is, backed into the warehouse and half unloaded. Something is definitely wrong. This is a setup!

I look at Sammy and Leo. *Brace yourself,* I'm thinking. *We are all about to be busted.* I have a sudden intense rush of fear and paranoia so powerful that for a moment I cannot move. I can't think. The warehouse is surrounded with Customs and DEA agents just waiting for me to show up before they make their move. *This has to be a setup.* My one overwhelming urge is to turn and *run, motherfucker! Get the fuck out of here. Now!* We are all about to get cracked, caught red-handed in a warehouse full of hash. Caught with the goods, a fugitive from another bust—I'm looking at decades in a federal penitentiary.

Sammy and Leo smile at me. They don't understand what is about to happen. Sammy's brother is there, and Bobby, Sammy's stash and wheelman. I wait as though in some state of stop-time for the doors to come crashing in and the place to be swarmed with federal agents sticking guns in my face and screaming: *Down on the floor, motherfucker!* And these guys are smiling.

Nothing happens. Nothing . . . happens. Moments pass and there is no bust. The guys are still grinning at me with these goofy looks on their faces like I'm the only one who doesn't get it. "Are you guys fucking crazy? What're you so happy about? You picked up the wrong container!" In a daze, I walk to the rear of the loading dock, grab one of the cartons with the red straps, plunk it down on a table and rip it open. "Red straps! What does that mean?"

Sammy, still smiling at me, says, "It means, bro, we got the load. Or part of it anyway."

I dig under the layer of dates. There is the tin box full of hash.

"It was a crap shoot," Leo says. "They wouldn't let us choose which containers to pick up. They *told* us what ones to take. If we insisted, it would've looked suspicious." He takes me to the rear of the warehouse, points out three more containers parked outside in the fenced-in yard. One of them, I know by the numbers on the outside, also contains hash. "Three carloads of Customs inspectors. They put seals on the containers and escorted them back here." Leo shakes his head, smiles at me. "Go figure."

We go outside, Sammy and Leo show me the US Customs seals on the locked container doors. "They opened the one container and started inspecting the cartons. They musta opened a dozen, maybe twenty cartons, all with nothing but dates."

"Pure dumb fucking luck," Sammy says.

Right next to one of the cartons the agents opened and inspected is a carton with red strapping.

"Finally," Leo tells me, "like we figured, it's late Friday afternoon. The agents're tired, they wanna go home, maybe stop by the local bar, have a few beers with the boys. So they left, said they'd be back Monday morning to finish the inspection."

"And," Sammy says when we are back inside, "you're not gonna believe this, bro. *They had dogs.*"

"Get the fuck out of here!"

"Serious, bro. Dogs. Dope dogs. Two of 'em."

Leo nods, shrugs. "Luck."

"They came in and sniffed around. We figured we're going down for sure," Sammy goes on.

"I can smell hash," I say.

"They must'a been junk dogs," Bobby says. "They get 'em strung out on junk so they go nuts when they smell heroin. But they don't give a fuck about hash."

"They just walked around wagging their tails, happy as could be," Sammy says. "We were freaked the fuck out. You believe this?" He points to the sky. "Tell me someone up there isn't looking out for us."

We are all silent for a moment, praising God, and then we laugh, giddy, nervous laughter. It still seems unreal. I expect agents to storm the place and lock us all up. Each moment that passes seems like a gift.

"Here's the problem," Sammy breaks it down. "We take all the cartons out of this container, right? We remove our goods, okay? But when Customs comes back here Monday morning this container is going to be light by about a third. What we gotta do is take the hash out and replace it with something that weighs about the same, and then put all the boxes back in, way in the back of the container. And hope they don't open one of the boxes and see there's no dates in there."

"Or maybe we buy dates and put 'em in there," Bobby offers.

"Please, there are no dates. That's the point," Sammy says. "No, we'll use sand."

"That's only a third of the load," I say.

"Better than nothing."

We go back outside to one of the sealed containers and look it over. No way to break the seal without Customs knowing. Bobby is a welder by trade. As my grandmother Ba Ba used to say: *Where there's a will, there's a way.*

Early the next day, Saturday, Bobby brings his acetylene torches to the warehouse. He cuts the hinges holding the locked and sealed doors on the rear of the container. Leo borrows a tow truck from a friend, we use the rear winch and hook to lift the sealed door up and off the back of the container, guiding it by hand, and then set it on the ground without breaking the Customs seal.

It takes all weekend—working through the night Saturday and well into Sunday night and early Monday—to remove all the boxes with the red straps containing hash from two containers and replace them with boxes of sand. It's a grueling task, working against the clock, sweating our asses off, in fear of being busted at any moment. But there is the thrill and satisfaction of finding tin box after tin box of hashish and loading our goods into a rental truck to be hauled off to the safe house. The hardest part of the whole operation is locating paint on a Sunday to match the orange color of the container so we can replace the door, weld the hinges back together and make it look like it had never been touched. The paint is still sticky early Monday morning.

By dawn Monday we have ten thousand pounds of hashish and fifty gallons of honey oil safely stored in a stash house on Staten Island. There is still one more container to pick up and the customs inspection to get through. If they find the remaining five thousand pounds in the container left at the docks, no doubt they will go back and look through all the cartons and find the sand. We will be busted. But at least we'll have the income from ten thousand pounds of hash to pay the lawyers and provide for our families while we ride out the bust.

I'm asleep in my room at the Chelsea Monday morning when the phone rings. Every muscle in my body aches. I wake in a panic. *What now?* It's Sammy, calling from a pay phone down the street from the warehouse. "Relax, bro . . . go back to sleep," he says. "Give yourself a big hug. You're a rich motherfucker."

"What happened?"

"Customs just called. The supervising agent said they're satisfied with the inspection. Told us we should go ahead and break the seals on the containers in the yard and come down and pick up the remaining the containers."

"No shit?"

"Serious . . . after all that," he says and we both laugh.

Later that day, I meet with Sammy for a walk-talk along Twenty-third Street. He tells me the dates were rejected by USDA. The infestation rate is too high. "Fuckin' A-rabs," he says. "Can't do anything right. But it's no big deal. The old man says we can ship 'em to Canada or England, where the bug count isn't as tight. Sell 'em there."

He hugs me. "How does it feel to be a millionaire?"

"We still gotta sell the load."

"From what I've seen so far—shit, man, it's primo. We'll own the market. C'mon out to the island. We're doing the inventory."

"Give me a day or two to decompress," I say. "I'm exhausted."

Back at the Chelsea, I pack my bags. Time for Dr. Lowell to check in to the Plaza.

10

DOCTOR LOWELL, I PRESUME

THE LOAD IS in. We did it, against all odds, snatched seven metric tons of hashish from under the collective noses of half a dozen Customs officers and two dope dogs. The mother lode has landed and is safely stashed. Finessed through a secondary Customs inspection. It hardly seems possible, and yet it happened. For two days I wander around the city in a mental bubble, barely able to comprehend the magnitude of our good fortune. Surely, the hashish gods are smiling. Now the real challenge begins: to turn 15,000 pounds of hash and fifty gallons of honey oil into $15 million in cash without getting popped.

I'm trying to act like none of this happened. It still feels too good to be real. There was a time not even a week ago when it looked like we would lose everything and wind up in prison. Sammy was ready to leave the load at the docks. Biff fled to Amagansett. Sammy and Bobby are so pissed at him for bailing on us they want to cut him out of his end. But I'm feeling benevolent. Let the good karma of this trip prevail. As I move about the city, I feel a strong urge to fade into the background and disappear. My job is done. The merchandise has been delivered. Now it's up to Toranaga, Rosie, Val, Benny in Wellesley, and whoever else to cash it out. I have to assume Wolfshein and the Feds are actively seeking to find me and lock me up for jumping bail in Maine. It would be foolish to draw my Heat to the trip. So I ride the subway down to Bowling Green and take the ferry to Staten Island—not a potentially wealthy fugitive outlaw, just another straphanger commuter blending into the multitudes.

Bobby picks me up at the ferry landing. He's still riding the adrenaline rush from the weekend. Talks nonstop, still in awe of how we managed to pull this off and how our lives have been changed virtually overnight. He offers me a bag of Sammy's top-of-the-crop indoor hydroponic homegrown, but I'm saving my head for a bowl of the Double Zahara. That's the real reason I've come out here, to visit the load, see it safely stashed stateside, and get my share of the dealer's choice—ten kilos of the very best slabs for my personal stash.

The safe house is a three-bedroom rental in a quiet, middle-class neighborhood. It has never been used to hold any contraband until now. Bobby has been living here for the past six months, since we embarked on this trip, and paying his rent on time, keeping a low profile. He has his welding business as a front; he comes and goes with tools and torches at regular hours. Sammy purchased a fully tricked-out, heavy-duty camper van and outfitted it with a built-in hidden compartment that can hold up to 200 kilos. We have dealers coming into the city from the West Coast, the Midwest, and Canada to look at samples and place their orders. I contacted Mohammed, through Nasif, to let the Lebs know the load made it into the country. They are already making plans to meet me and collect the $4.5 million that is their end: a third for Sammy and his father; a third for me; and a third for the Lebanese—minus what they've already been paid.

I walk in the front door and down the stairs to the basement where Sammy sits on a stool before a small table on which he has placed an adding machine that prints out little slips of paper with the totals of the figures he's entered. He has a baseball cap on his head and is hunched over like an accountant in a sweatshop. The whole basement is filled with cardboard cartons—not the date boxes, new boxes. This is the first time I have been present in one room with the entire load, and it is massive. Boxes are stacked from floor to ceiling; it's a room full of hashish. There is one whole wall of slabs that have not been packed in boxes and yet have very little odor. Sammy has an industrial vacuum sealer with heavy-duty plastic bags he uses to seal the slabs. He wipes down each sealed bag with alcohol, then seals it in a second bag. He's been at it for days, immersed in his work, weighing and inventorying the entire load.

Sammy defies the stereotype of the lazy, sloppy, spaced-out pothead. He's a workaholic who happens to stay high, a fanatic for details and organization. Clean, a neat freak, and always well groomed. A family man, he lives in a mansion in the exclusive Todt Hill section of Staten Island. His wife is also a stoner. She has a good job and looks and acts like a straight person—until you get to know her. The only thing that gives them away is their appetites: the best cannabis; fine wines and gourmet foods; loud rock music. They're undercover freaks. What I love about working with this guy besides the energy he brings to everything he does is the pride he takes in a job well done.

He takes me for a tour of the load, grins, and says, "You did this."

"No, bro. *We* did this."

Here are the cartons containing the Double Zahara. The Zahara and the Number One—whole sections of the basement devoted to the different grades. Each carton has a little plastic envelope stuck to the outside that reads *Packing slip enclosed*. Sammy has tallied the weights of the different grades and divided the load evenly. Half for him and half for me. We will split expenses and each contribute to Mohammed's end.

"It's a beautiful thing," he says, marveling at the load.

I am flashing back to the Bekaa, the days and weeks of riding from one plantation to another with Abu Ali in an effort to amass all of this hash, and now here it is, sitting in the basement of a home on Staten Island. The hairy weeks and months of captivity in Beirut. Eating, fucking, arguing with Mohammed. Val and I narrowly escaping getting blown up in the war. All that risk—and it worked. Now it's time for the payoff.

"How's your old man feeling?" I ask Sammy.

"Well, listen . . . he's fucking relieved, man. Are you kidding? He was about to lose his business. This trip saved his ass."

SAVED MY ASS too. Yet Dr. Lowell doesn't seem capable of swallowing his own medicine. The doctor will become the patient. Instead of receding into the shadows and keeping a low profile, I live like a rock star, or some combination of rock star and fugitive outlaw dope smuggler. I move into a three-room suite in the upper reaches of the Plaza and begin spending money with guilty abandon. In the shops and bars and restaurants I hand out hundred dollar bills. My assortment of guests and I are treated like royalty.

"Dr. Lowell." The maitre d' in the Oyster Bar rushes up to seat me. "How many for dinner this evening?"

"There will be two. Possibly four. Or more. You never know."

I order oysters, a vodka martini, and a bottle of champagne. Biff has insisted on an appointment. He arrives with a screenwriter and two women, sisters I met briefly in LA some years before. The older of the two, in her early thirties, is an actress who has a role in a film the screenwriter wrote and directed—his directorial debut—which is about to be released. So they are in party mode as well. The younger sister immediately gets my undivided attention. I fixate on her. She has green eyes, straight, lustrous reddish-blond hair to her waist. She reminds me somewhat of my older sister—also a strawberry blonde—with fine features dappled with freckles.

As we move to a larger table, Biff whispers that the screenwriter would like to buy an ounce of cocaine. "I don't have any cocaine. You know that. What have you been telling these people?"

"See what you can do. Make some calls. You won't regret it."

I met the older of the sisters, the actress, at a party during an extended stay at the Beverly Hills Hotel when Mailer hired me to do research on the circumstances surrounding Marilyn Monroe's death.

We became friends, the actress and I, never lovers, though had I been single at the time it might have gone that way. Her sister, the redhead, I saw only briefly at the home of a friend in the Hollywood Hills. But she made an impression then, as now.

After dinner at the Plaza we move our party to Elaine's on the Upper East Side. I call my friend Goofy John, who always has blow, and tell him to meet us at Elaine's with an ounce to sell—hypocrite that I am, facilitating a coke deal with the ulterior motive of getting into the redhead's pants. Goofy John is the guy who traded me his Toronado for my four-wheel-drive pickup he and his friends loaded up with Colombian pot in Maine and drove back to the West Coast. In town to buy hashish, John's been partying heavily and shows up at Elaine's with four other people and the ounce of coke he sells to the director in the men's room after we all do a couple of lines.

Biff keeps talking obliquely about the hash trip, like he wants to brag in front of these citizens, impress them and possibly interest the writer/director in doing a movie about smuggling dope out of the Middle East during a war. I act like I don't know what he's talking about. What hash? What smuggling venture? Beirut? I prefer to stay focused on the redhead. She says she knows me; I'm trying to figure out exactly what she means by that. She's a strict vegetarian, a vegan, wears no makeup, a willowy whole earth mama with strong looking haunches. She says she's into hiking and horseback riding. I'm thinking of hiking up her skirt, mounting from the rear, and riding her bareback.

By this point in the evening I have no scruples whatsoever and almost no inhibitions. Pure lust. The alcohol and cocaine have dissolved my conscience. I'm quiet, secretive about my desires, though they shine through the gleam in my eye. My plan is to dispatch the film director with the bag of nose medicine and scoop up the sisters, carry them back to my suite for a threesome. As we leave Elaine's, I slip my arm around the redhead's waist. She looks up at me as if to say, *How presumptuous of you*. But she does not move away.

As the party relocates to the Plaza, before we go into the hotel, I take Biff aside and berate him. "Why do you keep bringing up the trip in front of these people? They don't need to know what we do."

"This guy—he wants to make a movie. I was just thinking—"

"You weren't even there. You put your tail between your legs and ran like a bitch at the first sign of trouble. Now you want bragging rights? Make a fucking movie? Just shut the fuck up, Biff. Take this guy and his bag of blow and get lost."

He looks at me, stunned. "R . . . Doc, I'm always there for you, bro. Shit, I didn't know you needed me . . . I mean—"

"Of course you knew we needed you. I told you. But you split as soon as shit got heavy and you thought we were going to get busted. You're a fucking coward, Biff. Sammy doesn't even want me to pay you. Now take this asshole and get lost."

Surprised by my own harsh words, I regret them.

"But what about . . . I mean, the two hundred and fifty grand . . . Are you still gonna pay me?"

"Maybe. If you earn it. Seriously, get this guy out of here. I don't want him coming up to the room. You've already said too much in front of him. Sammy may come by later. He'll freak if he sees you. Don't reach out for me. I'll call you."

He looks at me like a spurned lover. "I can't believe you're saying this to me."

His self-pitying attitude brings out the worst in me. "Believe it. You let me down, man. Here." I shove him a fistful of money. "Just go. Take your friend and get lost."

Biff slinks away. The screenwriter is not so easy to get rid of. He's wired and wants to party. I convince him we will all meet later at a club. Goofy John and his friends see the play and herd the sisters inside as I put Biff and his friend in a cab.

Office hours. It's a group therapy session. So much for maintaining focus. About all I'm focused on now is this redhead's ass. A lavish order from room service arrives. Caviar. Fruits and veggies for the vegan.

Wine, beer, and tequila. Champagne. Goofy John provides more cocaine. There is an ample supply of hashish and marijuana. Sammy shows up with Bobby and a bindle of heroin. "Doogie," he calls it. We have medications for all manner of mental disorders.

"Dr. Lowell, I presume," Sammy says with a grin when I open the door.

We heat the junk on a piece of tin foil and suck up the smoke through a toilet paper roll. Goofy John produces tabs of acid. He phones around town for call girls. This is going to be a long night.

Doctor Lowell, however, is mainly interested in examining the redhead. When I ask her what she meant when she said she knows me, she says she understands me, like she's the shrink and I'm the patient. I can't quite identify her. In a sense, she is every woman I have ever lied to, every woman I have ever cheated on and hurt. Colleen, my high school sweetheart, virginal Catholic girl, drove her daddy's white Chrysler. After I broke up with her, senior year one drunken night, I waited outside her house. Parked up the street in my '40 Ford. When the guy she was out with dropped her off, I ambushed them on the doorstep. *Admit it, bully, piece of shit.* I beat the guy up for no reason. I'm confessing now, to the redhead. Colleen pleaded with me to stop. Her mother never forgave me for deflowering sweet Colleen. For years she called my parents' home and left tortured messages. Then there was Kathleen, stacked, as we used to say, another Irish Catholic girl. Kept her virginity but gave me hand jobs and blow jobs and let me suck on those bountiful boobs. It's like Frank Zappa says, *There's nothing like a Catholic girl at the CYO when they learn to blow.* . . . . Peggy, classic blond beauty. Her father walked in on us while we were fucking at their summer place in Newport. He literally shit his pants. Drank too much gin, something about loose bowels. They were all good girls before they made the mistake of dating Rick Stratton.

Ah, I could hate myself, but now the redhead is sitting on my lap, whispering in my ear as I confess and give her ear a tongue-lashing.

She tells me this is therapy, a cure for my obsession with pussy. "I know how to make you happy," she tells me.

"How?"

"You need to grow up and you have to stop."

"Stop what?"

"Everything, acting like a fool, whatever it is you're doing that's making you so crazy. Just slow down and concentrate. Figure out what it is you really want to do with your life. And then—do that and only that."

We are on the sofa in the sitting room. One of the hookers waltzes through in an advanced stage of undress and with Goofy John in meandering pursuit. He's lost his glasses and walks into a closet. My hand slips up under the redhead's skirt, but she takes me by the wrist and places my palm on her face. I tell her, "I want to make love to you."

"No you don't," she says. "You want to fuck me."

"Well, that too."

"Why?"

"Why? What kind of a question is that? Why not? You're beautiful. You smell so good, I want to bury my face in your pussy. Tell me: Is the hair down there red too?"

"You want to hide from me. You want to hide in me. But you can't. Listen to me, Richard," she says. "You don't even know me. But I know you. You're not the kind of guy who is into wham-bam-thank-you-ma'am. And I'm not that girl."

She has touched a nerve. This is how I think of myself, and I know I'm fucking up. But tonight I want to be that other guy, the guy with the stiff cock and no pangs of guilt. I want to lose the alter ego that sits in judgment. I am so horny, all I can do is gaze at her with a stupefied look on my face. My dick is hard, hormones and pheromones blended in a heady mix more intoxicating than any drug known to man. And then there is THC, cocaine, heroin, alcohol . . . LSD. I feel like I'll jump out the window if I can't get inside her. I'll buy her a home and fill it with children if that is what she wants. Wait a minute now, that was Val's wish. I'm confused, loaded, delirious.

"I think you're really a nice guy," she tells me. "At least you listen when I speak. You're basically a quiet guy, kinda shy. This is an act. You want to be the naughty boy. That's how you get attention. You want everybody to fear you and yet love you. But it's only going to hurt you in the end. You need to settle down and think about how you really want to spend the rest of your life. 'Cause the way you're going, you're gonna be dead or in jail very soon."

Her prophetic words pierce my puzzled consciousness. I know she's right, if only I had the presence of mind to take heed. Some part of me senses she has found me out, seen through my act, but it does no good. I am nibbling on her neck like some infantile vampire. There is a nerve there that if you bite just right, they melt.

"So how are you going to make me happy?" I ask. "Why don't we go to bed and figure it out? I will follow your every command."

She smiles and kisses me. We are making out, hot and heavy now. The heat is rising. I'll get her naked yet. I have an intimation of the crack in the universe through which I might slip to eternity. But not this night. The junk has my orgasm waiting in the wings like a patient understudy. This might yet constitute some elaborate regimen of sexual healing. A woman such as she could fuck me sane.

Then the door opens, and Val waltzes in. There are two ways the night might go from here. From good to better: Val could take off her clothes and join us. Or from bad to worse: She could go ballistic. She is tired. Been traveling all day. In no mood to play. She drops her bag, walks over, and stands before the sofa with her hands on her hips.

The redhead, seeing the look on Val's face, gently eases off my lap.

"You dick!" Val says and smacks me hard across the face.

* * *

WORD IS OUT. A massive load of high-quality Lebanese hashish has hit the continent. There are only a handful of smugglers who are in position to have managed such a scam—and my name is near the top of any such list. I am certain Wolfshein and his CENTAC agents are aware I am in action and working diligently to track me down. I grow a beard, dye my hair, take to wearing hats and shades.

Val creates such a scene at the Plaza, throws everybody out of the suite, that we move the next day, relocate to an apartment in the May-flower Hotel on Central Park West. She forgives me, attributes my behavior and excessive horniness to not having had her for two weeks. This is a girl who likes her powders. She confiscated all the drugs in the suite at the Plaza, and over the next few days we proceed to smoke the heroin and snort all the coke in our Mayflower digs. For three days we don't leave the apartment. We get high and fuck for hours, grateful for the fact that there is only a drug war going on outside. Then Sammy calls and says he needs to see me; it's important that we meet. We go for a walk in Central Park.

"Not good, bro," he tells me. He's got his Rottweiler, Rufus, on a leash walking with us.

"What's the problem?"

"I can't sell this shit, man. Can't even get most of my people to look at it. The town is flooded with some black Afghani. No one wants to hear about Leb after all the bogus slabs that were around last year. I keep telling them this is different. It's better than the Afghani and cheaper. But they don't want to hear it. Everyone wants Colombian or Thai sticks. Nobody's willing to put up any money for hash. Your friend John took a couple hundred kilos on the arm. At this rate, we'll be sitting on this load next year, still waiting to get paid."

"*Fuck.*"

"I know. It sucks. You work your ass off. The product is right-eous—and no one will even look at it."

"So we'll take it up north."

"That's what I'm thinking. We're gonna have to move most of this in Canada. You game for that?"

The longer we sit on the load, the more we run the risk of getting busted. Nasif calls every day; they want to get paid. Sammy's father needs money to keep his business from going under. Even Biff has the audacity to bug me for money after the disappearing act he pulled. And I have my own ongoing extravagant fugitive lifestyle to sustain: new smuggles in the works; airplanes, boats, trucks, motor homes, cars, and multiple homes to maintain; workers from Hawaii to Maine who depend on me for their daily bread; and people all across Canada— *Canada.* Of course. Land of the hashish eaters. Canadians love hash. They smoke it in cigarettes like Europeans. There is a dearth of reefer in Canada. The Canadian dollar is trading higher than the almighty buck. So what the fuck, sell the load—or most of it—in Canada. Which is okay. That means we make more money. It also means I have to go back to work. Which is good. I don't know how to handle myself when I'm not working. I spend money crazily, I drink to excess, I fuck my brains out. Work, as Mailer always says, is a blessing.

JD DRIVES DOWN to the city in the Global Evangelism motor home. We load it up with five hundred kilos that Val and JD then drive out to a stash house she has rented in Snowmass near her place in Aspen. She starts working her people in Kansas City and Alaska. Sammy's guy, Bobby, loads the camper van with two hundred kilos and takes it upstate to a campground on Wellesley Island in the Thousand Islands region on the St. Lawrence River. I'm comforted; it seems like an auspicious sign that the name of the island is the same as my hometown. I may be a fugitive and a wanderer on the earth, but part of me wants to stay connected to home.

I fly into Rochester and rent a car. From where Bobby is camped you can practically cast a fishing line across the US-Canadian border— an imaginary demarcation drawn somewhere in the middle of the St. Lawrence River. Rosie and I are on the horn pay phone to pay phone. One of his boys rented a summer place on an island on the Canadian side. The Canadians come across by boat and we load them up. Miraculously, once the slabs pass over that man-made line in the river, they go from being a sluggish, burdensome inventory to a highly sought-after commodity. This is the lure of smuggling: how the value of something can change exponentially simply by moving it from one place to another. I thank world governments for coming up with the concept of international borders.

The trip has become a double smuggle. Within a week we have landed a thousand kilos and all of the hash oil in Ontario. I consider the huge amount of free-flowing energy released all across North America. People who are not skilled or disciplined at handling money suddenly find themselves with more cash than they know what to do with, myself included, and are more likely to crash and burn. Success can be as big a pitfall as failure. Bigger. Trickier. It's a shape-shifter. Comes on looking like some gorgeous piece of ass who only wants to party and fuck you stupid. Ends up a raving crack whore babbling to the Heat.

I know it's insane to push my luck back in Maine, but I have two airplanes sitting around doing nothing but costing me money. Jonathan Livingston Seagull has the Aero Commander parked somewhere in Oklahoma. While I was in Lebanon, he was supposed to go to Jamaica and make arrangements to fly a load of ganja out and land it at an airstrip controlled by a Chicano friend of mine in South Texas. I reach out for the Seagull, call his wife, Avril, my sister-in-law, on a secure phone in Toronto.

"I thought he was with you," she tells me. She goes on to say she was planning to drive down to New York, to a safe house we rent in Millbrook, with her six-year-old son. She's bringing over a million dollars in cash. Rosie is moving the hash as fast as we can get it to him, and the money is flowing. Avril wants to get the money out of her possession. My plan was to have Jonathan fly half the money out to the Bahamas and turn it over to Nasif, give the other half to Sammy and his father, maybe hold on to a hundred grand. Give something to Biff. But now I can't find the Seagull. I'm also thinking I'll use him to fly a load of hash into Quebec for our Montreal people, who are desperate for more product.

Where is this guy? The Seagull is still on my shit list for the stunt he pulled in Texas, but I need him. I know he needs to make money—he's another one who blows through cash. And now he's MIA. I figure he probably shacked up with the divorcée. But when I call her, she says she hasn't seen him for ten days. Finally, I get a message to my Chicano friend in Houston. He calls me back at the Millbrook house.

"*Huero,*" he tells me, "we got to talk." He gives me a coded pay phone number, tells me to call him at his "office" in two hours.

This is not good. I get through one crisis, and here comes another one. I feel uneasy as I wander around the Millbrook property trying to take stock and organize my thoughts before setting out to find a pay phone. Millbrook, New York, county seat for the wealthy elite of Duchess County, has history in the drug subculture. It was here in a mansion on the Hitchcock Estate owned by the Mellon family that acid guru Timothy Leary was busted in a raid orchestrated by then district attorney G. Gordon Liddy, later of Watergate infamy. Leary had been holed up at the mansion conducting experiments with LSD when Liddy and his posse of local and state cops raided the joint. "Turn on, tune in, and drop out," was Leary's mantra. They busted him for possession of a small amount of pot. LSD wasn't even illegal then.

Sometimes they won't let you drop out. Not when it's *outside* the law. Not when you are proselytizing to the youth of America. Leary got popped again crossing the US-Mexico border in Texas with a small amount of pot hidden in his daughter's underwear. He took the weight and was sentenced to thirty years in prison. While out on bond, Leary relocated to Southern California, where he hooked up with Val's people, the Brotherhood of Eternal Love hippie mafia family. Val got her start in the business as a teenager smuggling hash and acid for the Brotherhood. She never trusted Leary; she saw him as a phony opportunist. The Brotherhood was bringing in Afghan hash hidden in surfboards. Leary got arrested again, for possession of two roaches. He was locked up, and then he escaped from prison with help from the Brotherhood and the radical wing of Students for a Democratic Society, known as the Weathermen, as in Dylan's line, *You don't need a weatherman to know which way the wind blows.* Leary was eventually run to ground in Afghanistan. President Richard Nixon labeled him "the most dangerous man in America." Huh? Val called Leary a rat; said he gave up some Brotherhood people to get himself out of prison.

Who knows what a man will do when faced with prison time?

I'm trying to occupy my mind until it's time to call my Chicano friend and hear what he has to tell me—which, from the tone of his voice, I already know is not good news. My wife, Anaïs, leased the Millbrook property from a Swiss German couple who live in Europe; I never met them. I've spent only three nights here in the year we've had the place, last night being the third. It's a rambling, four-bedroom, gray gables kind of house with a big, open banquet room—a later addition with an arched cathedral ceiling built in an L off the main house. The driveway winds up beside a brook, past the barn, and comes to a circle in front of the house. Just above the barn there is a man-made swimming pond built by damming the icy-cold water in the brook. I sit on the rocks beside the pond and light up a spliff of Sammy's hydroponic reefer sprinkled with Double Zahara to try to settle my nerves.

"*HERMANO*," MY CHICANO friend says when he picks up after three rings. Miguel is his name; I met him through some Mexicans from the Rio Grande Valley who worked on the ranch in Blanco. He's got a bad scar on his face, always wears tinted glasses, lives in Austin. We've done a couple of trips together, importing high-altitude Mexican weed across the Texas border.

"Where's Jonathan?" I ask him.

"*Hombre* . . . shit, man. I don't know how to tell you . . ."

"What?"

"*He's dead.*"

I'm standing at an outdoor pay phone at a gas station watching a man probably around my age, mid-thirties, drink a can of soda as he fills his gas tank. He's wearing a tie, short-sleeved light blue shirt straining at the buttons, no jacket. He has big pit stains under his arms, man-tits, and a prodigious beer belly hanging over his belt. He's got a crush-proof box of cigarettes in his shirt pocket. I'm thinking, in a self-satisfied way: *Thank God that's not me*, imagining how boring the guy's life must be—the hours spent drinking beer and watching TV—when Miguel's words register.

Hold it. *Dead?* Did he say Jonathan Livingston Seagull is dead? How can this be? The straight guy I brought into the business, who is married to my wife's sister. Involved them all in crime, didn't I? And now he's dead?

See, this is how it plays out, Dickhead Stratton. In your mind you're some kind of hotshot outlaw movie star defying the Man, breaking laws that are stupid and unenforceable. Un-American. You see yourself as a folk hero. You glorify what you do. But the truth is people die before their time. Or they molder and waste years of their lives in prison. Families are destroyed. For what? So you and your friends can live like rock stars and addle the brains of America's youth with high-grade illegal herb?

Yes, true, all true. But fuck it! People die of cancer and heart attacks and strokes, like that fat guy filling his gas tank, filling his belly, trying to fill the empty place in *his* life. Yeah. People die and kill innocent women and children fighting illegal wars in foreign countries supposedly defending a way of life that has more to do with drinking soda, smoking cigarettes, and pumping gas than with preserving freedom. It's all bullshit. America, land of the free. My ass. *My country 'tis of thee, sweet land of hypocrisy.* Land of the brainwashed. Land of the fat. Land of the mindless consumer. Land of the—

"Dead? How—"

"Ah, man . . . shit, brother . . . *Huero* . . . I been trying to reach you."

"What happened?"

I have a vivid picture in my mind of Avril, the Seagull's wife, a statuesque, good-looking honey blonde, and her young son. They are on the road in a car traveling from Toronto to visit me with a million plus in colorful Canadian bills. She's nervous but outwardly appears calm, straight looking, fits no money courier profile, and has her act together as she crosses the border. She's a very cool lady in her own way. Smarter, more sensible than her . . . now dead husband. And how am I going to break the news to her that her husband is dead? And then how is she going to explain to her son that he's never going to see his daddy again? She's always been so careful; she has good nerves. She took to the business right away, and never let it change her.

But now it will.

"He crashed, man . . . Went down with a load," Miguel tells me.

Then it all blubbers out. The Seagull and Miguel tried to pull one over on me. Miguel confesses that he and Jonathan embarked on a trip of their own, using my plane, the new Aero Commander. "You were away so long, *hombre*; we didn't know if you were ever coming back."

Jonathan flew down to Guadalajara in the big, turbo-charged Aero Commander and picked up eleven hundred pounds of sinsemilla. "Something went wrong. . . . I don't know what happened, *hermano*. He got lost on the way back. *Tu sabes?* He crashed, man. Ran out of gas. *Lo siento.* He was only like a hundred miles from the strip when he went down. There was another guy with him. Mexican dude. They both died. I know. . . . It's fucked up, man. . . . I'm sorry . . . I'm really sorry."

There is nothing to say. As I hang up, I know I will never speak to Miguel again.

IT'S LATE WHEN Jonathan's wife arrives with their son. The boy, Jason, is asleep. I carry him in from the car and put him in bed. She takes a shower, changes. I open a bottle of wine. She's relieved to have made it in safely with all that money, glad to have it out of her home in Toronto even as her sister is there taking in more cash from Rosie. "He said to tell you he needs more," she says, crossing her long legs, sipping her wine.

"Yeah . . . I'm working on it."

"Have you heard from that asshole husband of mine? He's with that woman, isn't he?"

She's angry with him for his affair with the divorcée. There was even talk of divorce. They have never been a particularly loving couple. Jonathan complained she was cold. But they had decided to patch it up, stay together for the sake of the child, and for the business. Divorces are ugly enough when the couple splitting is legit. When outlaws divorce it nearly always ends in someone ratting on their former spouse.

I take a deep breath, sigh, and shake my head.

"What is it?" she asks.

There is no way to tell someone something like this except to say it.

"He's dead," I tell her. "He died . . . in a plane crash . . . in Texas."

She puts down her glass, looks at me with wide blue eyes. "When?"

"A couple of days ago. I just found out this afternoon—after I spoke to you."

"Oh, God . . . *I knew it.*" She shakes her head and fights back tears. "I knew something like this would happen."

"He was flying a load out of Mexico. I'm not sure what happened. They think he ran out of fuel."

He had no ID on him, that much I know. The plane was registered to a shell company. Miguel told me they altered the plane's registration numbers. It will take some time for the Feds to figure out who he was and contact the RCMP and next of kin. Once the various agencies connect all the dots, they will no doubt pay a visit and keep an eye on comings and goings from the house in Toronto. I'm trying to think of the gentlest way to tell her she had better clean out the house and prepare to be questioned. I've already contacted Rosie, told him to change the plan up there given what went down.

I want to tell her Jonathan was not working for me when he crashed, to relieve some of the guilt I feel, when she says, "Mexico? I thought he was supposed to be going to Jamaica."

"He was. From what I can gather, he decided to go off on his own, with . . . a friend of mine. I . . . I didn't . . . I had no idea what they were up to. First I heard about it was this afternoon when I called looking for him."

She's crying now, quietly, tears welling in her eyes and rolling down her flushed cheeks. "I knew it," she says. "I knew it! *God damn him!*"

"*Don't—*"

"No! *I told him.* I knew he was planning something like this. He said he was fed up working for you. He was going to do this trip on his own and quit working for you. Bragging about how much money he was going to make . . . We had a big fight. I made him promise he wouldn't do anything without talking to you first. *He's such an asshole!*"

She's full on weeping now, tears of pain, anguish, sorrow, and anger, her body rocking back and forth. I hold her, let her cry it out. "How am I going to tell Jason?" she says between sobs.

I have no answer.

* * *

THERE IS WORK to do. Lots of it. Indeed, work is a blessing. Takes one's mind off the apparent meaninglessness of life. And the inevitability of death. There is hashish to move. Tons of it. Money to distribute. Hundreds of thousands, even millions of dollars to receive from distributors, get converted into large bills, and turn over to the various partners. And there is considerable Heat to avoid. Agents from the DEA, RCMP, US Marshals service, FBI, IRS—Bernie Wolfshein and CENTAC—out there trying to locate me and lock me in a cage. As Uncle George would say: a man has got to do what a man has got to do. Stay focused. Keep moving. Stay a step or two ahead of the Law and the Grim Reaper.

This is how I have managed so far to avoid any prolonged periods in a prison cell, or permanent residence in a grave—I keep moving. I keep changing the game plan, altering my modus operandi. I start out early each day with no idea where I will rest come night. That makes it much harder for the agents to track me. I smoke my morning joint, write out my list of things to do, people to call, and go from pay phone to pay phone, meeting to meeting, city to city, hotel room to hotel room, always ready to alter my plans based on the outcome of the next event, the next pay phone assignation.

I leave Avril and Jason at the house in Millbrook and head down to Long Island to visit Biff. Avril said she needed a few days on her own with the boy to break the news about his father. Anaïs knows now too, and plans are being made to bury Jonathan's remains once they are returned to Canada. The sisters' unspoken decree would seem to be: *That's what you get when you fuck around.*

The hash is moving, slowly in the US but picking up, particularly on the West Coast and in the Midwest. Goofy John paid his tab and re-upped. The fickle, competitive New York market has yet to fully embrace our product. To boost sales, I place a centerfold spread in *High Times* with a blurb in their Trans-High Market Quotations section. Boston is stepping up, always a good market with all those institutions of higher learning. Val and Judy have got action in Alaska. But this amounts to dribs and drabs, a few hundred kilos every week or two compared to what Rosie is capable of doing. And we have tons still sitting in the basement of the house in Staten Island waiting to be moved. Canada is where shit is happening. Toronto. Montreal. Vancouver. We're moving half a ton a week north of the border.

Biff is staying at his place in Amagansett. He invites me to go mako shark fishing on a charter boat. I'm thinking I'll go out there, strangle him, and throw him overboard. I reach out for a pilot Sammy turned me on to who keeps our Cessna Single Engine at an airstrip on Long Island. Weird dude. We use him to fly small loads into Canada. He got into some kinky sex scene with Fred Barnswallow and one of the strippers who frequents Fred's place. Fred would smoke coke and watch them fuck. The pilot told me about these warts he has on his asshole, anal warts, he called them. It was more information than I needed. I have never been able to get that image out of my mind. Whenever I see him, I look at his face and I see an asshole with warts all around it. For me, his name would always be Wart Hog.

It's odd about pilots. They may be the single least stable element in a way of life that attracts the human equivalent of quarks and neutrinos. Yogi Bear: that guy flat-out disappeared. I heard he got involved in some deal with The Happy Hooker, Xaviera Hollander, and fled to Amsterdam to avoid federal fraud charges. And Jonathan, he is never far from my mind. Poor dead Jonathan Livingston Seagull. His body, what is left of it, is on its way to Toronto in a box.

Twice that fucking Seagull nearly killed us both. Once we were landing in Provincetown, going down to visit Mailer. No contraband in the plane, Jonathan's Aero Commander, not the new big one that he demolished in Texas. After we landed, instead of putting up the flaps, he hit the wrong lever and retracted the landing gear while the plane was still rolling along the runway. The plane did a hard belly flop and scraped to a stop in the middle of the strip. My head hit the roof. Try explaining that move to the guys hanging around the airport lounge. It cost Jonathan everything he made flying a load to repair the plane. We were lucky a spark didn't ignite the fuel tanks and burn us both to a crisp.

Another time, we were bringing a load of reefer back from Mexico, had it safely in the States. We stopped to refuel in Tennessee. I was monitoring the weather heading east. There was a large, nasty front moving in from the northwest. But we had time to get where we needed to be in Massachusetts and unload well ahead of the storm—if we kept our asses in gear, fueled up, and moved on. But Seagull was dithering around the airport, bullshitting with the guys hanging out at the private aviation terminal. He decided he needed to take a look at a small plane called an Ultralight, thought he might want to buy one with all the money he was making. He was feeling good about himself, cocky after having brought in the load, but irresolute about seeing it through, as though he didn't want the excitement to end. I kept trying to impress upon him that there is no guarantee of safety until we arrive where we're going and unload. We still have to stash and then sell the shit. Then we can relax and think about how to spend the money.

Once we were back in the air, sure enough, the weather turned ugly—ominous storm clouds filled with rain and lightning. Jonathan freaked out. His face was flushed; he was sweating. We both were scared. I was convinced we were going to die. The plane was being tossed around in the sky like a toy. He made some comment, "See, I told you we shouldn't have taken off." I lost it. I grabbed him and was ready to choke him when I realized that if there was any hope of getting this plane safely on the ground, it was up to him. He tried to take us higher to get above the weather. Ice began to form on the leading edge of the wings. We were both suffering from oxygen deprivation. Pounding headaches. Hearts racing. Hands ice cold. Getting light-headed.

I looked out the window and saw sheets of ice building on the wings. I am not an experienced pilot; I had taken a number of flying lessons, passed the written test, soloed, flown on any number of smuggling ventures with pilots who knew what they were doing. So I understood enough to know that ice accumulating on our wings was not a good thing. When I mentioned it to Jonathan, he went into a total panic. His brain seemed to freeze. He stared straight ahead into the stormy sky, hands in a death grip on the yoke. I was thinking, *This is it, I'm going to die, we are both going to die tonight in this plane with a load of weed.*

Then, thankfully, as happens to me in moments when I perceive extreme, life-threatening danger, a clear, out-of-body calm took hold. This may be the one solid attribute I have as an outlaw. It's as though I can step outside myself to a place beyond the immediate peril, and my brain starts to focus on a way through the situation. It is a tremendously satisfying feeling and a good part of what keeps me coming back, sanctions putting myself in the crucible when that other self takes over and leads me to safety, or at least to some medium ground where all is not lost. It is, ultimately, fun. A terrifying variety of fun and dumb. Like when I was a kid jumping off the cliffs at the rock quarry into a small, deep pool, and knowing I had to land just right or run the risk of breaking my neck. Tempting death. Exhilarating. Thriving on the juice, the energy of the moment when anything can happen. And the rejuvenated feeling I'm left with when I know I'm still alive.

Jonathan's brain didn't work that way. He used to drive his Porsche way too fast, and he didn't have the nerves for it. Or the skill. He would have been better off if he had never learned to fly. He should have taken a desk job and kept his ass in a chair on solid ground. Whenever we were getting ready to take off, as I watched him go through his preflight check, I would see the high deep crimson flush rising to his cheeks and know this made him way too anxious for him to be a good pilot.

If nothing else, the ice thickening and misshaping the wings would surely cause the plane to crash. But wait, wasn't there some device, some switch one could flip that would activate heating elements beneath the black rubber leading edge of the wings and melt the ice? I seemed to remember talk of this, or reading something in the manual.

"De-icers?" I shouted. "Aren't there de-icers?"

Of course there are. And it was as though one of those lightning bolts flashing outside the plane struck the Seagull's brain. He flipped a switch to turn on the de-icers, and another switch in his head snapped into place and he understood that only by his continued efforts were we going to be able to live through this night. Action. One must act. One cannot quit and allow death to enter. He got on the radio, made contact with the tower at an airport in Pennsylvania. He was instrument rated. The air-traffic controller in the tower talked us down. The visibility was so bad we couldn't see the ground until moments before the landing gear touched the runway.

Later, in the hotel room, I attacked him. I wanted to beat the shit out of him, but I couldn't do it. We both started laughing.

After the debacle with the dive-bombing incident in Blanco, when the Seagull had moved in with the divorcée and was causing all kinds of internal family strife, I was on my way to kill him one night. Yes, I was driven to contemplate murder. I had a Browning 9mm automatic, fully loaded, under the seat of the car, and I had every intention of blowing his brains out. I was going to shoot him and then dispose of his body in Canyon Lake. Of course, I had been drinking—the only time murder enters my mind with any marrow is when I've been drinking. Jonathan got in the car and before I could reach for the gun he started crying, bawling his eyes out about how he fucked up his life, betrayed his wife, ruined his family. I don't know if I could have killed him in any situation; but it's hard to shoot a guy who's weeping about how he's a total fuckup. I know the feeling only too well.

In my mind's eye, I can see him in the new Aero Commander. He's running low on fuel, still off course. Someone hasn't done their due diligence on this trip and arranged for radio contact or some infallible means to guide him to where he needs to be. Whatever they did or didn't do, they fucked up. It is the attention to detail and careful planning that separates professional smugglers from amateurs. Planning. Planning. And more planning. As General Eisenhower, supreme commander of Allied Forces in Europe during World War II, once said, "Plans are useless but planning is indispensable." And effectuating those plans, seeing them through. It's like those guys who pull off sophisticated bank burglaries as opposed to desperate holdup men. It's what Mailer always says about his writing: "I am, after all, a professional." There is no room for these kinds of mistakes if one is a professional. I see Jonathan has that frozen-in-fear look on his face, his cheeks flushed scarlet. He's staring straight ahead as though waiting for someone to say something that will snap him out of it. Panic has short-circuited his powers of reasoning. He can't figure a way out of this one. And the Mexican sitting in the copilot seat is no help. He's crossing himself and saying his Hail Marys, preparing to meet his maker. The engines sputter and quit. The plane loses altitude, goes down fast. The ground comes up faster. Jonathan Livingston Seagull is about to fly off into the hereafter.

I'll miss the fucker. People would ask me, "Why do you keep working with this guy? He's such a fuckup." Benny, my partner in Wellesley, in particular, couldn't understand it; he had no tolerance for the Seagull. JD loathed him. Val too had serious misgivings about Jonathan. "He's a Heat score," she would say. She doubted he'd stand up if he took a fall. Rosie found him amusing and useful to a point but complained he was flaky and talked way too much. He kept trying to take over the operation. But he was family. And it was because of him, because of the bet we made in P'town those many years ago, that I got back in the business. At times we had a lot of laughs together, when I wasn't looking to kill him.

Biff is shocked when I tell him about Jonathan. They knew each other fairly well. Biff often delivered or picked up money from him in Toronto. In many ways, they are a lot alike, though neither of them would appreciate the comparison. Both Jewish guys married to blond shiksas; in their forties and with no discernable careers to maintain expensive lifestyles; willing to break the law but petrified of the repercussions. For my selfish purposes, to look at either of them, it worked. You would never guess they were involved in criminal activity—that is, until Jonathan started flaunting it.

Biff gets fidgety and asks me for money. I give him twenty-five grand in Canadian. He seems disappointed. Fuck him. Let him work for his end helping launder some of this Canadian money. He gives me that sheepish look, says Nasif has been calling him every day, several times a day. Fuck them too. Let them wait. After all they put me through, and the time they kept me waiting in Lebanon while they tried to pull one off behind my back with the Wizard. *Shit.*

"Tell him I'll meet him in Nassau in two weeks," I say. "With at least a million bucks. And remind him: It doesn't pay to be impatient. Look what happened to that fucking Seagull. Now his kid's got no father. All because he couldn't wait."

11

MONEY CHANGES EVERYTHING

A BODY IN motion, always harder to track. For over a year now I have been on the run. Running from the law, from Bernie Wolfshein's sharp intellect. Running from the consequences of my renegade life. Running from my fear of exposure. Running from my fear of mediocrity. It seems I never stop traveling, moving from place to place—a day here, two days there—as if I sense that to cease to move would be to fall under the shadow of death that follows me. Or succumb to stasis, locked in the prison cell I know awaits me. Revealed as a fraud, a mere criminal.

Jonathan's remains have been returned to the earth. I am bound to Toronto—no matter the risk—to visit the family sitting shiva. There is death all around. Yesterday I learned from my friend Jake's sister that Jake had been murdered in Mexico. A scorched VW minibus was found in the desert of Northern Mexico with Jake's and his Mexican wife's burned bodies inside, riddled with bullets. He had taken the money he made selling hash and invested it in a load of weed from Michoacán. Got as far as Chihuahua and ran into the wrong people. Before he met me, Jake was into armed robbery. I turned him on to the nonviolent world of marijuana trafficking.

I am brutally hungover. Haven't slept all night. Last night was spent in Philly cavorting with Doctor Kato, indulging my preference for dark women. As if fucking a fiercely alive black African American female could gentle death. Back to the roots, back to where it all began millions and millions of years ago. I doze in the car as Kato speeds me to the airport in his BMW. Through the mists rising in my brain I am trying to remember my name. *Who am I today?*

On the plane—Air Canada to Toronto—I memorize my alias profile. Reason for visiting Canada: funeral. That much at least is partially true. The funeral is over. I'm here to offer condolences to the mother and wife, assuage my guilt, show my face to convince them—and me—it is not my fault the Seagull croaked. *I regret that your son had to die such an asshole, and fuck this whole thing up, bring down intense DEA and Royal Canadian Mounted Police Heat on the family here in Canada. Now we are all vulnerable. The Mounties, as you know, always get their man.*

Won't even mention the hundred and fifty grand plus for the new Aero Commander the Seagull crashed. Plus another forty or fifty grand to upgrade the avionics. Seems like he should have installed some long-range bladder fuel tanks. Who knows? Maybe he did. I can't keep track of these things. They come to me and ask for money for this or that, I give it to them. Who cares? It's only money. But no, there is more—a crack in the chalice. Energy seeps away. I can feel it as the plane lifts above the clouds and enters Canadian airspace.

Rosie. Got to love that man, the marijuana martyr, done more time for herb than anyone else in the history of this nation. He glories in the role, loves to rub his defiance in their faces. Last time he was sentenced, to fourteen years, the Rosebush spoke for an hour and fifteen minutes to the court and showed no remorse. On the contrary, he told them all what for. How they are a bunch of unenlightened fools, reactionaries at the beck and call of Uncle Sam, and how men like him who dare to defy laws that are stupid and not in the common interest will one day be seen as heroes, whereas the judge, the Crown prosecutor, the cops and Mounties who busted him will all come to be regarded as anal repositories of everything that is counter to growth and freedom and intellectual curiosity and art and passion. Evolution! It was a beautiful speech, even if it rambled on too long and he repeated himself. The same self-justifying rant I play over and over in my head. The point was well taken by his supporters in the courtroom. The judge, however, was unmoved and gave him the maximum available under the law. Rosie vowed he would continue doing what he did and never give in to their repressive and totalitarian impulses.

He meant it; he did and does carry on undaunted. Fourteen years don't mean shit to the Rosebud. I would go visit him at the penitentiary in Kingston, Ontario, smuggle him in a vial of honey oil he would slip up his ass with the practiced ease of a proctologist inserting a suppository. We planned and schemed. He got fatter in the joint. Most people lose weight and lose money. Not Rosie. He hooked me up with his man, the Squid, we call him. Squid has a wandering eye and a raspy voice. He's a numbers man—low profile, smart—and we made a lot of money while Rosie did time. And Val, who came to be my partner and lover, she was Rosie's connection as well. Also his girl. Rosie was making more money locked up than he did on the street. Then there was the whole Nervous Nick trip, the New York bust in '78 that nearly resulted in my going to the joint for what could have been a long jolt. Rosie did just under seven years on that bid, not quite half the sentence. The Canadians are liberal with good time and early parole. Unlike American correctional authorities, the Canadians still hold some belief in rehabilitation. Fat chance for that when you are dealing with R. W. Rose. He caught a new case in a holding cell while waiting to be released; like catching the flu, the man was vulnerable, his immune system was compromised. He felt he had some catching up to do. The Crown's rat infected him with extravagant conspiracies. The judge just shook his head. *Won't you ever learn, Mr. Roseblossom?* But there were no overt acts, just a lot of blather, and Rosie spun it back on them, claimed he was checking the guy out, setting *him* up—a bald-faced lie but it worked. He did another couple of years and came out to start a new life as the don of Sprout House. He and his partner, the Squid, have this legitimate enterprise where they grow all kinds of sprouts and sell them to health food stores.

Come to find out, the RCMP is up on a wire in the office at Sprout House. Rosie had the place swept and found it infested with bugs of the electronic variety. He left them unmolested so he could disseminate misinformation. They have a pen register installed on the phone to track outgoing calls. Rosie makes his illegal business calls from pay phones in the vicinity of the office. So the Mounties bug half a dozen or so pay phones within easy walking distance and are slowly picking off our lines of distribution. Just days before I arrive in Canada, the RCMP cracked the Thousand Islands route, took down 500 pounds of hash and three of Rosie's people sitting on the stash in the house on the island in the Saint Lawrence River. That means of access is blown. Another fifty kilos got popped in the city. Toronto is flooded with our Lebanese hash, as is Montreal, Vancouver, Quebec City. Despite the Heat, Rosie still manages to move one thousand pounds a week all across the Great White North.

Bobby got away from the Thousand Islands bust unscathed and relocated to Alaska. Last I heard, he shipped out on a salmon fishing boat. It feels like time to shut down the whole northern theater of operation. There is so much Heat it's melting the polar ice cap. My wife has already left the country. She flew to the Bahamas with a satchel of money for the Arabs. It could be argued Toronto is the last place in the world I should make an appearance given my fugitive status and the mounting temperature. But that is precisely why I am here. One must obey the risk.

The plane's wheels bite the tarmac with a screech and bump that jerks me awake. My clothes are rumpled, I smell like dark pussy, and residue of booze is oozing from my pores. It is one of those hangovers that feels like an altered state of consciousness. Like doing acid or mescaline or psilocybin mushrooms. Everything is painfully clear and fraught with sharp, pointed edges and fears like invisible razors and daggers shredding my nerves. Move the wrong way and get stabbed in the heart. Indulge the wrong thought and disappear down a rabbit hole of paranoia and guilt.

That and the fact that I got tangled up in some apocalyptic fucking last night. The lady in question, and she is every bit a fine African princess, manages one of Doctor Kato's shoe stores. Imagine how cunning this guy is: a proprietor of stores that sell ladies' shoes. We know how they all love shoes. And to have their feet rubbed. If the way to a man's heart is through his stomach, the way into a woman's cunt is through her feet. Kato, with his true calling in laying pipe, knows all this and opened shoe stores catering to young ladies. Brilliant. An endless supply of female feet padding in and out sampling his wares. He gets down on one knee, genuflects before the altar of their spread legs, and, like a prince slipping the glass slipper on Cinderella's foot, tries it on for size. It's the instep, he tells me, the arch, you can tell everything about how a woman fucks by her arch. If it is delicate and finely curved, expect deft, gymnastic, catlike coupling and a pussy with a mind and muscles of its own, the kind of cunt that clings to your cock and tugs on it like a sucking mouth. If the feet are wide and flat with splayed toes you are in for a hard, serious drubbing—like being worked over by a 200-pound German masseuse. Boot-knocking, ass-slapping, bed-breaking sex. Either way, according to the good doctor, pay attention to her feet and she will treat you right.

I can go on about this, and probably I will, later, because cunt is never far from my mind. Pussy is like any other source of solace: the more you get, the more you want. I'm ready to fuck my way across Canada. Even as I inch closer to the counter and computer where Canadian Customs and Immigration officials will examine my phony ID, run it through their system, and ask me a set of questions designed to reveal any inconsistencies or tension in my rap, I'm thinking about two French girls from Quebec, using them to take my mind off what is going on before me so I don't invest it with too much stress.

These government people are trained to sense nervousness and pounce. I'm so nervous my heart is sweating, my balls are huddled together in my scrunched-up scrotum. I know these fuckers would love to get me in their clutches. Not that they believe what I do is so wrong. Hell, no. Half of them smoke the shit themselves. They want to dominate me, they want to make me beg: *Please don't lock me up! I'm scared. I don't want to go to prison.* We are like a pack of dogs. Who's gonna hump who? Who is gonna roll over and expose his genitals? In all my comings and goings, at no moment am I more exposed and vulnerable than these few minutes when I stand in the portals of officialdom. So I focus on the land of cunt from which I have recently departed and will hopefully soon return.

The Customs guy is young, looks like a hockey player, the kind they call an enforcer who would hip check you and kick you in the ankle with the blade of his skate. Immediately, I want to smack him, punch him in the gut, tell him to take his miserable civil service gig and choke on it, bend him over and kick him in the ass. One thing you don't want to do with these people is appear too friendly or upbeat. Look bored, mildly pissed off, unhappy to be away from the little lady and the kids. He looks me over, scans the driver's license, glances at the landing card I filled out on the plane.

"US citizen?"

"Yes." I'm thinking, *Ah, yeah. No shit. Didn't you look at the card?*

"What's the purpose of your visit to Canada?" he asks. "Business or personal?"

It's all there on the card, but I tell him, "Personal." *Asshole. I am here to pick up money from the illegal drug business.* Never give them more information than they ask for. I can tell he wants to know more, but I wait to make him inquire. He doesn't like me any more than I like him. He resents my Americanness, the contained Yankee arrogance, the expensive, conservative if rumpled suit, the beard, the fact that I do not appear to live a nine-to-five life like his. The fact that I look happily fucked and he is an onanist.

"Visiting friends? Relatives?"

"I'm going to a funeral."

Ah, yes, death. The inquisition stopper. He stamps the landing card and allows me entry. I confirm the identity I'm using is still good—or, possibly they are allowing me to enter unmolested so they can follow me. There is little sense of relief as I walk from the international arrivals terminal and head for the exit and queue of taxis parked outside, for I expect that at any moment they could appear, flash badges, take me roughly into custody. Or they could lurk among the throng of expectant relatives and friends and lovers, watching me, murmuring into hidden radios: *There he is. Pick him up at the exit.*

It makes me feel important.

In the cab on the way into the city my mind wanders back to black pussy. The lady bathed me in her juices, anointed me with her essential oils. I reek of cunt. The fecund animal smell rises up mingled with my nervous boozy sweat. Must take a shower and change before I appear at the shiva. I don't want those old Jewish ladies to pick up the *shvartz* scent.

It's curious. The older I get, the more attracted I seem to have become to a certain kind of woman who is near to my opposite physically. I've had a hankering for black women since I first laid eyes on Dionne Warwick; since I first heard Billie Holliday, Dinah Washington, and Diana Ross sing; since I first saw Lola Falana nude and caught an image of her bushy twat as she ran through the otherwise hairless pages of *Playboy*. Maybe it's because there were no black girls in the town where I grew up. Jews were about as exotic as we got in Wellesley Hills, and only a few of them, mostly with names changed, trying to be WASPs. A smattering of Italians from the other side of town. We had to go into Boston to see black girls who oozed sexuality like sap from a slippery elm. Man, the way they walk. The way their asses move when they walk. Forget about it—their asses, period. Where do you see asses like that except on black women? Brazilians. Puerto Ricans, maybe, but that's because of the African blood. And it's their attitude I like. The way they look me over and smile. Sassy like. As if to say, *White boy, come with me. Let me show you something so pink and succulent, something redolent with scent you never get a whiff of from those fey girls out there in the suburbs.*

You know I'm going. I'm already gone, headed into Boston driving my grandmother's '54 Chevy, the Blue Racer we called it, and singing "Satisfaction" along with the Stones on the radio, *I can't get no . . . oh no no no . . . no girl reaction . . .* I've already crashed all my other cars. Totaled my mother's baby blue Dodge Phoenix, blew the transmission in the '40 Ford. Grandma Ba Ba gave me the Blue Racer when they took away her license for too many speeding tickets. I'm with one of my craziest high school friends cruising along Tremont Street in the South End, a beer in one hand and a smoldering roach in the other, steering with my left elbow, we pull up in front of the Estelle's Musical Lounge with no idea how we got here. Maybe I saw some blurb in the newspaper about a private party for Dionne Warwick and thought that sounded like fun.

Eighteen, nineteen years old, white as the lines in the street, white as the priest's collar, white as milk, white as the White House, white as the Founding Fathers and the slave owners, white as a Klansman's sheet, white as the fluorescent light in the interrogation room where they give you the fifth degree on your bigotry.

How do you feel about them black folk, son?

Oh, Daddy, I don't like 'em, they scare me. They got big muscles and bigger cocks. But the women . . . mmm-mmm, now the women . . . they sure can sing . . . and dance . . . and fuck . . . Yes, subject to all that crap. And living through it. Attracted to everything I was not. But with one advantage: I never believed shit they told me. And certainly, once I got high, it was all about putting the lie to the test. I would go there, follow them down, and find out what was real and what was bullshit.

This is how we happen to trip down the stairs into the private room and even more private birthday celebration of Mr. William Elliot thrown by Dionne Warwick. You know, someone must have told me about this. Maybe at our usual haunt on Mass. Ave. near the juncture with Columbus where the pros hang out, where you can score a nickel bag, where very few white boys from the 'burbs would dare to show their faces. Someone told us about this, had to be. There's a party, they tell us, down the street at Estelle's. Private party. Just ask for Bill. Tell 'em you're friends with Bill.

Bill who?

It don't matter, just Bill.

The guy at the door looks us over. What the fuck're you doing here?

You know, we're friends of Bill.

He just laughs. Bill, how you know Bill? Bill! You know these white boys?

Bill is playing the piano. Singing. An elegant, slim and handsome young man, he looks over and smiles. Sings like it's a lyric from the song: "*Never seen 'em before in my life.*"

Man, you boys got to be crazy. You think you can just walk in here and join this party? Look around. You see any other teenage white boys here?

But that's exactly why you should let us in: We're not like any other white boys. We can dance! Yeah, man, I can dance like Elvis. Like James Brown. And sing like Chuck Berry. Bo Diddley and Fats Domino. Fuck all that white boy stuff, man. I am the blackest motherfucker in the room!

Of course they let us in. I'm sitting at the bar with Dionne Warwick, put my arm around her and whisper in her ear, *I love you. Marry me.* This is some kind of dream come true. She smiles. A mouth full of gleaming teeth.

What's your name?

You can call me Ricky . . . you can call me Rick . . . you can call me Richard. *Just don't call me Dick.*

You hear that? she says to Nancy Wilson. He says, *Just don't call me Dick.*

Nancy Wilson says, You're cute. I'm gonna call you Ricky.

They call over Bon Bon DeLoach, "*Just don't call him Dick.*" They are all laughing and cuddling me. "*Call him Ricky.*"

I'm dancing with Dionne Warwick, holding her in my arms. She's singing in my ear, *Don't make me over. . . . Now that I can't make it without you. . . . Accept me for what I am. . . . Accept me for the things that I do. . . .*

It is Thursday, June 3, 1963. I'm nineteen years old, and I'm smitten. I love my country in all its diversity. Fuck the flag. It's not about the flag. All that patriotic bullshit. It's about the people. Black yellow red brown white mestizo mulatto octoroon: the great melting pot.

God bless the American people.

* * *

I GET OUT of a cab a few streets away from the family home of Jonathan Dead Seagull. Not the home where he lived with his wife and child, but his mother's home in the Forest Hill section of Toronto. Earlier, I checked into the Windsor Arms Hotel in Yorkville, five-star digs under yet another name, using a clean credit card to break the paper trail in case there is some flag on my ID and they are surreptitiously tracking me. Spruced up, deodorized, I walk past the house, eyeball the several cars parked along the quiet residential street. There does not appear to be anyone staked out on the home. Still, I stand at the end of the street watching the house as an elderly couple leave, get into a car, and drive away. Can't be too careful these days.

I am so exhausted I feel like weeping. I want to lie down on some strange lawn, cower in the hedges, hide my face in the turf, and just disappear. It all feels so pointless and futile. *Why bother? Who gives a shit?* We are all going to be dead anyway. Fade away, cease to exist, wiped off the face of the earth like the Seagull. Disintegrate like spume on the tide. Go to ashes like Jake. In my mind I conjure an image of him and his Mexican wife, their bodies stiff and black as burnt logs, faces like grinning charred masks. The words *crispy critters* come to me, and I choke on them, a grim guffaw. Dead, dead, dead. *You'll be dead too one day, Stratton. Maybe sooner than you think. And no one will give a shit. Not really.* Life goes on, such as it is. Thousands and millions and billions of people on this teeming ball of matter spinning through the universe. *What the fuck is it all about?*

Seagull, Seagull, where are you now, you motherfucker? Why couldn't you just be patient? We were making shitloads of money. Isn't that what you always wanted? No, you wanted to prove to me that you were—what? Smarter? Braver? Tougher? That you could drive faster, redder automobiles? That you didn't need me? That's nonsense. That's a lie. We all need each other, or what's the point in doing anything? Standing out here in this street alone, I feel your presence. Without me, without you, there is nothing.

I see figures moving in the windows of the Seagull family home. A flock of Jewish mothers alight on elegant chairs and settees like a jury. Am I afraid of their recriminations? Probably. And just as probably that is why I am here. I came to hear them say, "You killed our son. You led him astray. Fucking goyim bastard. It is always you Gentiles killing our sons, leading them off to war, leading them off to concentration camps and to the ovens. Leading them off to mad adventures in strange lands. Leave us alone!"

What is my karma with the Arabs and the Jews and the Italians, the Blacks and the Hispanic people? White man. Anglo-Saxon. It has to be blood guilt. Genetic guilt. Guilt that goes back centuries. A barbarian, a conqueror, a Crusader, a slave trader, a colonist. I'll pay for it all in this lifetime. I have a horsewhip in my spine. Brass knuckles in my handshake. A vault for a brain. My balls are made of amethyst. *You want trouble, trouble is my real name. You can't take it, get out of the game.*

Thus encouraged, I march up and enter the grieving household. Truth is, it's the kid I don't want to see. Don't want to see the accusation in his eyes: *You killed my daddy.*

"Thank God you came," my sister-in-law says and holds me briefly as I kiss her cheek and tell her, once more, how sorry I am that her man is gone. "I have something for you," she says, focused on the present, on life. "I've been worried sick about it. It's here. I had to get it out of my house. They're watching me. They come every day. They don't even try to hide."

The room is full of people I don't know. Thankfully, the boy is already asleep somewhere upstairs. Mrs. Seagull senior, who I met only fleetingly before at the wedding, seems equally beyond grief. She is a frail, sharp-featured widow in her seventies. The line, *No mother should have to bury her son*, comes to my mind as I walk to her, but I do not say it. There is no reproach in her touch as she takes my hand. I get the sense she doesn't know, or care to know, the details of how her son died. Plane crash is enough information. She never understood why he had to fly around in his own plane anyway. Leave that to the others. Stay home. Get a real job. Doctor. Lawyer. Professional man. Accountant. Like your younger brother. Like your father, may he rest . . . like Aunt Bea's sons. Take care of your family. Enough with this running around.

The gathering feels like something between an Irish wake, where everyone's drinking and flushed with relief that the son-of-a-bitch is dead, and an Italian funeral, where the women are dressed in black and wallow in sorrow while the men stand about calculating their losses and gains. Here there is plenty to eat. Food for the living. Which is a good thing because I am famished. And some alcohol. I help myself to a stiff glass of vodka and scarf up a plate of hearty victuals. *And death shall have no dominion*—Dylan Thomas resounding in my brain.

"I told her it was just some stuff of Jonathan's I had to get out of the house," Avril says as she opens the hall closet and drags out two suitcases. "But I think she knows. This is everything." She looks at me steadily. "I hope you told him not to bring any more." There is something in her that enjoys the criminal. She will miss it, her eyes say.

"I did. But you should hold on to whatever you need."

"Don't worry, we're okay. I just want this out of here in case . . . something happens."

She calls me a cab and I lug the suitcases out, heave them in the trunk. At the hotel I don't want the bellman to handle the bags because they are abnormally heavy. "Bring me the cart," I say and hand him a fifty. "I've got these." In the room later I open them. Two point six million mostly in brown hundreds and red fifties. A ledger with Rosie's careful accounting. In the minus column a notation: five hundred. And another: fifty, the shit that got busted.

Who's gonna eat that?

I put the suitcases in the closet and forget about them, fall into a deep, dreamless sleep. No dead bodies to dispose of. The Seagull is at peace in his grave.

In the morning I rent a car, one way with a drop-off in Montreal. This is what I'm made for: a man of action. I reach Squid pay phone to pay phone. It is imperative I rendezvous with the Rose, I tell him, but equally critical that he not draw his Heat to me—I have enough of my own. He must use all his skills as a veteran outlaw, a seasoned ex-con, an intelligent if outrageous dope dealer to make absolutely certain he is not followed to wherever we meet. I buy more luggage, clothes, underwear, wrap the money and split it up so the individual bags aren't so heavy. I check out, greasing palms along the way, drive downtown and park the rental in a garage near the Royal York Hotel.

The Squid has rented a suite for our meeting. He answers the door when I knock. He's ordered a lavish breakfast from room service: omelets, French toast, coffee, tea with milk and honey for Rosie. I give Squid the keys to my rental car, the location and the parking ticket. The Rosebud, he tells me, will be along presently.

There are a few men in my life I can honestly say I love. Men I believe would lay down their life for me, and I want to believe I would do the same for them. Men to whom friendship and loyalty mean everything. Even more than money. Call them brothers, but they are closer than kin. Brothers are bred for rivalry. Friends of this rare caliber are bound together in some vista of the soul where past, present, and future events are clearly understood without need to express where one stands.

Norman Mailer is such a friend. As is Rosie. They are alike in many ways. Both men of large intellects and unbridled appetites. When I introduced them at the farm in Maine some years back, it was like bringing together two rogues of equal but disparate nature. They sized each other up warily like wrestlers approaching one another in the center of the mat. Mailer testified as a character witness at Rosie's trial. He compared him to Errol Flynn and Robin Hood. An apt comparison since the Rose is as Celtic as the crown jewels, as British as Blackbeard. Descended from a long line of pirates and horse thieves.

Rosie is even fatter than the last time I saw him. He smokes cigars when not burning herb. His teeth are stained brown with resin and tobacco tar. Prosperity is not sitting well on him—or on me, for that matter. What is wrong with us? We work so hard to accomplish this, why can't we enjoy it? Or be satisfied with it? Why don't we use the energy to make us better? Stronger? Healthier? Instead of crazier and more dissolute.

"I need more," he says. "I'm gonna run out by the end of the week."

We go over the books, balance our accounts.

"Who's gonna cover the five fifty that were lost at Thousand Islands?" I inquire.

"Split it?" he suggests.

"Explain to me why I should eat any of that loss. It went down on your side. We agreed. Once it crosses the border, you own it."

"Okay. Give it to me for cost. But I need more to make up for the loss."

"That doesn't seem right. You know Sammy and the Arabs are gonna take it out of my end."

He shrugs. "I'm making you guys a fucking fortune."

"We're making you a fortune."

"So we should split it. Everybody takes a piece of the loss, it doesn't hurt as much."

There's truth to this. Why be greedy? But it's not about that. It's about security. And responsibility. He's too fucking flamboyant. I love the guy, but he troubles me. It's like he needs to get caught to validate who he is and what he does. Squid told me the story, how they were having a party recently, Rosie and a whole tribe of freaks and hippie dope dealers in a public park, all puzzled up on reefer and Heineken, carrying on like a bunch of nymphs and satyrs at some Dionysian rite when the Metro Toronto cops rolled up and took them all downtown. The cops seized two slabs stamped with the Flower of Bekaa seal. Doesn't take Sherlock Holmes to solve this mystery. Rosie argues the gathering was like a corporate picnic where the worker bees get to mingle with management and let off some steam. Good for company morale. It's like anything else, he says, somebody has to get out there and hustle. A happy salesperson is a productive salesperson. It makes them feel good to frolic with the bosses. The Squid got hauled in as well. No wonder the Law went up on a wire at Sprout House.

There're these two cops, Rosie tells me, Metro Toronto drug squad, who have a hard-on for him. They want to make their reputation by taking down Canada's hippie godfather. He gives me their names, Carter and Mason—in one ear and out the other. I've got my own Special Agent Bernard Wolfshein and his crew to worry about. I say, "Fuck these guys. Don't make their job any easier."

Rosie is like one of the old-school mob bosses: He hates to leave the neighborhood. He has his set routine, his daily stops like going to the social club. He can't fathom the anonymity of a life on the lam. We settle on a compromise. The Heat seems to be concentrated in Toronto—naturally, on him—so we'll spread it out, ease up distribution here and focus on his West Coast market. If he wants to send some of his best local customers out there to score, so much the better, as long as they don't bring the Heat with them. And we will not store any more product or accumulate large sums of money anywhere near Rosie's operation. He is to profess he's gone into semi-retirement, let his underlings handle the business, while he spends his days thinking of ways to frustrate the Man. I urge him to take a holiday, go on a trip and relax; but he says he can't, he's still on paper from the last bust and is not allowed to leave the Metropolitan Toronto area without permission from his parole officer.

"So get permission and go away."

"Maybe I'll go to Vancouver," he says with a lopsided smile.

"Great . . . no, stay here."

"What do you want me to do with the . . ." He consults his ledger. "Four hundred K plus I still owe you?"

"You mean, not including what you owe me for the five hundred and fifty pounds you lost?" I remind him.

"You're hard. . . . You sure you're not Jewish?"

"Swamp Yankee."

"Same thing."

"I'll send someone to pick it up. Whatever you do, don't bring it to Avril."

"How's she taking it?"

I shrug. "Right now, I think she's so freaked by all the Heat she hasn't had a chance to miss her old man. It's like it hasn't sunk in."

"Who could miss that guy?"

"C'mon, you liked him."

"Some people are better off dead," he says.

"That's cold."

"He brought this Heat."

I shake my head. "No, brother. This is your Heat."

"And yours. You're the fucking fugitive. You think they don't know who brought in this load? It's got your MO all over it."

Each in our own way, we love rubbing it in the Man's face.

THE SQUID RETURNS with the keys to my rental and a new parking ticket from a different lot. He says there is an additional eight hundred sixty grand in the trunk. Mostly large bills. Two hundred and sixty thousand in American. They have buyers from Detroit and Madison, Wisconsin, coming over to buy hash in Canada and smuggle it back into the States. "The Weather Underground," Rosie says. "We are helping finance the revolution."

"So we're smuggling it into Canada so they can smuggle it back into the States. That doesn't make sense. Tell them we will deliver stateside and save a lot of aggravation and risk."

"But I still get my price," he says. "I don't want them to meet anybody. I'll send one of my people down to handle the exchange."

"As long as whoever it is doesn't bring the Mounties with them."

We readjust the books. The eight hundred and sixty grand was supposed to be an even million. That's another hundred and forty grand that goes back on his tab. "Plus the—"

"I know, the five fifty. You'll talk to Sam and see what kind of a number you can get me on that. What about Thai weed?"

"What about it?"

"Can you sell it in New York?"

"Sticks?"

"Loose. Comes in bales."

"Any good?"

"Squid. Show him. It's beyond good."

Squid hands me a Ziploc full of lush dusty green buds veined with red hairs and clustered with furry, seedless bracts. I pinch a bud and hold it to my nose. Smells like exotic Eastern incense. "It's expensive," Rosie tells me. "Fourteen hundred a pound in Vancouver. But there's a lot and we can make a deal if you can handle transportation. . . . Keep it," he says when I go to hand him the bag.

I'm leery of carrying any quantity of reefer while transporting cash. But this is too nice to pass up. I roll one up for the road and stuff the bag in my crotch. We hug.

"You fat motherfucker," I tell him. "What is it with this belly? You're gonna have a fuckin' heart attack."

"Don't worry about me. How's Val?"

I've been wondering when he would ask this. "She's good. Busy."

"She keeping her nose clean?"

"She better be."

"Watch out for that, bro. You still fucking her?"

"Whenever I can."

"Yeah, well, tell her when she gets tired of that Yankee needle dick and wants a real man, she knows where to find me."

"I'll tell her to look you up in the fat farm for worn-out, old hippies."

"Bend over an' spread 'em, I'll show you how worn out I am."

Rosie's vices have never included powders or pills. He did a lot of acid as a kid and now consumes cannabis like a Rastafarian. More. His cells are drenched in THC. He reminds me of a pot plant. No wonder they call him Flower. His long, thinning reddish hair is like pistils and filaments, and his gangling appendages wave in the breeze like branches. His big, bulging, rheumy, and bloodshot eyes are like luminescent disk flowers at the center of the ray. When he dies and they bury him, a whole field of sativa will sprout with Rosie's face in the bud.

Rosie rolls up a towel from the bathroom, places it along the space at the bottom of the door to keep the odoriferous ganja fumes from drifting out into the hallway and mesmerizing the hotel staff. We fire up a joint of the Thai weed. I take a couple of hits—all I need. I feel the twinge of pain as my lungs expand. Rosie sucks it down to the roach. We embrace again, clasp hands in the Brotherhood handshake. Bid adieu. Commend each other to the gods of cannabis. I leave first.

The rush assails me even before I reach the elevator bank. Suddenly, I have no idea where I am, how I got here, who I am, what I am doing, and where I am going. I'll be lucky if I can find the elevator and press the right button to get me to the lobby. I've lost my moorings to reality, such as they were. I don't even know my name or any of my names. I'll never find this car with the three and a half million dollars in the trunk. I'm going to spend the rest of my pathetic life wandering around this strange city babbling to myself like a schizophrenic homeless person trying to remember who I am and what I'm doing here. If agents of the law stop me and inquire what I am up to, I will be reduced to a blubbering idiot, I will sink to my knees and beg them to lock me up for the rest of my life. *Save me from myself!* A wave of fear and paranoia grips me in a mental bear hug. I can't move, I can't think. I'm too high . . . way too high.

What horseshit. I am in complete control. Never been more on top of my game, never felt better. I hear gongs from distant Buddhist monasteries resounding in the Thai jungle of my mind so spaced out it's like a week passes between each blow with the padded mallet of my heart on the membrane between the hippie campus and the hippopotamus, with the preferential corex sopping up the brain leakage until elephants lumber out from of the hinterlands, those dead elephants in the Beirut penthouse come to life beating a path to little brown men in loincloths who take me by the arm and lead me to a clearing where I am presented to the Headman. Who looks exactly like me!

"Dick?" he asks, "Is that you?"

Not on your life. I am Richie Rich. I am Batman. Archie and Jughead in one. Elvis. Scrooge McDuck. Popeye. Al Capone. Tarzan. Frankenstein's monster lurching through the woods calling out, Friend? Friend? Friend? to the angry villagers seeking to capture me. I am Joseph Kennedy marijuana mogul coming down now, hours later, on the highway tooling along the 401 with the radio on, past Belleville where the Rosebush took root, and Kingston where he was placed in confinement, heading up the river to Montreal, French Canada, back in my right mind, if such a space exists.

Man, that is some good reefer.

But now it is time to get totally serious. Not that I have been the least bit goofy or lackadaisical in my altered state of consciousness. Just the opposite. Herb heightens my awareness to every possible pitfall. I'm like a brain surgeon operating on myself. One false move and I am paralyzed.

I check into a motel northeast of the city on the outskirts of Drummondville. I'm now within one hundred miles of the US border. My Cannuck friend, Giles, drives down from Quebec and joins me for a late dinner. Two bottles of good wine. French cuisine. Good to be back in the civilized world. We discuss riding into Montreal to feast our eyes on the best strippers in North America. No, I can't go, not with all this dough to babysit. Giles gives me another hundred and fifty grand and wants to know when he can get more hash. This is the way we like it—the money flowing freely, everyone wanting more product. I call our pilot, Wart Hog; he calls back from a pay phone—supposedly. Everything is in motion now.

Alone in my seedy motel room with six suitcases stuffed with money, three and a half million plus in cash, I take a few final hits of the Thai weed and lapse into a feeling of utter peace and contentment. At last I have figured it all out. I understand life—at least my life and exactly what I need to do with what is left of it. I place the suitcases on the twin beds, open them, and gaze at the contents. All these stacks of dyed and printed paper signifying amounts of an abstraction. It has no intrinsic value, and yet we define who we are in terms of its measure. Money is man's greatest abstraction next to time. Money means nothing beyond what one does with it, also like time. How simple and yet how profound: Time means money and vice versa. If you squander it, you lose it, you blow it, and you lose time. If you use it productively, not just to make more money, but to do something useful, to build or create something that has real value to yourself and others—something of beauty, something that will bring joy and inspiration and good fortune long after you have gone—then it's time and money well spent. You are an artist, a creator. But if you use it to buy booze and hookers and trucks and boats and airplanes, homes on three continents and more dope; and if you don't do anything useful and creative with your money and your time, then it don't mean shit, son. You are a fool, and you might as well douse all these suitcases with gasoline and set a match to it for all the good it will do you and the world you walk in.

You are, Mr. Stratton—now look in the mirror and get this straight, for at this moment and in this chemically altered head you are finally seeing yourself clearly, as you really are, and what you are is—say it: *You are a fucking asshole. A genuine, three-hundred-and-sixty-degree, wizened but wartless, puckered, quivering, stained-brown, stinky bunghole who ain't got no sense.*

But wait. An asshole who knows he's an asshole can become something else. A better asshole. Or even a new man. I can change. I can stop drinking so much. Stop spending a fortune in bars and restaurants. Stop fucking all these lovely young ladies—well, maybe not all of them, just most of them, save a few, and drink a good bottle of wine once in a while. But get back in shape. Stay off the vodka martinis. Work out. Meditate. Chill. Relax. Think. Use my brain for something besides a testing pad for adulterants. Stop running around the world like a lost soul. Be a man. Settle down and have a family. Maybe even be a father someday.

12

BETTER THAN SEX

NORMAN MAILER GOT a visit from Agent Wolfshein and a deputy US marshal with the fugitive task force. This I learn in an early morning pay phone to pay phone conference with Biff. From what Norman told Biff, the agents were polite and seemed mildly amused to be visiting the famous author on police business. Wolfshein informed Mailer that they believe he was one of the last people to speak to me before I split. The Wolf went on to say that the United States Attorney's office in Portland, Maine, was distressed to see that Mailer's signature was missing from the bail surety bond putting the farm up as collateral. He told Mailer that the government might be required to sell the farm and give him half of the proceeds. Mailer should expect to hear from the prosecutor's office. Did Mailer have any idea where I might be? No. Was he aware of the penalties for harboring a federal fugitive? He was not. Wolfshein informed him that even knowing the whereabouts of a fugitive and failing to inform the government could constitute a harboring offense punishable by imprisonment. Mailer thanked the agents and told them that if he heard from me, he would be sure to pass along their concerns.

Wolfshein has moved in to occupy a substantial piece of real estate in my head. While I was in Lebanon, I rarely thought of him. Now he is never far from my mind. I'm sure his intelligence has informed him that North America is experiencing a glut of high quality Lebanese hashish that has the Stratton/Rosie freak family imprint all over it—our telltale stamp, both marketing contrivance and slap in the face to the authorities.

Be that as it may, there is still work to do. And running around with suitcases containing nearly four million dollars in cash is risky business indeed. Stressful. I hate the idea of getting caught with all this money. Losing any amount of money is anathema to me: the embarrassment, the ridicule, the shame. And the satisfaction it would give the Feds. The loss. I don't mind spending money like an Arab sheik, but allowing it to be seized by the Heat is worse than losing a load. One can always get more product. Money is never easy to come by, and once it's lost you can never get it back.

Giles shows up with another forty grand to balance out his account. We pack all the suitcases into his car, then he follows me to Montreal where we return the rental. Wart Hog lands in our Cessna 210 at the municipal airport in Trois-Rivières, Quebec, and calls me at the motel. He has filed a legitimate flight plan, informed the authorities he is picking up an American businessman and returning him to Bangor, Maine. Giles drives me to the airport, where I greet Wart Hog and board the single engine Cessna, carrying only one small overnight bag and my briefcase. When we taxi to the far end of the runway, with Wart Hog on the radio filing his return flight plan, Giles pulls up along the access road, I throw open the rear door, and we quickly load in the suitcases containing the cash.

And we take off, up over the mountains of western Maine well ahead of the weather that tends to gather along the plains of Ontario, picking up moisture from the Great Lakes, which builds into banks of dense cumulonimbus by mid-to-late afternoon. The joy of flight lifts my spirits. It's a great feeling to be suspended midair in a small plane, airborne above the earth like some minor deity looking down upon the firmament. After the geometric designs of family farms arrayed like postage stamps in shades of green and brown and auburn give way to

wooded mountains and vast expanses of nearly uninhabited pine forest, crystal blue lakes and green ponds, frothy rivers and boulder-strewn
streams, there is America—the great beast lies beneath us slumbering,
dozing in the summer heat, unaware of our gnatlike intrusion.

Wart Hog is quiet, perturbed by the potential fallout from Fred's
having flipped. He also makes it clear he expects to be paid more for
this trip, since there is obviously something illegal in the suitcases. He
knows it is most likely money, having done this a few times before. Or
some exotic weed. I tell him not to worry, of course he'll be adequately
compensated. I have a few days work for him; he could make himself
twenty grand.

"Does that work for you?" I ask over the drone of the 210's engine.

"Yes, that's fine," Wart Hog says. He's a precise guy, a good pilot,
gets the job done, but he's suspicious, acts uptight like he believes
everyone is out to cheat him.

"I thought you told me Fred never knew your real name," I say.

"He doesn't."

"So what are you worried about? You have no record. It's not like
they can show him mug shots."

He unloads. He met Fred's "friend," the corrupt cop, a couple of
times, once at the airport after returning from ferrying a load of pot
into Canada. And another time at the bar and restaurant Fred owns a
piece of in Sanford, Maine, the town where he lives, the joint where
Fred would hang out and party with his stripper friends, one of whom
Wart Hog fucked in the ass while Fred smoked coke and watched,
playing with himself, trying to get his dick hard. Wart Hog seems to
take perverse delight in telling me this.

I shake my head and sigh. "Does she know your real name?" I ask.
"Who?"

"The hooker. The stripper. What's her name?"

"Oh, Piper . . . I don't think so."

"Yeah, Piper. You don't think so. But she might."

"Well . . . I caught her going through my wallet once."

"Why the fuck didn't you tell me this before?" I want to know. "You think she's a snitch for this cop? You think this cop is really bent? Or is he playing Fred?"

"He asks a lot of questions," Wart Hog says, and I sense in his voice that he fears the worst.

"So you think you might be hot?"

"I don't know. I'm just saying."

"Change of plans," I tell him, enraged but keeping it to myself. "Drop me in Rangeley. Then go on to Augusta instead of Bangor and leave the plane there. Check in to a hotel and call the service in New York. Leave a pay phone number where I can call you tonight at ten. Don't leave the area code. Just the number."

I was contemplating doing this anyway. Nothing like a sudden change of plans to confound the Man. I know the little airport at Rangeley well. I took flight lessons there, did my first and only solo takeoff and landing. I'm friendly with the sole proprietor of the flight school, a taciturn local who comports himself with typical Yankee reserve: Ask me no questions and I'll tell you no lies. People in these parts make it their business not to stick their noses in other people's business. Particularly when you pay in cash. With any luck, there won't be anyone around the airfield this time of day. It consists of a three-thousand-foot paved runway, a windsock, a small shack, and a pay phone and is situated at the foot of a range of mountains overlooking the magnificent vista of Rangeley Lake. The only hazard is the unpredictable crosswinds.

We land. I load the suitcases into the shack, and Wart Hog takes off alone and empty. I call the farm down the road from my place where JD stays with my neighbor's wife. No answer. Then I page my nephew, Carlos, who lives with my parents in Wellesley, and leave the pay phone number. I'm stranded with nearly $4 million in six suitcases. But better that than busted. When Carlos calls back from a pay phone fifteen minutes later, I tell him to pick up the truck with the camper from my partner, Benny, retrieve 300 pounds of hash from the stash in Cambridge, and drive it to Maine, near Farmington, check into a hotel, and leave the number on the service in New York.

"No area code, just the number," I repeat the instruction.

Still no call back from JD. I reach a local taxi service and arrange for a ride from the airport in Rangeley up through Stratton, Maine— the town named for my intrepid forebears—past Sugarloaf Mountain, where there is some sort of summer music and arts festival going on, to Kingfield. The taxi driver, who picks me up in a station wagon well past its warranty, is a talkative sort with a deep, backwoods Maine accent and a ponytail. He's got a USMC tattoo and, I learn, knows fellow ex-Marines JD and Father Flaherty. He tells me they are both probably up at the Sugarloaf Mountain music festival with the rest of the local freaks and hippies and bikers and dopers. So I give him some buds from the bag of Thai weed as an added tip and ask him to track down JD and have him meet me at the bar in the Herbert Grand Hotel in Kingfield. He drops me at a motel on the outskirts of town. I check in, leave my luggage, and then walk to a local upscale inn and tavern owned by a friend in a large restored Colonial mansion set on a hill in the middle of town.

Something about the way the taxi driver eyed those suitcases when he dropped me off and my general heightened paranoia at leaving all that money unattended will not leave me alone. Even as I walk around without the suitcases, in my mind I'm still carrying them. I need to put this burden down. Where the fuck is JD? I need him. And Father Flaherty, I could use them both with a couple of guns to sit on that money until I can get it out of my hands and safely into Sammy's hands, Nasif's hands, even Biff will get another taste of the cake. Pay some bills. Hide some in an offshore account.

My resolve to stop drinking hard booze evaporates. At the bar in my friend's tavern I order a Patrón margarita prepared by a friendly bartender who is astounded to see me.

"I heard there was some kind of trouble down there in Phillips," he says. "No salt, right?"

"No salt."

"Something about a big plane that crashed. Then you took off. That was like . . . over a year ago." He eyes me with a glint of humor and pours the lime green liquid into a chilled glass. "What was that all about?"

"You know how these things get all blown out of proportion," I say and slake my thirst first with a cool glass of water and then sip the margarita. "There were some problems, yes. Someone did leave a wrecked plane on the strip."

"It was in all the papers," he goes on. "There were pictures of the plane. Fucking huge. I read that you got arrested in Farmington. And then . . . split. I heard the government was going after your farm."

I shrug. "Fuckers. I heard that too."

"Man, why don't they just leave people alone?"

"Exactly . . . listen, can I borrow your truck? Just for half an hour. I'll give you two hundred bucks. I need to pick up my luggage, and I can't find JD or Flaherty anywhere."

"My wife has got my truck," he says. "She should be by here any time now."

"Can you call her?"

"This is urgent?" he asks.

"It's not that. I just want to get changed, clean up, and settle in."

"Let me speak to Michael, the owner. He knows you. Maybe you can borrow his car."

Michael knows me only too well. He's a weed head, gets his herb from Father Flaherty, and he's close to my friend and attorney Channing Godfried. Part of me had hoped to keep my presence in these parts known to a bare minimum of low-profile residents lest word get back to law enforcement and some state cops decide to take me down. I wanted to stay clear of Michael; he's a compulsive gossip, loves intrigue. My visit will be all over the county within a few days.

The other side of me, the side that has a penchant for notoriety, enjoys it when Michael walks out of his office and says, "Jesus Christ! Look what the cat dragged in!"

He's an Irish guy, dapper and well fed, always wears red suspenders. He has a ruddy face with a graying, carefully trimmed beard, handlebar mustache, and arched, startled looking eyebrows. We hug. He slaps me on the back, then looks around suspiciously, goes to the door, and peers outside. "Fuckin' Legs Diamond," he says. "Any G-men on your tail, Legs? Should I close the place down?"

"That's not a bad idea. We could have a party. But Mike, first I need to borrow your car. Just for a few minutes. I want to pick up my luggage. I'll be right back."

"Pick up your luggage where?"

"It's just down the street."

"C'mon. I'll drive you," he says.

"Where's Godfried?" I ask as we head down the hill from his place and out to the motel on the road to Sugarloaf. I'm feeling better already. Safer. It was the right thing to do, always is—to trust in friends.

"He's around, been in town most of the summer. He was down on the Cape at Mailer's. You going down there?"

"I can't. Mailer already has enough Heat because of me."

"You got one rolled up?" he asks.

"Yes."

"What the fuck're you waiting for? Fire it up."

"It's not four-twenty yet."

"It is somewhere."

I light a joint of the Thai weed, take a couple of hits and pass it to Michael.

He gazes at the burning joint. "Shit smells good. What is it?"

The car is veering off the road.

"Thai weed. It's excellent. Watch where you're going."

"Can you get me an ounce?"

"I don't have it right now. There should be some coming through soon. Stay in touch with Father Flaherty." I make a mental note to reach Rosie and order as much of this herb as I can get. Now that my head is used to it, the high is extraordinary.

Michael takes a couple of deep hits. "What's going on, man?" he asks. "I've heard so many crazy stories. All this crap in the papers. Biggest drug bust in the history of the state, or some shit. And I'm thinking, What the fuck did they really get? A few hundred pounds of pot? I heard they found nothing at your place. And the plane was empty. You're like some fuckin' Robert Vesco fugitive kingpin, for fuck's sake. Man, this is some good dope," he mumbles. "It was even on TV, the bust, I mean. I hear the government is trying to seize your farm . . . sell everything. Wow! I'd take a quarter pound of this. How much is it?"

"It's expensive. The guy from down state rolled over."

"So I heard. The guy from Sanford, right? Fuckin' scumbag. You can't trust them city folk. I heard he was in a head-on collision and killed two people."

"Yes," I say and let the wave of guilt and dread wash over me like nausea.

"Not good," Michael says

"Not good at all," I agree. "He's hurting a lot of people."

"Miserable fuck. So what're you going to do?" Michael asks as we pull into the motel parking lot. "I'm fucking loaded," he announces. And then, "Why the fuck are you staying in this fleabag joint?"

"I'm not. It's a decoy. I have these bags. You know, there's stuff in them. Not drugs. But . . . stuff I don't want to lose. I'll give you five grand if you let me lock them up in your office until I track down JD and he can take care of them for me."

"Stuff?" His eyes light up with a conspiratorial twinkle. "Five grand?"

"Stuff. I'll give you another five grand to shut down the inn for the night and we'll have a party."

"I have a few guests."

"Are they cool?"

"They ain't cops," he says. He's smiling, happy now. The thought of money and a party cheers him up. We get out and fetch the bags.

"So invite them."

"Throw in a quarter pound of this weed and you're on," he says and helps me load the suitcases into the trunk and rear seat of his Volvo.

"Stuff," he mutters and grins. "This is some good weed. I'm fucking hallucinating."

It's like energy, I'm thinking, remembering my illumination of the previous evening. Paper. Dope. It's as if there is some mysterious force emanating from these bags as we ride back through town that has me uptight and Michael excited. I'm sure he knows what's in the bags. We load them into his office. He puts the CLOSED FOR A PRIVATE PARTY sign on the door to the inn and gets on the phone, calls Godfried's farm, leaves a message with the housekeeper. He calls around and invites a few other mutual friends—a poet and a sculptor, some musicians—to come by for a dinner party later but doesn't mention there might be a mystery guest. I give him a few fat buds of the Thai weed, take ten grand in Canadian hundreds from one of the bags and give that to him as well.

"Canadian," he says. "Better yet."

"You can tell your banker you had a family of Canadians come through and pay cash."

"Always a pleasure doing business with our neighbors to the north," Michael says and puts the ten grand in his desk. "Now I can pay my mortgage for the next six months and take the little lady on vacation this winter." He locks his desk drawer and taps me on the chest. "Just don't forget my quarter elbow."

Seriously high, I lope down the hill to the bar at the Herbert Grand in the middle of the village. Even as I assure myself that I know what I am doing, I feel like one of the characters in the *Fabulous Furry Freak Brothers* comics. Each step seems impossibly long, my legs are like wet noodles, I imagine a posse of baton-wielding cops in hot pursuit while I whistle *toot toot*.

No one knows me at the Herbert Grand. I use the pay phone in the lobby, check the answering service. Wart Hog called and left a number, as did Carlos. I call Carlos in Farmington and tell him to head over. At the bar, sipping Patrón on the rocks, I question this move: Why bring the hash into proximity of the cash? That's a fundamental no-no in this line of work. Never put the dope and the loot in the same locale. But I won't; I'll keep them well separated. I just need a hand here, and JD and Father Flaherty are still MIA. I try my neighbor's farm again and finally reach the stable hand who confirms they are all up at the mountain at the music festival and not expected back until late.

This town is like something out of the Old West: one dusty main street through the middle of a cluster of wood-frame buildings; a railroad line long out of use; and some stately mansions set on the outlying streets. Sitting at the bar in the late afternoon with a mellow tequila and reefer buzz on, I look up as my nephew, Carlos, steps through the door and stops, framed in the sunlight, backlit like some young-buck gunslinger who just rode into town and strode into the local saloon looking for trouble. He blinks, sees me, and takes a seat at the bar beside me.

"What're you drinking?" I ask.

"I'll have whatever you're having."

He's a good kid, Carlos, as I call him, half Dominican, fathered by my older sister's second husband. Just out of high school. We've been close for years, since he was a child. Some would argue I destroyed any chance this young man may have had for a normal adolescence or even a normal childhood by introducing him to the outlaw lifestyle at an early age. Maybe so. He lived with me one summer after my freshman year at Arizona State when I was working as a lifeguard—one of the few straight jobs I have ever held, and I got fired from that position midway through the season. Carlos was four or five years old. My sister, Gi Gi was off working as a model at the World's Fair in New York. I rode a Harley Davidson Sportster bought with money I made smuggling weed from Mexico. I used to tie young Carlos around my waist, climb on the Harley and take him to work with me at the Wayland Swimming and Tennis Club, where nubile, bikini-clad girls would look after him while I dozed in the lifeguard's chair.

I lived in a rented house that summer with a few friends. On any given night, you never knew who might be crashing there. It was a nonstop party with a revolving cast of characters and a keg or two of beer on tap in the garage at all times. My friend Ronnie, the guy who first turned me on to pot, showed up one evening with a giant snapping turtle. He discovered the beast trying to cross the street and tossed it in the bed of his pickup truck. Prehistoric-looking creature. Take your finger off with one snap of his wedge-shaped jaw. We filled one of those basting tubes with gin, stuck it in the turtle's mouth, and squirted gin into his gullet. The turtle got completely fucked up. He staggered around the party that night on all fours so drunk he was snapping at the dancing barefoot girls in slow motion. Then we chopped his head off, stuck a set of those wind-up chattering teeth in his mouth, and mounted him in the refrigerator. Childish, and cruel, I know, but we were kids.

A few of those summer nights after we closed the swimming and tennis club down for the day, I opened the pool back up for skinny-dipping parties for my friends. Nude teenagers, boys and girls, cavorting in the pool, drinking beer and Southern Comfort, smoking a little weed, making out when one night the place was raided. A couple of local cops and one of the owners, the guy who had hired me, surrounded the pool area and then lit the place up with spotlights. My friends hurriedly pulled on their clothes. We were busted. Trespassing. Underage drinking. I stashed the weed. The owner was flabbergasted to find that it was his head lifeguard who was responsible for the intrusion. He called me the next morning and said I should not report for work until they had a board meeting and decided what to do. I told him I would save him the trouble by quitting. At the end of the summer I sold my motorcycle and everything else I owned and took off for Europe and parts unknown instead of going back to college.

Years later Carlos came to live with me again on the farm in Maine, and I put him to work. My sister had been married two or three more times since then. She was a serial bride. Her first husband she met while in her senior year at Wellesley High School. A beautiful girl, she had no trouble attracting boys. The one male she couldn't get to pay attention to her was our father. Her first husband, Oswaldo, was from a wealthy Venezuelan family. He was going to college at Babson when they met and eloped before my sister finished high school. They had one child, a daughter, who was born on my sixteenth birthday. The marriage didn't even survive the pregnancy. Next she married Carlos's father, a handsome playboy whose grandfather had been president of the Dominican Republic.

"I was wondering if I'd ever see you again," Carlos says as we sip our drinks. "Mimi and Grandpa have been going out of their minds worrying."

My parents. Another pang of guilt. "Let them know I'm okay."

"They were relieved to know you're alive."

"With all this Heat, I have to be super careful."

"I know. I keep telling them, if something bad happened to you, we'd hear about it," he says.

He's a smart kid, Mensa-level IQ, with an amazing memory for trivia and useless information and a soulful, complicated nature. It's as if the workings of his brain inhibit his ability to take initiative. He thinks too much and gets lost in a jumble of ideas undermined by sentiment and fantasy. He watches too many movies and too much TV. Too much pornography. Once he's given a task and instructions, he's fine. Left alone, he gets tangled up in convoluted cerebration and daydreams. I'm sure that's why he took to his uncle with my restless jones for decisive, dangerous action.

"Where's the truck?"

He nods toward the street. "Right out front."

"There's a parking lot in back. Put it there and then get yourself a room."

While Carlos is off moving the truck, the bartender gets a phone call.

"You Richard?" he asks me.

It's JD, calling from a pay phone at the base lodge at Sugarloaf. "Yo, what's up, kemosabe?"

"You know, taking care of business."

"Everything all right?"

"So far . . . I could use a hand."

We make plans to meet at Michael's inn for dinner. He asks if it's okay to bring his lady, Father Flaherty, and his date.

"Sure," I say. "Why not? It's a party."

The boxes containing the hash look legitimate enough with their packing slip enclosed envelope stuck to the outside. And there is no odor. Carlos and I carry them into the hotel through the rear doors and up the stairs, pile them in the closet of his room. We drive the truck up to Michael's place, where already people have started to gather. Michael is one of those hosts who, once he gets a buzz on, will go to extravagant lengths to show his guests a good time. He has a large banquet table set up with pitchers of margarita, bottles of wine, a feast of hors d'oeuvres. The main course is venison, duck, lobster, oysters, and shrimp with local vegetables, and corn on the cob. A guitar, drums, and violin trio plays country rock. Michael joins in on piano. The bartender's old lady sings.

Midway into the evening Channing Godfried shows up with his wife, a respected political writer and biographer, and a former classmate at Harvard Law School with his date. Channing is at first freaked to see me. "Rick!" he bellows when he walks in. He practically gasps and looks around to make sure it's not a setup. When he gets over the initial shock, he says, "I was beginning to think you'd been taken hostage by Hezbollah."

"Not quite. Almost."

As my attorney, Godfried understands the gravity of the situation. During a private moment he tells me Wolfshein and an agent with the Internal Revenue Service stopped by his home in Cambridge what must have been six months ago. When Godfried invoked the attorney/client privilege, Wolfshein made reference to the exclusion of knowledge of ongoing criminal activity as not protected and in fact possibly indictable. The IRS agent asked Godfried if he had accepted any large sums of cash money from me as a retainer. Godfried refused to answer their questions and told the agents he would have to speak to his attorney before he would agree to be interviewed.

"But what do I know?" he says to me. "This is the first time I've seen you in . . . what? Over two years."

Godfried is a cigar smoker, loves his Cubans. He has wild, bushy Groucho Marx eyebrows, skin pockmarked from adolescent acne, and an unkempt bird's nest of curly black hair. When we get up from the table to withdraw to Michael's office, Godfried doesn't so much walk as he lurches like a stiff-legged man on the deck of a ship in high seas. He's brilliant, graduated *summa cum laude* in his class at Harvard Law School and was recruited early on by the Kennedy camp when Jack was still a senator. The war in Vietnam eroded his political conscience. He's been holed up here in Maine, in Cambridge, and at times on the Cape writing his memoirs ever since retiring from the Lyndon Johnson camp. He once told me that for days on end the farthest he would go from his writing desk was to walk to his mailbox. He would open it, see it stuffed with bills, and close it back up. Return to the refuge of memory, the solace of the written word.

Godfried's wife, whose writing career has produced bestsellers, asks the inevitable question: "Where's Anaïs?"

Ah, yes . . . My estranged wife, dear Anaïs, known and mostly well liked, even loved by the people who meander in and out of this gathering. The question alone is enough to alter my mood. The simple answer is: Toronto, though that's not true. She is in Spanish Wells, a small island in the Bahamas, at our home there, waiting for me. I believe this to be so but choose to tell no one. "She's traveling," I say and leave it at that.

Anaïs has been on my mind ever since we touched down at the airport in Rangeley. She occupies a place just next to that section reserved for Wolfshein. There is some connection between them I haven't figured out yet. Anaïs used to drive me to the airfield in Rangeley; she would sit on the hood of her Land Rover and watch while I took flying lessons. Memories of our best years together take form and dissolve around random thoughts like reflections of a familiar face seen fleetingly in a hall of mirrors. I see her here or there and then she is gone. I can't quite hold on to her image or the feeling evoked by our remembered good times together. The sense that I let her down, that I failed to live up to the promises we made to each other is so strong it overwhelms any other feelings I have for her. I hurt and drove away the woman who loved me and wanted only to have my children and be my wife. Because I was too selfish, too consumed with my own desperate need to prove myself and impress others.

Was that it? Maybe I am following a path that I absolutely must pursue, overcoming some karmic debt to reach that place where I will meet my higher self. A life of crime, if that's what this is, will deliver me—where? I know the answer to that: to a small space from which I can no longer run, or a hole in the ground. And no one will be there except me. I will be alone with my guilt. But not yet, not now, not so long as I still have fight and flight left in me. And Val, waiting for me in Hawaii . . .

LATER IN THE evening when the band takes a break, Michael puts on the Steely Dan album *The Royal Scam* and plays the title song. Almost on cue, Jimmy D and Father Flaherty walk in with their babes on their arms and the outlaw bravado of John Dillinger and Baby Face Nelson in their swagger. They act like it was only a week or so since they last saw me. Good to see they are flush, wads of money give a man élan. This is what it is all about—the rush, the feeling of living outside the law. Music. Dope. Money. Food and drink. Song. All energized by the awareness that the Heat would love to crash our party. If only they knew where we are. It's like we are back in high school; the bullies and the hard-ons are out there riding around trying to find out where the cool kids are getting down.

JD gets with the program immediately. This is business disguised as gaiety. No questions asked, just get the orders and carry them out. That's what I love about these ex-military types. The good father eats. As a former gunnery sergeant, he has assumed command. JD and Carlos remove the suitcases into the rear of Flaherty's truck. They take the kid, and the three of them are gone for nearly two hours as the rest of us party on.

I should say the party continues mostly without me, for I have withdrawn, first into thoughts that follow the men on the road into the night to my neighbor's farm, owned by JD's old lady. I watch them like a voyeur. They stash the money in a sealed concrete compartment we built beneath the floorboards of a horse stall. They work by the light from a single bulb smeared with bat shit. The boards of the stall floor are heavy with horse piss. The horse, tethered outside the stall, watches them work and flicks his tail from side to side impatiently. Flaherty gives the animal a handful of oats in a black rubber bucket. JD works with an unfiltered cigarette hanging from his lips. His long hair falls from under his Boston Red Sox baseball cap. My nephew is thrilled. This is the real deal. Crime. Better than sex in that it lasts longer. Certainly more real than pornography.

When the loot is safely put away, they return smelling of horseshit. I can relax at last, for a minute. But I don't. Instead I recede further, I take leave to my room at the inn—the bridal suite. Now I have rented five rooms, counting Wart Hog's in Augusta, Carlos's two rooms, and the empty motel room on the outskirts of town. Finally, this room, with a large four-poster canopied bed where I curl up alone on my honeymoon without even my cash-filled suitcases to keep me company.

My marriage is over, I feel it now, feel it in the marrow of my lonely bones. Married to myself, I am married to this life. Curious how I had to come back here, where we were so close, to let her go. I rest my head and know the comfort that at the end of the day when lovers, husband

and wife, mother and child, loosen their embrace and roll over into the land of sleep, they are as alone in their dreams as I am.

* * *

IN THE MORNING Carlos and I load the boxes of hash back into the camper on the rear of the truck and head out to the Sugarloaf Regional Airport to rendezvous with Wart Hog. Giles will meet the Cessna 210 in Trois-Rivières, and the Canadians will have their appetite for hashish replenished. But not so fast, for as we pass by the motel on the outskirts of Kingfield where I first checked in last night, a state cop car peals out in front of us and speeds off in the direction of the airport. There are two more Maine state trooper cars and a black unmarked federal cop sedan parked in the motel lot. The door to the room I occupied for all of fifteen minutes is open and cops and plainclothes agents mill in and out.

"Fuck," I say. "*Holy shit.*"

Carlos has spotted the police activity. "What do you want me to do?" he asks.

"Just keep driving."

I left nothing in the room. Registered under a phony name. Paid cash. Made no calls. A clean break. But the Heat is obviously hip to my presence in the area. This truck has Massachusetts plates and is not traceable to me, so presumably still cool. There is a diner across the road from the airport. The state cop who pulled out in front of us is parked in the airport lot and is out of his car looking around.

How the fuck . . . ? I'm wondering. Wart Hog must be hot—or busted. That would not explain how they got hip to my decoy motel room. The ponytailed taxi driver? Good thing I moved out of that room and secured the money. See, always listen to that still, small voice within. If the taxi driver gave me up, that would mean JD and Father Flaherty are hot as well.

"Pull in to the diner," I tell Carlos.

We park the hash-filled truck and go inside.

Sitting at the counter in the diner, with the front windows behind us looking out at the airport, we can see everything going on there. More cop cars arrive and a couple of pale green US border patrol vehicles. The airport is swarming with cops and agents. Two vans pull into the diner parking lot. Half a dozen long-haired freaks descend on the diner, and I'm thinking, *Fucking DEA. We are busted.* But they are not. They are a rock band that played a gig at the mountain music jam the night before. Carlos and I strike up a conversation with the musicians, trying to blend in, trying to disappear. I go to the hallway outside the restrooms and call JD from a pay phone.

"How's the weather?"

"Everything's cool here," he tells me.

"We're hot," I say. "Stay tuned."

When the band gets up to leave, Carlos and I follow them outside. As we walk through the narrow entranceway to the front door, two beefy state troopers enter. We have to turn sideways to let them pass and are face-to-face, eyeball-to-eyeball with the Heat. I nod and say, "Good morning." The cops ignore me, and we keep walking, say our good-byes to the musicians and get into the truck with the three hundred pounds of hash in the bed. At each passing moment I am relieved not to be arrested.

"Where to?" Carlos asks.

"Just drive. Don't go back to Kingfield. Head up toward Stratton."

If I'm going to get busted, might as well be in a town with the same name, I'm thinking—just for the record: *Fugitive drug smuggler Richard Stratton was arrested this morning in Stratton, Maine.* What? But then, as we approach the entrance to Sugarloaf, two more state cop cars speed up behind us. *Here it comes*, I say to myself and wish I hadn't involved my kid nephew.

The cops pull out and race past.

"Shit, man . . . what the fuck is going on?"

"Jesus!" Carlos says. "They're everywhere."

I'm sure they are looking for us, scouring the area but not seeing us. It's as if we are invisible. Soon, no doubt, they will set up roadblocks, and we will get stopped. They will search the truck, and all will be lost. Got to land somewhere and wait this out.

"Here. Pull in," I say, indicating the entrance to the Sugarloaf Mountain ski resort. Already cars carrying concert-goers for the continuation of the music and arts festival are heading into the road to the base of the mountain. They are lined up at a team of parking attendants directing them to fill up the parking area. Best to try to get lost in the crowd.

Carlos pulls in and parks in the lot with cars and trucks and campers from all over New England and the East Coast. We walk up to the lodge and take a seat in a booth in the bar and restaurant with a bird's-eye view of the parking lot. The place is alive with festival ticket holders, college kids, young couples, aging hippies, backwoods freaks, and tie-dyed flower children. We order breakfast and Bloody Marys.

"I don't know if I can eat," Carlos says when the omelets arrive. "My stomach is in knots."

"Eat," I advise him. "It may be the last decent meal you have in some time."

Fool for coming back to Maine, I chastise myself. Returning to the scene of the crime and tempting fate. I'm wondering if it's time to call Godfried. No, best not involve him yet. Even as I am trying to formulate a plan to get us out of the area without getting busted with a truck full of hash, the cops arrive. State troopers. Border patrol. Plain clothes federal agents. My balls shrivel up inside me. I'm looking around, expecting to see Bernie Wolfshein appear at any minute. Or that other guy, the blue-eyed stranger who ignited all this Heat and seems to act as Wolfshein's forward scout.

Barnswallow! Fucking Fearful Fred. This is all his fault. Wart Hog must have been popped. Trace it back, follow the thread, look for the loose ends, and unravel the net. The Cessna 210 is hot. Probably seized by now. Another airplane gone. The Wart Hog flipped and told them I deplaned in Rangeley. It took them all day, but they eventually located the taxi driver who took me to the motel outside Kingfield. But he apparently protected his fellow ex-Marines, JD and Flaherty, who do not appear to have picked up this Heat. Or maybe the cops are laying back, watching them, hoping they will lead them to me.

Best to distance myself from any of my close associates in case the Man is onto them. I go on rubber legs to a phone booth downstairs from the bar and call the local guy who worked for me on the farm as a cabinetmaker, a skilled craftsman and quiet, mellow, the dude we call Mild Bill. Bill's old lady used to bug Anaïs to urge me to throw some of the more lucrative work Bill's way. They were broke and needed money to pay their mortgage before the bank foreclosed. I used him a couple of times to load planes for the smaller trips into Quebec. He made a quick ten grand and was thankful. And he was there on that memorable morning when the DC-6 crash-landed. Bill was one of the recruits who turned tail and ran before JD ordered them back. His wife answers the phone and is obviously upset when I ask for Bill. Bad idea, I'm thinking as I wait for Bill to come on the line. I decide to change plans. I tell him to go up to the neighbor's farm where JD is living, give him the number of my pay phone, and tell JD to call me from an outside line in half an hour.

"If I don't answer, tell him to call Hef in Boston. You got that?"

"Yeah."

"Everything okay?" I ask.

"Yeah, I guess so."

But I don't like the tone of his voice. He's alarmed, sounds perturbed to be asked to lend a hand. Oh, but it was okay to beg for my help when you needed money. Now I'm putting you out by asking for a favor. What the fuck is that? Straight people. *Fucking citizens!* You never know how they will react when the Heat comes down. Of course, that can be said for pretty much anyone. Some crooks roll over and spread their legs like bitches. The JDs of the world are few and far between. JD took a beating at the hands of the cops when we got cracked in New York and stayed strong, gave them only name, rank, and serial number.

While I'm waiting for the call back, I survey the parking lot from the ski shop windows on the lower level. Cops everywhere. But they do not appear to be in bust mode. No guns drawn. They are looking for something. A vehicle, obviously. But apparently not the truck we are driving with the Massachusetts plates and hash in the rear, for they walk right past it, not ten feet away, and are on radios conferring with other cops or agents elsewhere. I'm searching my mind trying to figure out how they knew to come here to the mountain to look for whatever it is they are looking for—apparently me.

There he is. Lord above, it's Wolfshein. Or am I hallucinating? No, it's him. He drives up with Blue-Eyes in a government sedan. They get out to confer with the state troopers and border patrol agents. I am almost glad to see the Wolfman—a familiar face. At least I know he will try to stop the more excitable cops from shooting me. *Fuck*. If they believe I am here, they will search every square inch of this place until they find me and drag my ass to the slammer. I'm thinking I should grab Carlos and hightail it, just run up over the top of the mountain and head off into the vast Maine woods. Leave the truck. Just go. Run. Get the fuck out before they hit the lodge.

Adrenaline pours into my bloodstream. My heart is racing. My mouth is dry. I'm speeding my brains out. *Relax, calm yourself*. Think this through. This is happening right here in front of me, I am on top of this situation, I see them—cops and agents who look like toy soldiers from my vantage point. *Think. Come up with a plan, Dick. This is where you shine. In the crux of the matter, in the vital moment, at the turning point*.

I'm thinking I could go to the locker room and squeeze into one of the lockers until they've made their search and moved on. Not likely. I'm too big and too claustrophobic. Where else to hide?

And then I have it, my boldest, wildest idea yet. I go back to the pay phone and call information, ask for the number of the DEA office in

Portland, Maine. Once I get through to agency staff, I identify myself as a concerned citizen who would like to report suspicious activity. "Some men just landed in a small plane on a private airstrip in Phillips, Maine. They're loading the plane with what I suspect to be drugs. I live in the area and know for a fact these men use this airstrip to smuggle drugs," I report in a voice imbued with the authority of truth.

"Can I have your name, please sir?" the DEA functionary asks. "I'll put you through to the agent in charge."

"No, sorry," I say. "I don't want any trouble." And I hang up before they can trace the call.

I go into the locker room, into the bathroom area, into a stall, drop my drawers and sit on the shitter—even though the last thing I need to do at this moment is to take a crap. *Scared shitless* are the words that come to mind to describe how I feel. I bury my face in my hands and try to calculate how many minutes have passed since I asked Bill to relay my message to JD, and how long it will take for JD to go out and drive to a pay phone and call me back. I'm watchless, as I hate to be encumbered by anything around my wrists. It has been at least ten minutes, I estimate, maybe fifteen. I'm not happy about leaving Carlos alone upstairs. He must be wondering what happened to his insane uncle. But I'm not excited about the prospect of going back up there and running into Special Agent Bernard Wolfshein of the Drug Enforcement Administration either. Yes, I'm hiding. Admit it. I'd like to flush myself down the toilet like a big turd and swim away into the deep underground septic system of America.

Calm . . . calm. Relax, Dickhead, I tell myself, though my heart is pounding so hard it aches. *This too shall pass.* What's the worst that can happen? I get busted. They can't know about Carlos. He'll walk. So I go to jail. Been there. I don't relish the prospect, but as long as they don't shoot me, I'll be okay. There are worse things that could happen. I could get sick and die of some excruciating, long-drawn-out disease. I could lose my nerve and end up cowering in the corner, pissing and shitting myself, begging for mercy. Roll over and give up my best friend. Become a rat, a coward—a fate worse than death in my mind.

Some men enter the room and relieve themselves, splashing their waters into the porcelain for what seems like too long. I sneak a look under the stall to see if they are shod in cop shoes. No, sneakers and sandals. They leave. Minutes drag by. *Carlos, Carlos . . .* I'm sending him thought waves. Sit tight. Eat, drink, and remain calm in the eye of the storm. Let the excitement swirl around you like the weather, but be as the mountain—unmoved. You think the mountain gives a shit about any of this? No. I keep telling myself with each slow-moving shift of the planet that this moment will not last or alter anything in the cosmic order.

I creep out of the stall and climb into a utility closet to squat among the mops and buckets. More minutes crawl into the endless moment. I visualize Wolfshein getting the call from headquarters in Portland. He's excited as he strides to his car and wheels off in the direction of Phillips, to the so-called Amascontee Lodge and Flying Club, with glimpses of Stratton in his sights. Must be our boy, he's thinking, marshalling the troops. In my vision, the squad of cops races off behind him. Yes, please, dear Lord, carry them away on this wild goose chase. Here I go, praying again.

A stringy-haired, bearded-and-tattooed old freak is startled when I stumble out of the closet. "Hiding from the old lady," I say, but he stares back at me as though he knows who I'm avoiding.

Step by step back to the pay phone. I bear only a slight resemblance to my last available mug shot. My hair is long and bleached blond, my beard full. I'm wearing a baseball cap and shades. The Wolf has never seen me looking anything like this. But that warty asshole Wart Hog would have clued them in to my changed appearance. But maybe not. The one advantage we have in this chase is that the Heat doesn't know what we are doing; they know only what their rats tell them, which is not always accurate or complete. Rats make shit up. They embellish. Or they conceal things for whatever private reasons.

I sit in the phone booth, turn my face to the wall, pick up the receiver and act as though I'm engaged in conversation, but with my hidden hand pressing down on the plastic lever that disconnects the line. Chatting away to no one, I nearly leap out of the booth when there comes a rapping on the folding wood-and-glass panel door. But it is only Carlos.

"What's going on out there?" I ask.

"I don't know," he says. His face is ashen. "A bunch of them took off."

It worked! Did it? Something happened. . . . I feel giddy, though not quite relieved. "You okay?"

"Some guys in suits—"

The phone rings and I release the lever.

"What's up, chief?" JD asks.

"Hold on a second." And then to Carlos, "Yeah?"

"These guys, they just, you know—they're not here for the concert."

"Are they still here?"

"I don't know," he says. "It's fucking weird."

"Go back up to the bar and wait for me. I'll be there in a minute."

I tell JD to come pick me up in his old lady's car.

"Get here as fast as you can. But be careful. The whole area is crawling with cops."

Back in the bar, I take another look out into the parking lot. Many of the cop cars have gone. If there were seven or eight counting the border patrol units, there are now no more than three: a state trooper's car, a sheriff's department car, and one of the fed cars. Wolfshein's car? I don't know, but I suspect not. If they went for the bait, which it appears they have, Wolfshein would not have allowed himself to miss the bust. I almost smile, imagining the Wolfman standing in the middle of the airstrip. He looks around with that quizzical, befuddled scowl, pushes his glasses back up over the bridge of his nose and inspects the strip for signs of recent use. Then he shakes his head and leaves, knowing he's been outflanked.

My omelet is cold, but I eat it anyway. Anything to carry on with whatever is required to stay alive. Eat. Breathe. Drink. Think. Carlos is looking at me as if he expects some explanation. I don't want to jinx the ruse by mentioning what may have happened. All we know for sure is that the cops seem to have gone—most of them, anyway. I say "seem to," for there is always the possibility that they have merely moved and set up a roadblock at the entrance and are checking everyone who leaves the area. Time passes. More Bloody Marys. Two guys in suits who are not here for the music festival come in and take a seat.

JD pulls up in his woman's Saab. I pay the tab, and we leave. It's the oddest feeling each step I take, expecting at any moment to be confronted with agents wielding weapons and screaming, "Down on the ground, motherfucker!" Each step is charged with every ounce of freedom I can bring to bear. Walking to the hangman's noose or to the edge of deliverance.

I never felt so alive.

We walk outside, meet JD in the parking lot. "You run into any roadblocks on the way?" I ask. My hands are trembling, yet I know I appear calm. I look around. No cops anywhere.

"No, but I saw plenty of cops. They're all over the strip and the lodge."

I can't suppress a guffaw, more a sputter of relief.

"What's so funny?"

"I'll tell you later. Right now, we gotta get out of here," I say.

"Carlos, stay here." I give him a few hundred dollars. "Buy a ticket and go to the concert. Relax. Enjoy yourself. Keep an eye on the truck, but don't go near it until you hear from me. I'm going to call you at the phone booth downstairs—the one I was using—at . . . let's say seven tonight. We'll check the roads, make sure it's cool, then you drive the truck out of here."

"Where to?" he asks.

I look at JD. "Take it to Father Flaherty's?"

"Yeah. His new place. It's cool."

THE ROAD BACK to Kingfield is cop free.

"You did *what?*" JD says when I tell him about the bogus tip that drew the Heat. "That is fucking *crazy.*"

"They hit that place this morning," I say when we pass the motel. I'm feeling good but still vulnerable. All this good fortune must be balanced somewhere. You either win or lose. We are both laughing. This is the feeling I live for: the rush. The thrill of getting over on the Man. This means more to me than all the money in those fat bags stashed under the horse stall. More to me than the juiciest piece of ass. And yet it is every bit like a blast of cocaine or a win at the blackjack table or a loveless fuck, for almost as soon as you get off and reach the peak of the high, you are already starting to come down, thinking about the next hit, the next flip of the card off the deck, the next scent of pussy, the next brush with the law. And in the private hell of your habit, you sense the empty feeling that is still there at the bottom of the well of your being.

"Fuck it," JD says. "It's not like they don't know about that place. So they fell for it. They must be apeshit. Standing around with their dicks in their hands."

We laugh again, but in my mind I am already moving on. I don't want to alter good fortune with derision. JD confirms state troopers contacted the taxi driver. They checked the trip log to learn he had taken a passenger from the airfield in Rangeley to the motel, but he told them nothing more. "He's cool," JD says. "Ex-jarhead."

I figure the answering service in New York is burned, since Wart Hog used that number. Wolfshein will check with the service and subpoena the records of every message I received. That will take them back to Carlos's hotel in Farmington and provide them with his name. So it's safe to assume my nephew will pick up Heat. My instructions to the nine or ten people who used the service were to never leave a home number, only pay phones and times. But people get sloppy. I'll have to notify everyone that the service is no longer good and get some new means of receiving messages.

The rest of the afternoon JD is busy getting the cash that was hidden in his old lady's barn and putting it on the road to Boston, New York, and points beyond. Nasif is in Nassau clamoring for money.

Anaïs is in Spanish Wells with money from Rosie. I hang out at Father Flaherty's waiting for Carlos, while JD drives the cash-laden suitcases to a motel in Revere, near Logan Airport. We're in gear now. Sammy sends a driver up from New York to Boston to retrieve two million. I call the charter service in New York and arrange for a jet to meet me at Logan and take me to Nassau with the rest of the money.

But first I need to get Carlos and the truck full of hash out of Sugarloaf, out of the area. Send the kid on a long vacation until things cool down. Let everyone who needs to know that Wart Hog is no good.

Another fucking rat has jumped ship.

13

ISLAND UNIVERSE

ANAÏS LEFT A message on the New York answering service. *Damn.* I had no way to reach her to let her know the service was burned. When I tried to call her at the house in Spanish Wells, the phone rang and rang. I picture her out walking on the empty, white-and-pink sand beach, the phone ringing through the empty white-and-pink wood-frame house. Her message was characteristically circumspect. Sometimes I think women make better criminals than men. Their egos don't get in the way, though their emotions do. Still, so few words, so much information: *Nassau Beach Hotel, room number 23.*

She is not in her hotel room when I try to reach her. I pump more quarters into a pay phone and call Avril in Toronto. She calls me back pay phone to pay phone.

"Have you heard from Anaïs?"

"Yes. She's—"

"I know. Tell her to move. The service in New York is no good. Tell her not to use it anymore. She should call Biff and leave a message with him once she relocates. I'm on my way there now."

Carlos and I are in a contraband-free truck, on the Maine State Turnpike heading south, when we hear an alarming grinding of metal on metal coming from one of the front wheels. Carlos pulls over into the breakdown lane. The right front wheel is smoking and looks like it is about to fall off. The axel appears to be broken. We're stranded. All I can think is: *Thank God there is no hash in the truck.* If this had happened yesterday while we were driving around loaded, we would have been busted for sure. But I have got to get to Boston to catch my ride to the Bahamas. Both Nasif and Anaïs have been waiting for me for nearly a week. Every impulse I can decipher tells me to flee the country before the hammer comes down. Wolfshein has probably already contacted DEA agents in the Bahamas, or he dispatched someone to Nassau to watch Anaïs. She will unwittingly trip them to Nasif. Nothing to do but march into the blast furnace.

It is a good mile and a half, maybe two miles to the nearest exit—the tollbooths at York, Maine. I grab my bag and jog to the end of the highway. There, soaked with sweat, I call a tow truck service for Carlos and the stranded pickup truck, and a taxi to take me to the motel in Revere where I rendezvous with JD and pick up 1.5 million in Canadian to take to Nasif. One third for the Arabs, plus a third of whatever Anaïs brought; a third for Sammy and the New York crew; and a third for me. I'll bank mine in the islands. There is still another seven or eight million in hash to distribute and cash out.

The aircraft is a Cessna Citation 500. One of the pilots knows me and does not question it when I ask him to change his flight plan and take me to Eleuthera. A diffident Customs and Immigration guy at the small island airport glances at my phony passport and almost misses the gratuity—a sepia Canadian $500 bill in diminishing circulation folded into the visa section. He smiles broadly when the bill flutters out onto his desk. A taxi delivers me to the narrow channel between Eleuthera and Spanish Wells, where I ferry across in a small motorboat.

Spanish Wells is an anomaly in the Bahamian archipelago. The local inhabitants are mostly white descendants of British fisherman who emigrated here from Bermuda in the 1700s. A few extended families living on this tiny island still produce the bulk of lobster, grouper, and conch exported from the islands. As well as the legitimate fishing industry, some of the islanders have flourished in the square grouper trade—off-loading mother ships from Colombia and ferrying the hefty, oblong, pressed bales of pot to Florida. The square grouper gets its name from bales jettisoned from smuggling ships pursued by the Coast Guard. The plastic-wrapped bales wash up on Florida beaches and lie there like fat, square, headless-and-sightless creatures until discovered by some fortunate beachcomber.

I catch a ride to the house from one of the islanders in a golf cart. Anaïs's parrots squawk raucously when I enter the small, two-bedroom bungalow. The home is elegant in its simplicity, clean, open, warm, and bright. The furnishings are comfortable, utilitarian, and tasteful. Standing in the house, looking around at the uncluttered surfaces, the burnished wood floors, and vivid local art on pastel walls, I am taken by the order and sense of Old World decorum Anaïs brought to our life together—and reminded of all I lost when I ruined our marriage. I lock the money in a bedroom closet and set out on foot to find someone who'll take me by boat to Nassau.

It's a little over an hour by speedboat, fifty nautical miles from Spanish Wells to the Bahamian capital of Nassau on New Providence Island. I go by taxi to West Bay Street on the north shore of the island, get out half a mile down the road from Anaïs's hotel, and walk along the beach to the rear entrance. How to find her and my tall, plump Lebanese friend without stumbling into whatever Heat they might have emanating from the mainland? I wonder. Having donned a Panama hat and wrap-around shades and dressed in a white guayabera shirt, white linen slacks, sandals, I look like some character out of a Graham Greene novel.

The beach is littered with oiled bodies searing their flesh in the harsh sunlight. There is no answer when I ring Anaïs's room using the house phone. Room 23 is on the second floor. I walk up the service stairs and along the hall past the room. No curious characters lurking in the hallway. The front lobby also appears agent free. I collar a bellman, palm him a twenty, and ask him to check on the status of the guest in room 23 while I wait in the bar. He returns minutes later to tell me the room looks to have been vacated, the guest apparently checked out. So she got my message.

No answer at Biff's in New York. He's probably out in Amagansett soaking up the rays, working on his melanoma. But there is no answer there either. Finally, I reach Avril, who tells me to call her back in half an hour and gives me a coded number. Even in paradise, I spend half my day going from pay phone to pay phone. "I spoke to her. She moved," Avril tells me what I already know.

"Did she say where?"

"No. But I gave her your message."

My only alternative is to check into a hotel and keep trying Biff. This fucking jerk-off, the one thing I can depend on him to do is to disappear when I most need him. I take a suite in an historic downtown hotel and go shopping to relieve my anxiety. Diamond stud earrings for Anaïs and Val. A platinum Rolex for Sammy and a gold Presidential for Nasif. Drop a quick sixty grand and then wander around this former pirate haven pretending to be a tourist.

* * *

AT THE BLACKJACK table in the casino on Paradise Island, the cards are good to me. Stacks of red and blue chips are piled on the table. I'm up somewhere around forty grand when Nasif settles in beside me. "Mr. Richard," he says and hugs me.

I look around. He nods, and I spot Anaïs across the room at the baccarat table. It was always her game, chemin de fer, the iron road. She is lovely in a black dress, her thick, dark hair halfway down her exposed back. This woman is too good for me, I'm thinking, gathering my chips. Too sophisticated, too civilized. No wonder it didn't work.

"Richard," Anaïs greets me, using the French pronunciation, and gives me her cool, moist hand. "*Mon ami,*" she says with peck on the cheek, a squeeze of the hand. And then the now familiar line: "I was beginning to think we would never see each other again."

"That would be a pity," I say. "You look beautiful."

I even become more refined around her, or so I would like to believe.

She smiles. "I never would have recognized you."

"Good. Let's go."

She and Nasif have checked into bungalows at Club Med. The three of us walk out to sit by the pool. Nasif orders a bottle of champagne.

"Everything all right?" he asks.

"We need to go to Spanish Wells," I tell them. "I left the money there."

"No business tonight, please," Anaïs says. "Tomorrow." To me she asks, "How have you been? How is your mother? And Emery? Please give them my love."

My parents adore her, particularly my father. "I haven't see them," I say.

"Of course . . ."

There is a void between us. I don't know her anymore. It has been nearly three years since we spent any time together and she has moved on. We would meet briefly in Toronto during the first year after she left, then not at all once I went on the lam. Jonathan's death stands stiffly in the gap like a tombstone.

"What happened?" Nasif asks when Jonathan's name is mentioned.

"Plane crash," I say. "I don't have any details."

"It's the curse of this life," Anaïs says quietly. "Why I never wanted it for you. For any of us."

"People die all sorts of ways," I remind her.

Nasif cannot contain himself. "How much longer before this business will be finished?" he asks.

"Tomorrow, Nasif," Anaïs says and puts a hand on his shoulder, gently pushes him, urging him to go.

He stands, a bit embarrassed. "What time will I see you?"

"I'll call you in the morning," I tell him. "Tell your father everything is fine. We'll be done soon."

"How much should I tell my father to expect?"

Anaïs laughs, a deep throaty chuckle. "Tell him—a lot."

"He asks when we can make another shipment?"

"Go to bed," she tells him in French. "Leave us. I haven't seen this man for a long time."

"They don't quit," I say after Nasif leaves.

"Like some people I know," she says.

"I can't. Not until this is over."

"And then?"

I shrug. "Some day it will be legal."

"Not in our lifetime," she assures me.

In the years we have been apart she has become even more bewitching. It's her eyes and the elegant curve of her neck. She makes me think of the French actress, Anouk Aimée. The way she crosses her legs, wraps one leg around the other, and leans into the conversation, with her large dark eyes looking up at me. We would sit like this for hours playing chess and talking of everything but the here and now: religion, philosophy, literature, movies, music. I have never known another woman with whom conversation flowed so easily for so long and was so enjoyable. It was during those intimate talks that I fell in love with her.

"For us, it's over," she tells me, and I'm not sure if she is speaking of us as a couple or the business. "Avril and I don't want to do this anymore," she goes on. "There is so much Heat in Toronto, it's too dangerous."

"I know. I spoke to Rosie about it."

"Rosie doesn't care. Prison means nothing to him. But Avril has a child, who now has no father. He must not lose his mother too."

"Enough said. I understand." I hesitate but can't stop myself. "No one forced you to—"

I don't finish the sentence. She scowls at me, nods, takes out a Gauloises and I light it for her.

"I am so glad he wasn't working for you when he . . . crashed," she continues on the subject of Jonathan's death. I can see it has spooked her, spooked Biff too. I don't tell her about Jake and his Mexican wife. Or the rocket that hit Saad's building in West Beirut. Death dwells in the shadows just beyond the soft-colored lights of the patio. "The insurance company refuses to pay because he was involved in illegal activity when he died," she tells me and exhales a cloud of cigarette smoke.

"You and Avril should hold on to whatever you need."

She nods, smokes, sips her champagne. "We'll be all right."

"I should go."

"Stay," she says. "Finish your drink. Tell me about your life. It may be a long time before we see each other again."

I MET ANAÏS in what seems like another person's life on another enchanted island—Mallorca, in the Mediterranean. I was running couriers out of Spain with false-bottom suitcases filled with hash from Morocco and Lebanon, trying to put together a transatlantic sailboat smuggle. During the crew's stopover in Palma, as they waited to journey on to Larnaca, Cyprus and off the coast of Tripoli to on load four hundred kilos—at the time the largest load we had attempted—the weather turned against us. One delay ushered in another. I was stranded on Mallorca for weeks, waiting for the weather on the North Atlantic to improve. For a time, with the crew back in the States over the Christmas holidays, I stayed aboard the sailboat, *La Petite Mort*, docked at the marina in Palma. Then, when the weather grew too cold, I relocated to a small flat in the basement of a monastery in the mountain village of Valldemossa. The place had history; Chopin and George Sand had both once lived in the monastery. It should have been a peaceful time for me, but we were losing money daily as the smuggle ground to a halt.

I met Anaïs and her younger sister, Avril, at a party at the villa of a British documentary filmmaker and smuggler who lived in the village of Deyà on the north coast of Mallorca. Trevor, the filmmaker, had invested in the hash trip. The sisters spoke fluent Spanish with French accents. Lapsed Catholic girls. Russian and Belgian, brought up in France, their mother is from the Walloon part of Belgium. Anaïs and Avril hardly resemble each other and may actually be half-sisters; they never spoke of their Russian father except in the most general terms. Avril is tall and blond; Anaïs has black hair with a widow's peak. She's average height and has a stunning figure, delicate features, and a way of fixing you with her big, dark eyes and asking serious, pointed questions. "What do you do?" she asked when we met. "Why are you here, in Mallorca? You don't seem like a tourist."

I lied, made up a story about being a journalist, said I was writing a magazine article on Trevor and his latest project—a film about a notorious British punk band. Actually, I was in correspondence with the editor at *High Times*, who was interested in the punk band, and even more interested in the hash Trevor and I were moving piecemeal to London and New York. Anaïs and Avril owned a small pension in Deyà. When it began to look like the sailboat trip would be postponed indefinitely, Trevor drove over to Valledemossa one evening with Avril and Anaïs. At dinner, when the ladies excused themselves, Trevor and I discussed rethinking the trip. This was before I began working with Mohammed. At the time my Lebanese connection was a Christian middleman out of the village of Zahlé, a guy named Fariz who spoke only Arabic and French, and who was putting a lot of pressure on me to finish the business. Trevor proposed, referring to the sisters, "These two are looking to make some money. Why don't you suggest they help you get the rest of the hash out of Lebanon?"

"I should suggest it? Why me? I don't really know them."

"Yes, you see, that's why—I know them too well. Rather, they know me too well. If anything should happen . . . Besides, they suspect that's what you do, while they don't know of my involvement. And I prefer keep it that way. *I must.* They are my neighbors, after all. They're friendly with my wife. You know, got to keep it away from home, that sort of thing."

"What makes you think they're game?"

"Believe me, they dropped hints. You know, 'What does Richard *really* do?' And with you passing out bits of hash. Pockets stuffed with money. I can tell you, they are intrigued."

It took me another two weeks of getting to know them better—and in particular, Anaïs—before I got up the nerve to broach the subject. I bought a motor scooter and began riding over to Deyà in the evening to dine and hang out, mostly with Anaïs. She had a boyfriend, a Frenchman, who worked as a translator in Paris and visited infrequently. Anaïs is an avid chess player. We would sit out on the patio at the pension, or in the sitting room by the fireplace on chilly nights, drink cognac, and play well into the early hours when I would ride the ten miles back to my room in the monastery. There, in my lonely bed, I would hug myself to sleep and know that I was falling in love with her.

One day soon after the New Year we drove together in Trevor's Citröen to Palma on the other side of the island to do the monthly shopping for the pension at the central marketplace. She was a good driver, told me she had once had a job driving an ambulance in Paris. I took her to the marina to show her *La Petite Mort*—which translates as "the little death" in English, a euphemism for orgasm. As I was helping her aboard, when she stepped from the dock to the boat, I took her hand. We had touched before, casually, or I shook her hand—but this touch was different. It was electric, a current of energy passed between us, and we both felt it, both knew it as a magnetic force that would draw us closer and closer until we came together, though it would still be months before we kissed. Sitting aboard the boat, sharing a bottle of wine, I finally told her what I really did for a living.

I bought a used diesel Mercedes sedan, had it outfitted it with stash compartments that held up to 150 kilos. The sisters registered the car in France. Posing as photojournalists, they drove from Paris to Beirut and back twice and removed all of the hash Fariz had on hand. Trevor had the hash concealed in his film gear and the band's sound equipment and shipped it to New York. Sammy and Rosie sold it all without losing a gram. We did well that winter and spring as civil war in Lebanon broke out. Early in the summer of 1975, we finally managed to load up *La Petite Mort* and land another 400 kilos in Montauk, Long Island.

Anaïs and Avril continued to work transporting money from the States to Europe and Beirut. I would meet them in Paris or London, then one or both of them would go on to Beirut and deliver money to the Lebanese until the war made it too dangerous. They set up bank accounts in Lichtenstein, Austria, and Hong Kong, became adept at managing international wire transfers and money laundering. I began to live for those meetings with Anaïs. When we were apart I wrote her poems and love letters. And still there had been no physical expressions of love between us. She and her boyfriend were in some protracted process of ending their affair. There was an unspoken feeling between us that we would find each other when the time was right.

Then, one evening in a London hotel after we had said good night, she came to my door. "What do you need?" I asked.

"You," she said and came in. "Hold me." We didn't leave the room and hardly left the bed for three days. She and Avril sold the place in Deyà and moved to New York. Promises were made—and broken. By me, never by her.

Now, looking at her, I wonder why what I felt for her—and still feel for her—strong as it was and continues to be, was not enough.

She picks up on my thoughts. "Are you happy?" she asks.

"I don't even think about that. I'm on the run."

"I mean, your girlfriend. Is she good to you?"

"She is. Although I don't see that much of her. It's basically—it's about the business."

"That's you," she says. "All about the business."

"I spent almost a year in Lebanon."

"You were lucky to get out of there alive."

"And you?" I ask, not willing to mention her new man.

"All I want now is some peace. I want to wake up in the morning without the fear of the police breaking down the door. And pick up the phone and not be terrified to hear someone has been arrested. Or worse yet—killed."

"You deserve that."

"What is it?" Anaïs asks. "Why can't you give it up, Richard? What are you trying to prove?"

"Who knows? It doesn't matter."

"What does matter?"

"Maybe if we'd had kids . . . a family, I would have settled down."

She shakes her head. "No, that would not have stopped you. That would only have brought more chaos into our lives. And you still would have been . . . gone somewhere . . . doing whatever you seem to think you must do."

"How can you be so sure?"

"Because, I've always known—yet I would not admit—there is something in you. I don't know what it is, but something is forcing you to keep pursuing this mad dream of yours. It's as if you're not happy unless you're risking your life. What is it? What do you want?"

I stand and sigh. The conversation is making me uneasy. "Who knows? Who knows what they want in this life? You think you do, and that's great. I wish you luck. But that life, what you're talking about, the thought of it bores the shit out of me."

She laughs, stands with me, and I walk her to the door of her bungalow.

"Shall I come in?" My cock stirs at the thought of making love to her. "We may never see each other again."

"No," she says. "That won't do." She puts a hand on my chest, over my heart, as though to keep from hurting me, and says, "I loved you. Very much. Some part of me will always love you. But . . . our timing was off. It wasn't meant to be," she tells me. "I knew it when we first met, that you would take me away from everything I knew. And then you would leave me. But you were like the Pied Piper; everyone just wanted to follow you." Her fingers clutch ever so slightly at my chest, pushing me away and pulling me closer at the same time. I want desperately to kiss her.

"I don't blame you . . . for anything," she says. "Even being unfaithful. If that's what you needed." She steps back and reaches in her handbag. "But I don't want to be alone the rest of my life. I want a divorce."

We lived together for years before we finally got married. We had a townhouse in Knightsbridge, in London, then leased a farm in Marlow in the Thames River Valley. While living in Marlowe, I came home one day with a furry white puppy in a cardboard box. Anaïs was reading *The Brothers Karamazov* and began calling the puppy her little Karamazov. We moved to Boston, then to Cape Cod. After I was arrested in New York in '78, Anaïs was deported as an undesirable alien. She returned, flew into Montreal, and we married in the basement home cathedral of a justice of the peace in rural Quebec. Anaïs was nervous and high and fumbled her vows. "In richness and in death," she said instead of, "In sickness and in health." It seemed appropriate then, more so now. Our witnesses, Avril and Jonathan, cracked up. The wife of the justice of the peace who married us had a whole display cabinet filled with these shrunken head–like figurines made from dehydrated apple cores. I smuggled Anaïs back into the States, and we bought the home in Provincetown.

"We'll do it Arab style," I say. "I divorce you. I divorce you. I divorce you."

"No, I want a real divorce. I'm getting married." She takes a packet of papers from her handbag. "You can take care of the whole thing in one day in Santo Domingo. I have all the information." She hands me the papers. "Will you do it?"

I walk back to my hotel. Hurt much more than I understand. I brought this upon myself, and yet it feels unjust. Maybe I need to feel sorry for myself. Yes, that's it. I wanted to fuck her for old time's same, and she rejected me. Cock and balls walk along the iron road. Cunt sleeps wrapped around herself. The dawn of a new day seeps along the horizon. And it doesn't matter. Nothing means shit. Life is just one pointless, unsatisfied lust after the next. I could walk until I fell off the edge of the world. Keep stepping. Find out when I arrive that there is nothing and no one there, just more empty space. And chaff blowing in the galactic winds.

* * *

NASIF TURNS A tannish shade of green on the boat ride back to Spanish Wells. Later, walking on the beach, he complains of chapped thighs where they rub together when he walks. "That's because you're too heavy," I tell him. "You need to lose weight, you fat fuck. You'll end up like your father."

"I got accepted at the university in Miami," he says gleefully.

"Congratulations. You'll enjoy it there. Lots of blond girls."

When we return to the house, Anaïs has discovered both pairs of diamond stud earrings. "Which are hers?" she asks and cocks her arm as though she will pitch the offending pair out the window. Then she laughs.

We charter a plane back to Nassau. Nasif leaves on a BOAC flight to London with a connection to Zurich, $2.7 million in cash in his luggage. I'm relieved to have another big chunk of money out of my hands. Anaïs books a flight back to Toronto. We say good-bye at the airport.

"God bless you and keep you safe," she says and walks off.

I hold the charter plane and carry on to Grand Cayman with four hundred grand in Canadian money to deposit in the bank. Val arrives the next day with another quarter million US. With the bulk of the cash safely put away in an offshore account, we charter a flight to Jamaica and check into the Half Moon in Montego Bay. I am determined to fuck every vestige of Anaïs out of my heart and soul and into Val's writhing, heaving, sweating, welcoming body.

"Damn, daddy. What got into you?" she says.

"I thought you wanted to have a kid."

"Yeah, I do. But I want to be able to walk too."

The reggae SunSplash festival is in tribute to Bob Marley, recently dead from cancer. Rita, Bob's widow, and half a dozen little Marleys are staying in the next bungalow at the Half Moon. Val befriends one of the departed star's sons, who looks like a mini version of his dad. We take the boys out on a fishing excursion one afternoon. Mini-Bob has a crush on Val; she has a way with kids, still a kid herself.

On the evening of the concert, I hire a taxi to take us to Jarrett Park. Our dreadlocked, stoned driver is speeding, driving like a maniac, passing trucks on curves. I tend to be fatalistic in these situations; it's all about the experience. If I'm meant to die in this taxi with this crazy, red-eyed Rasta, so be it. Maybe my ego won't let me admit fear. Val, sitting behind the driver, has no such restraints. She tells him to chill, slow down, we're in no hurry. He grins and says, "No problem, mon." But doesn't change his driving. Val grabs him by the dreads. She yanks his head back and says, "Slow down, motherfucker, or I'll break your neck."

It's a long night. Takes these folks hours to get the show under way. Endless sound checks. Soon come, mon . . . soon come . . . "These fuckin' Rastas," Val says. "They drive so fast and do everything else so slow."

Stevie Wonder comes on at dawn. When we return to our room at the Half Moon, along with fresh flowers and chocolates on the pillow, I notice the message light on the phone is blinking.

"Dr. B. called. Please call him back."

"What's up, doc?" I ask when he picks up.

"Bad news, bro," Biff says when I reach him.

"Tell me."

"Ah, well," he hesitates. "Now?"

"Yeah. Now."

"Okay. They arrested Anaïs when she landed in Toronto. Avril, Rosie, Squid, something like sixty people all across Canada have been busted."

My stomach drops and then cramps. I feel sick. A jolt of pain through the center of my being says: *You caused this.*

I hang up and call the lawyer who handled Rosie's past cases. He assures me he'll have Anaïs and Avril out on bail in a day or two. It was a massive sweep, coordinated by the Metro Toronto drug squad working with the RCMP, he says. They got some money but very little product. It's essentially a conspiracy case. My soon-to-be ex-wife and sister-in-law have been charged with violations of the recently enacted Canadian currency control statutes—basically laundering money in furtherance of a drug distribution conspiracy. They are facing five years in prison.

"Tell me the cops' names," I say. "Metro Toronto drug squad cops."

He tells me, "I only have one name. Carter, Sergeant Terrence Carter. He's had a bee in his bonnet about Rosie for some time now."

"Carter arrested Anaïs?"

"Well, Immigration Canada detained her when she landed at Pearson Airport. Then Carter came along and lodged the formal charges."

"Where are they?"

"The Don Jail in Toronto."

"You got a phone number for Carter?"

"What're you going to do, Richard? Don't threaten him."

"No . . . of course not."

Later, from a public phone in Montego Bay, I place a person-to-person call to Sergeant Terrence Carter. He comes on the line. "Sergeant Carter, Metro Drug Squad."

"Carter . . . you feeling pretty good about yourself?"

"Who is this?"

"Richard Stratton."

Silence and then, "Oh." His voice registers surprise. Then contempt. "What do you want?"

"I want to know what kind of punk asshole cop you are. You can't get the man, so you arrest his wife."

A longer moment of silence and then, "Don't worry, Stratton. We'll get you too."

I'm sodden with guilt, anger oozing from my pores like sour sweat. Angry at myself and directing it at Carter. "It'll take more than a couple of lightweight Toronto cops to get me," I say and wish it made me feel better. Instead, I feel foolish. Childish. A naughty boy who thinks he's a big shot. Yet I can't restrain myself.

"Suck my dick, Carter."

Next I try Wolfshein. I know how stupid this is, and yet I can't help it, I feel I must vent to release my guilt.

"Special Agent Wolfshein," he answers.

"I thought you had more class that that."

"Who is this?"

"Stratton . . . You go after the wives?"

"That's not me, Rich. That was the RCMP."

"You telling me you had nothing to do with it?"

"I'm telling you it was not my decision," he says.

"It's a punk move."

"It's the law. When are you gonna get it through your thick skull? People break the law, they go to jail. You want to put a stop to this? Come in, give yourself up. It's not too late."

"No, that's not gonna happen. You're gonna have to catch me," I say and hang up.

Val leaves the next day. "Fucking Rosie," she says. "That guy just can't stay out of his own way."

I kiss her good-bye at the airport, tell her, "Be careful."

She nods, smiles. "You too, Dad."

We're in crisis mode. With sixty people in custody in Canada, a US sweep can't be far behind. Other than Anaïs and Avril . . . and Rosie . . . and Squid, I'm trying to think of any other link to Sammy, JD, Biff, Benny, the whole American organization. There is whatever intelligence Wolfshein has gleaned, but where can this go? If the sisters hold up . . . I have no doubts about Rosie; he can handle jail. Squid? He could lead them to Biff, but I doubt the Squid will roll. He's tight with Rosie, and as a first-offender he'll be out on bail and won't be looking at a lot of time. The security shield between the borders seems secure. Val will make the rounds, she'll pick up cash and let anyone who needs to know about the situation up north.

I take a commercial flight to Santo Domingo. At night, painfully alone in my hotel room and recently divorced, I dwell on the boy, Avril's kid. First his father eats it in a plane full of pot, now his mother is in the can.

Pied Piper all right, leading everyone off to jail . . . or to the grave.

14

END GAME

AT LAST THE Lebanese trip is winding down. I'm in Maui, alone at the house in Ulupalakua. All fifteen thousand pounds of hashish and fifty gallons of honey oil have been distributed, most of it going to Rosie in Toronto before he got cracked. Jimmy Chagra's commercial Colombian weed is all gone as well. Capuana sent someone to inspect the contaminated tonnage, then JD borrowed a backhoe and buried it. I have visions of a forest of mutant marijuana plants oozing diesel fuel cropping up in the wilds of Maine.

The Kansas City Kid's DC-6 load of primo gold Colombian is long gone and paid for; I personally made sure Val delivered the money to Cartagena. The last thing I need is a bunch of disgruntled Colombians on my trail. Hard enough eluding DEA and the US Marshals. The Colombians don't play. You stiff them, you die. Val tells me they want to hook us up with another load. I'm tempted but still have an inventory of some several hundred pounds of Jamaican sinsemilla in Boston and New York to move, and a couple of other trips in the early-planning stages. Mostly, however, over the past weeks I have been obsessing about how it is all to end, trying to devise a feasible exit strategy to avert the obvious one.

Now it's all about cleaning up the aftermath. Dealing with lawyers, bail bondsmen, families of the incarcerated. Finding and collecting the rest of the hash money. Balancing the books and distributing the profits. The Arabs in Lebanon are beseeching me for more money. So are the Jews in New York. And the Mexicans in Texas. The Rastas in Jamaica. Val has been managing the final stages of the trip. She is the public face, traveling to New York and Boston, Chicago, LA, San Francisco, Kansas City, Detroit, Austin, Lake Tahoe, Anchorage—where she and her partner, Judy, have their own thing going, selling slabs and pounds to dope-starved, dollar-heavy Alaskans for twice cost. She picks up money and delivers it to me, to Sammy in New York, Nasif in Nassau or Cyprus or Paris. Makes deposits at the bank in Grand Cayman.

Val has been gone on this latest trip for over three weeks, almost a month. I've lost track of time living alone here in Maui, at the house she bought on the slopes of the volcano. My days are ordered and nearly identical. I meditate, work out, take long hikes, eat a strict raw food vegetarian diet. No booze. I've lost all the weight I packed on during my plush, overfed captivity in Lebanon. I feel good, strong. Lonely but good. It's curious how I seem to get stronger physically, mentally, and emotionally when I am alone, dwelling in a self-contained and private headspace. Like I have come to port after a long and tumultuous voyage. It hasn't worked to assuage the guilt I feel over the destruction I left in my wake, but there is something to say for survival.

Given the time difference between here and the mainland, I make my first round of calls early in the morning. Biff has a new office phone in New York. Anaïs and Avril are out on bond; we don't speak. The Squid as well is out awaiting trial. Rosie the repeat offender has become Canada's most famous cannabis prisoner. He has his own radio show from inside the joint. He's on the cover of *Maclean's* magazine, the Canadian *Time*. There was a big spread on him in *High Times*. He's the voice of the marijuana subculture. The lawyers tell me Anaïs and Avril are going to cop pleas. No one, I'm told—except the recalcitrant Rosebud, who will no doubt go to trial—is expected to get more than a couple of years. They don't take pot offenses that seriously north of the border. It's almost a peccadillo. Except if you are the unregenerate hippie godfather.

In the evening I usually connect with Val. She's due back today. She has begun to worry me even more than usual. I know she's been doing blow; I can hear it in her hoarse, halting voice. She's partying. Sometimes she misses our calls. "Oh, sorry, I was running around," she admits. Yeah, running around. You couldn't sit your sweet ass down in a phone booth? At times I think she may be fucking some other guy. Biff saw her in New York and said she and her girlfriends were having a wild time. A lot of my questions go unanswered. "I'll tell you when I see you," she says. And then the trip gets extended. A week, ten days has become close to a month. I could get pissed off and frustrated, I could order her to return and explain herself. But to what end? She's an adult. She has a mind of her own. I can't force my will on her even if the money is my responsibility. She's my eyes and ears and already the connection is tenuous. The longer I spend alone, the further I withdraw from that reality, the more brittle our bond.

Meanwhile agents of the law, led by the indefatigable Bernard Wolfshein, plot my demise. I get messages from people who have been visited by the Heat. They have questioned my parents and sister. Everyone in the Maine case pled out. Freddy Barnswallow got five years. They've got him tucked away somewhere in the Witness Protection Program waiting to testify against me and the Colombians who supplied him with cocaine. For all my bravado and false posturing, I know my days are numbered unless I can make a complete break and reinvent myself. Cut all my ties to my former life and become a new person—a total metamorphosis. It's a challenge. One would need a whole new belief system. And that would entail denouncing the former me. Spin the globe, point my finger down on some distant land. Argentina. They take Nazis down there. Surely they would not mind a fugitive dope smuggler. Resurface when it's legal, when I am 150 years old.

Each day is like a precious stone in the mosaic I am constructing from my fragmented life. Out walking in the hills, stupefied by the beauty of this island in the Pacific, it's as though I can see the jail cell waiting for me: an empty, gray, steel-enclosed chamber suspended in the cloudbank beyond the horizon. I blame only me; this is the result of the choices I made. There is drug and alcohol-fueled madness, decadence and decay; there is death; or there is the monastic life of the prisoner. Yet I discern some other future if only I can find the pieces of the puzzle and put together a renewed vision.

As I walk, I think of a time sitting in the basement of a Greenwich Village apartment with Tom Forçade, founder of *High Times* magazine. I had brought Tom a sample of some class A-plus herb from high in the Sierra Madre del Sur out of Guerrero, Mexico. We agreed Mexican weed got a bad rap. True most of the commercial pot available in the country then (early '70s) was low-grade, heavily seeded pressed bricks. Colombian pot was just beginning to hit the market. But there is good, bad, indifferent, and superb herb available from wherever pot is grown. I've seen pot from Thailand that was as bad as the worst Mexican dirt weed. And the tight, lime-green-and-gold, lightly seeded colas I gave Tom took you as high as the mountain peaks whence it came.

"Good sticks," Tom said after we shared a joint. He was lean and intense, a good listener. The editorial staff wanted to hear all about the adventures I had getting the load out of Mexico and bringing it to New York.

The second issue of the magazine had just been published, the one with the cover showing a seaplane being loaded with bales of pot. The magazine was in their face, all a great lark, or so we thought. Anything seemed possible. *High Times* was a huge success from its first issue. Modeled on *Playboy*, with pictures of cannabis in the centerfold, it was brilliantly conceived and executed. The future looked bright. We believed that the government would soon see the folly of their War on Plants and free thinking and declare a truce. A few years later, Tom blew his brains out.

Anaïs had been with me when we imported the load I showed Tom, which eventually graced the spread of the *High Times* centerfold and announced a new legitimacy for premium-grade Mexican bud. The magazine became our advertising vehicle. We were living in a villa in Cuernavaca, where Cortes had gone to rest and recuperate with his Indian mistress after subduing Montezuma's Aztecs. Anaïs wanted to go with me to Xixila, the tiny pre-Colombian village high in the mountains of Guerreo where I bought my weed. We brought Karamazov along to keep us company. The plan was to drive up the mountain in our four-wheel-drive truck. In the village at the foot of the mountain, we were informed that a company of *federales* was on patrol along the single dirt-and-rock-strewn track leading up to Xixila. The presence of gringos in a big, American truck with a big white dog could mean only one thing: a load of *mota* was being readied for shipment; bribes, the *mordida*, the bite, were in the offing. It was decided we would climb the mountain on burros to avoid the soldiers.

It was incredibly hot. The sharp stones along the trail cut and burned and turned the pads on the dog's paws raw and bloody. He limped along valiantly until he could hardly walk. I had to dismount and strap him to the back of my donkey to continue the trek. As I walked along beside him, the dog looked at me with a pathetic expression as if to say: *Why are you humiliating me like this, tying me to the back of this inferior beast?* And he would snap at the animal's haunches. It was a grueling, ten-hour hike, but we made it undetected.

Adelberto, the village *jefe*, put us up in his adobe home. There was no electricity in the village, no running water. We ate stone-ground blue corn tortillas, black beans, chili peppers, and an occasional scrawny chicken leg. We slept on mats on the dirt floor. Adelberto was a prince in this primitive realm. Handsome, poised, dignified in his bearing, humble and yet bold. He had a young wife and five little kids who had never seen anything like Karamazov, this fearsome white giant, a god of a dog next to the skinny, mangy village mutts. It was Quetzalcoatl and Cortés all over again.

I gave Adelberto twenty-five grand, enough money to keep him and his whole village for a year. We stood on a precipice overlooking the nearly vertical stepped clearing where he had planted his next crop, and he pointed across the steep valley to the opposite mountainside. A patch of black like an oily smear or a blurred smudge on a photograph, marred the landscape. It looked like the earth was diseased. Nothing grew there, Adelberto told me. Not since the helicopters came and sprayed the mountain with poison. It was part of the American campaign to eradicate marijuana cultivation in Mexico by spraying the fields with a powerful, deadly herbicide called Paraquat. Adelberto went on to say that several villagers who had been in the fields tending the plants when they were sprayed had become ill and two young kids died.

Early on our second day in Xixila, Adelberto received word that the soldiers were coming to the village. It was believed they had heard rumors of gringos in the vicinity. Anaïs, Karamazov, and I were sequestered in a windowless storeroom beside the pigsty behind Adelberto's home. His wife delivered our meals. Our second morning there, Anaïs turned to me and said she had to "spend a penny," using the British colloquialism for taking a shit. Where, she wondered, was she to go? I told her I had been instructed to use a spot out behind a freestanding wall in the pigpen. She was to sneak out, squat behind the wall and relieve herself.

"Really?" she said, incredulous.

"It's that or hold it," I told her.

Brave lady. She did it, but came back horrified. Mortified. And covered with mud and pig slop. "The brutes knocked me over!" she said. The bigger pigs, in their haste to get to her leavings, rudely shoved Anaïs aside and gobbled up the excrement.

"Now you know why we don't eat pork," I said.

A moonlit night a few days later, a burro-train delivered the bales to the base of the mountain. We piled them in our truck and drove to the villa in Cuernavaca. The load sat there for two weeks. One morning I loaded the single-engine Maule on a lonely roadway in Morelos, delivered the load to the ranch in Goldthwaite, and took it to New York in the Global Evangelism machine. The pot sold in two days. That $25,000 netted not quite ten times the investment in profit, a little over $200,000 after expenses. We used part of the money to buy the place in Provincetown.

Of course, I should have quit then, maybe done the occasional off-load, brokered someone else's trip and invested my money in real estate, my other great passion. By now I'd be totally legit—and possibly a multimillionaire. But the feeling I got when I handed Adelberto that initial investment, and to see how good it made him feel; to know the whole village would benefit and be sustained, and the feeling I got from that vision, the burros silhouetted in the moonlight and sure-footing their way along the mountain trail, bails of fresh reefer strapped to their backs; the excitement I feel when I first hear the plane's engine and look up in the sky to see the aircraft approaching; the rush of landing the load on the US side of the border; and finally sitting and sharing the herb with a connoisseur like Tom Forçade, having him pronounce it good—I live for all that.

Now I'm a man on the run. Each day when I wake up I ask myself: *Will this be the day they catch me and put me in a cage?* The prospect of going to prison bothers me less than the thought that by arresting me and locking me up, they will win. The authorities will win; I will be the loser. Wolfshein and the other cops and dope agents will sit around gloating, go out for drinks, and toast their victory while I sit in a jail cell feeling like an asshole for having made one too many false moves.

Oh, well—*fuck it*. Like Wolfshein said after they popped me in Maine: "You had a good run."

Still running. It's all about the adventure, the experience. The game. And they haven't caught me yet.

I'M TOO PARANOID to go to the airport to meet Val. When she arrives, she takes a taxi to a hotel in Lahaina. Checks in. Chills. And when she's sure she has no Heat, she calls me. "Hi, Dad. Want a date?"

We meet at our favorite restaurant. One look at her and my suspicions are confirmed. She's got dark circles under her eyes, looks like she hasn't slept or had a good meal in days. "Let's talk biz later," she says. "I'm starved." Yet she picks at her food. She's nervous, can't look me in the eye. When she feels me looking at her, she gives me a guilty smile. She excuses herself and goes to the ladies room to powder her nose. *Yeah, right.* I can see her, looking in the mirror, scooping a little mound of blow out of the bag with her fingernail and whiffing it up those large, flared nostrils. When she comes back and sits down, she's full of that false sincerity and artificial chemical ebullience that comes with the initial coke rush.

Dog that I am, and horny after weeks of no loving, I'm thinking I'm not going to confront her until after we fuck. We drink a bottle of champagne and a bottle of red wine with the meal. She staggers slightly as we leave the restaurant. I slap her in the ass.

"What was that for?" she says.

"You know."

"'Cause you love my ass?"

"'Cause I'm gonna tear that ass up."

We step out onto the balcony of the hotel room and smoke some Hawaiian herb. It seems to straighten her out—for a minute. Back in the room, she sits on the bed and rummages through her handbag. Almost as an afterthought, she presents me with a business card: James Sullivan, embossed with the Department of Justice, United States Marshals seal. "He came to my mother's house with that other guy. You know the guy," she says as I sit staring at the card, expecting the hotel room door to burst open and agents to come crashing in at any moment. "He was at the restaurant that night when we had dinner with Norman. The one with the curly dark hair."

"Wolfshein. He's DEA."

"I thought they were comin' for me. Flipped me the fuck out. But they didn't even know I'm a fugitive. They only asked about you."

"Don't underestimate what they know." I'm looking around now, rushing with fear, imagining Wolfshein outside poised to make his move. I'm ready to get up and run. They didn't arrest her, I'm thinking, because they knew she would lead them to me. "What did you tell them?"

"Nothing. I said I hadn't seen you since that night in New York."

"They probably followed you here."

"No way, José," she says. "I've been lammin' it long enough to know how to shake the Heat. I drove to San Fran, flew out on fresh ID."

I hand her back the card.

"What am I supposed to do with this?" she asks.

I shake my head. When she reaches for her handbag, I grab her wrist. I take the bag, dump the contents out on the bed. There it is, the little glassine bag of glittering white powder. It looks inviting. Why not do a couple of lines? Drink some more. Get totally fucked up. Party my brains out. The evil twin urges me: Fuck the girl. Suck that pussy. Have fun! So when the Heat comes down, you go to jail all played out.

I pick up the bag of blow, dangle it in front of her.

"And this?"

"What?"

"You know what." I get up and start for the bathroom. "This is what you were doing over there when you were supposed to be taking care of business."

Val is beside me. "Where're you goin' with that?"

"I'm going to dump it down the fucking toilet."

"No, Richard, please, don't. Just . . . *give it to me.*"

"You—" I stammer, shake my head. "You're strung out."

She reaches for my hand holding the bag. "Give it to me."

I pull away.

"When it's gone," she says, "that's it. I'll—"

"You'll what? You'll find another bag somewhere."

"Don't get all self-righteous on me. Just give me the fucking bag."

"Here." I toss the bag back on the bed. "That's what you want, take it. I'm out of here."

"Ah, honey." She puts her arms around my waist, rests her head on my chest. "C'mon, Dad. Don't go. Love me up. I'll stop, I promise."

My cock jumps and twitches. It has no moral compunctions. It knows how well this girl gets it on when she's doing blow. She can go for hours. But the weed has sent my mind wheeling off on some flight of jealousy and anger and fear and guilt steeped with self-disgust. I'm imagining Val fucking other guys. I know how she is when she parties. One of the guys she does business with is a former boyfriend. She dropped out of communication for a couple of days while visiting him in Lake Tahoe.

The worm turns. Something inside me snaps. I just want out.

"Where's the money?"

"What money?"

"*What money?* What the fuck were you doing over there? The money. My money."

"I gave it to Sammy. And that guy, what's his name? The Lebanese guy. The taxi driver. For Nasif and Mohammed. And the other dude, in Texas. Like you told me."

I push her away, take her by the shoulders, sit her back down on the bed. I'm thinking, *I left my wife for this strung-out coke whore?* A cruel thought, and not true, but some part of it sizzles like fat burning in my brain. Static. Mental white noise. I can't get a clear, coherent picture in my mind of what I am supposed to be doing with this information, what I see and feel coming from this woman. What am I doing with my life? Something is definitely wrong. I enabled this: the money, sending her out on the road to hang with people who do blow. Every time this shit comes into our lives, it leads to one major fuckup after another. Treachery and deceit. *Let's talk biz later.* This is later. She's not telling me something.

"Our money," I say. "My end. The money you were supposed to bring back to me."

"Ah, well . . . I can get it back."

"Get it back? Who's got it?"

She says, "I gave it to Ally. She was going to take it back to LA for me. Because . . . I was worried. I had too much going on." Her girlfriend, Ally, one of her couriers, and usually trustworthy.

"So what happened? Where is it?" I ask, trying to contain my rage.

"She gave it to her old man. He *made* her give it to him. I mean, he just basically took it. He picked her up at the airport and . . . and kept the money."

"Two hundred thousand dollars? Some guy has it?"

"Yeah . . . something like that."

She opens the bag, does a quick whiff in each nostril. Hands it to me.

"No." I shake my head. "Give me this guy's name and phone number."

"I don't have it."

"I'm just supposed to forget about this? Is that what you're saying?"

"Honey, you gotta lay low. They're looking for you hot and heavy. It's only money. I'll get it back," she tells me. "Besides, Ally's good for it. We'll work it off. This guy, her old man . . . he's a bad dude. He just got out of the joint."

"Where's Ally?"

"LA . . . or, actually, Orange County." She snuggles up to me, reaches for my cock. "C'mon, Dad. Fuck me."

"Give me Ally's number."

"Not tonight. C'mon, baby—I've been away so long. I missed you."

She's massaging my cock now, reaching inside my fly. "Lemme suck it," she says. "I'm so horny."

"No. Get away from me." I push her off.

"Dad . . . don't—"

"Give me the fucking number!"

"What's the matter with you?" she pleads. "Not now. Be nice."

But I can't, I feel mean, hateful, hating myself and taking it out on her.

"*Now. Give me the number.* You think I'm going to just let this guy rip me off? Give me Ally's number and her address."

"You're fuckin' crazy!" she says and scribbles the number on a scrap of paper. "Here!" She balls up the piece of paper and throws it at me. She's in tears now. "If you leave," she cries, "that's it. It's all over."

Yes, it is, I think. All over.

I walk out, leave her in the room with her bag of blow.

BACK IN ULUPALAKUA, I cruise past the house once, twice, to make certain there are no agents staking the place out before I pull into the driveway. Inside, I grab an overnight bag, a change of clothes, and ten grand in cash. There is one late flight left from Maui to Honolulu. I check in to a hotel near the airport in Honolulu and book a flight to LA for the next day.

At a pay phone in the lobby, I make a call to Biff in New York.

"Jesus, Doc, it's like five in the morning. Where are you?" Stupid question to ask a fugitive. I don't answer. "I'm glad you called," he goes on. "The Captain is looking for you. You know—"

I cut him off. "Did he leave you a number?"

"Yeah." He gives me the number. "You know the area code. He said to call anytime."

I'm a man on a mission. It doesn't matter how much money I have salted away in offshore bank accounts. Or how much I have on the street still to collect. Some sleazebag thinks he's going to rip me off for two hundred grand? No, that's not happening. Fuck that and fuck him. I'll take the action.

"Don't worry about it," the Captain tells me when I reach him pay phone to pay phone the next day. "*I found Pierre*. I spoke to him."

"Really? Where is he?"

"LA. He doesn't know it, but I have his address. Where are you?"

Why do people keep asking me that?

"Oh . . . never mind," he says when I don't respond. "He told me he will pay. But he only wants to meet with you."

"Me? Fuck that. I want nothing to do with this creep. I told your father, it's not my responsibility."

"Yes, I understand. But you also said you would help in any way to retrieve the money. Pierre is afraid I'll kill him," the Captain explains.

"He wants to meet with you, only you, and give you the money, and let you deal with me, my father, and Abu Nasif."

Abu Nasif, which means father of Nasif in Arabic, is Mohammed. These guys are all still trying to involve me in a deal I wanted no part of in the first place. It's the fucked-up deal that won't go away. What is my karma that I keep getting sucked back into this mess? All that anger, all that brooding over being ripped off, and I'm no different. Why can't I just let it go? Because I can't; I'm no different than the Arabs.

"Listen, I have a plan," the Captain continues. "While he's meeting with you, to give you the money, I'm going to blow up his house."

"You're going to do what?"

"You heard me!" He's excited. "Blow up his house! Create a vacant lot," he laughs. "He comes home, instead of a house, all he sees is a pile of dust. Just like Beirut! That should teach him a lesson."

We are talking somewhere around three million dollars here. And payback to that rat fuck Wizard for all the grief he caused me in Lebanon. I make plans to meet the Captain in Los Angeles. I tell him I'll call him with a location. That afternoon, I leave for the mainland. My thoughts are to get there a day or two prior to the meeting, scope out a suitable spot to meet with the Captain before I set up a rendezvous with the Wizard. I want to meet with Val's girlfriend, Ally, and get a location for her old man, the tough guy who did a bid in the joint and figures that gives him the right to rip people off. After we deal with the Wizard, we'll take this other clown and show him he's not dealing with a bunch of spaced-out hippies.

On the plane on the way over, I read G. Gordon Liddy's book, *Will*. And I am struck, when I come across the line "And then began one of the most interesting phases of my life" that Liddy writes of his experience in prison. The words reverberate in my head. It all feels preordained, as though I am living a part of my life that has already happened in some other dimension. I don't even question the Captain's proposal to blow up the Wizard's house. It seems like a good idea at the time. He says he will make certain there are no humans or pets inside before he reduces the house to a Beirut-style pile of rubble. This is like some CIA shit.

I stay for two nights with friends of Val's in Orange County while I try to track down Ally and her boyfriend. No calls to Maui; I have no idea what Val's doing. Everyone, it seems, is strung out on blow, snorting it, smoking it, shooting it. I want no part of the scene. I am disgusted with what has become of the business, and with what I have become—greedy, self-indulgent, hunted, crazed. In good shape physically, I'm spiritually bereft, hungering for something inside and outside of myself, something pot and the high I get from fucking and risking my life can no longer satisfy. I'm angry at—I don't even know what—myself! Of course. Stupid for wasting my life. And still I keep pushing the boundaries, looking for my limits. Searching for the test that will bring me to my knees and ultimately define me.

"You better not fuck with me," Ally's old man says when I finally catch him on the phone.

"Oh, yeah? Why is that?"

"I just got out of Terminal Island. The federal joint," he says.

"And that makes you—what? A tough guy? You rip off girls," I say. "No. Listen to me. You ripped off the wrong people. We know where you live."

He hangs up. It's a lie; I don't know where he lives. I have the phone number. The Captain can use his government connections to get the address. This asshole is history, and he doesn't even know it. The Captain says he has the C-4 explosives. I'm thinking, after he blows up the Wizard's house, we'll go for Ally's old man and get my money back—whatever's left of it. It doesn't matter anymore. It's like Tamer said to me in Baalbek: It's about revenge.

I make plans to meet the Captain in the lobby bar of the Sheraton Senator Hotel at the airport in Los Angeles. I arrive there a day before the rendezvous, find a spot on the mezzanine where I can position myself out of sight while keeping an eye on the lobby entrance. Then, on the day, I get there two hours before the appointed time, sit in the mezzanine with a view of the front doors through which I know the Captain will enter, and pretend to read a book while I scope the hotel entrance and lobby bar where we intend to meet.

Nothing. No unusual activity. No signs of a stakeout.

The Captain arrives on time. He walks in carrying one of those bulky black cases like a lawyer might bring to court. I watch him come through the doors, stop to look around, then take a seat at a table in the lobby lounge and order tea. Wearing a tweed jacket and a tie, he looks more like a traveling salesman with a valise full of samples than a highly trained Delta Force anti-terrorist spook carrying C-4 explosives. I've never seen him in anything but civilian clothes, though I know he's still stationed at the base at Fort Hood and on active duty—doing what, I don't know. Chasing money for his drug lord dad. Shipping weapons all over the world. And now, blowing up rip-offs' homes.

After the Captain enters and takes a seat, I keep an eye on the front doors to see if he has been followed. Nothing, no shady-looking characters who might be undercover agents come in after him. Just a couple of women, who go directly to the front desk. Nor do I see any suspicious agent types lurking around the lobby. No sign of the Wolfman.

Satisfied the Captain is clean, I go down the escalator, walk over to where he sits. He has not seen me since I grew a beard and bleached my hair. When I approach his table, at first he doesn't recognize me.

"Ah, Richard," he says and stands. We shake hands. "You look different."

"Let's take a walk," I say. "My car's parked out back."

He leaves a bill on the table, picks up his black bag, and we start back through the lobby toward the rear doors to the parking lot. When we are in the middle of the lobby, near the front desk, I look over and see what looks like hotel employees vaulting over the counter. Bellmen are drawing weapons. Desk clerks, the concierge, they are all running toward us with guns pointed at our heads. It's as if the entire hotel staff is made up of armed agents.

This is it—the bust. I freeze, raise my hands. But the Captain, who is a serious martial artist, drops his bag and goes into a karate stance.

"GUN!" someone shouts. "He's got a gun!"

Who? I look around. The only guns I see are in the hands of the agents. I'm thinking, *Oh, shit. Any second now they are going to blow us away.*

"Take it easy!" I yell. "NO GUNS!"

I look around for Wolfshein. Three agents leap on the Captain and wrestle him to the floor in the middle of the lobby. A stocky, well-built blond stands before me flashing his badge. He needs no introduction. "US Marshals," he says. "You're under arrest."

"Where's Wolfshein?" I ask.

The marshal looks up, nods toward the mezzanine. Wolfshein stands alone above the fray. He points his trigger finger at me, cocks his thumb. Son of a bitch, he was there all the time, watching his play go down. The marshals cuff me behind my back, advise me of my rights, and then hustle me out the rear door. As I leave, I glance back and see a pile of agents rolling around on the lobby floor trying to subdue the Captain.

They take me to an LAPD satellite station at the airport, lock me in a small room. After about an hour, the blond marshal comes in and formally introduces himself. "James Sullivan," he says, "Deputy US Marshal with the fugitive task force." It's the guy who questioned Val at her mother's home. Now I'm beginning to wonder if she set me up. "You can call me Sully," he says. "I'm from Boston. Like you."

Big deal. What do I care where he's from? All I want to know is how he knew where I was meeting the Captain.

"We've been tracking you for a long time now, pal," he goes on, "and I gotta tell ya, I'm sorry to see it end. I was really enjoying it. I'd tell my boss, 'Hey, Chief. We got a tip, he's going to be at the place in Maine.' I'd take my fishing gear and spend a few days catching trout in that pond of yours. Or I tell him you were spotted in New York and get a couple of days hanging out in the Big Apple." He pauses, gives me a wry smile. "But I guess all good things must come to an end, huh, Rich?"

"So they say."

He nods. "Where's your girlfriend?"

"Who?"

"R———." He uses her real name. "She's pretty clever, but I knew she was lying. I knew she knew where you were."

He pauses again, longer, and looks me over. "What's up with the other guy?"

"What guy?"

"Your friend. Bruce Lee. He coulda got you both killed."

Sullivan sits down. "You know what he has in that black bag?"

"I don't know what you're talking about."

"Plastic explosives," the marshal says. "Rich, what's the deal? You goin' terrorist on us or something?"

So he did bring the explosives.

"Not only do we have you on the fugitive warrant for the Maine beef," Sullivan continues, "you and your pal are both facing new charges: illegal possession and transportation of explosives. That could get you another fifteen years." He shakes his head. "What the fuck were you gonna do with C-4?"

I say nothing. Sullivan shrugs, stands, walks out, and leaves me alone to ponder who set me up. Val? No way. I haven't spoken to her since I left her in Maui. Her friends had no way of knowing where I was meeting the Captain. The Captain? It *had* to be him. He was the only person who knew where we were going to meet. But then, why bring the C-4? Why resist arrest and risk getting us both killed? From what Sullivan said, it appears the Captain has been arrested as well. Obviously, they've seized his bag with the C-4. Maybe they have his phone tapped. But I was sure we never discussed where we were to meet over his phone; I made plans with him pay phone to pay phone. The agents had to have known our plan well in advance in order to position their people at the location posing as hotel staff.

I am bewildered, oddly relieved that the hunt is finally over, but totally stumped as to how they caught me.

About an hour later, Sullivan returns. Right behind him, Special Agent Bernie Wolfshein enters. He walks in, sits down, and looks me in the eye. "Rich," he says, "how are you?"

"Agent Wolfshein . . . I was wondering when you'd show up."

"Well, you know how it goes. I had some calls to make," he says, and then to Sullivan, "Did you advise Mr. Stratton of his rights?"

"Someone did, right, Rich?"

"I think so."

"Feel like talking?" Wolfshein asks.

"Not really. I'm tired. Just take me to jail."

Both Sullivan and Wolfshein laugh.

"You gotta love this guy," Wolfshein says to Sully. "You play the game, you lose. You go to jail." Then to me, "Right, Rich?"

"Do not pass go. Do not collect two hundred dollars," Sully chimes in. They are loving this.

"I guess so," I say when nothing better comes to mind.

"Yeah, well, let's see how well he holds up," Sullivan says. He looks me up and down. "You know you're lookin' at a lot of time."

I nod. "Yes . . . I know."

"All right, Rich," he says, "Now I really want to know: Who the fuck is that guy?"

"I can't help you, Sullivan."

"Bullshit . . . seriously, Rich. Off the record. Call me Sully. As one Irish guy from Beantown to another. Who was that masked man?"

"I'm not Irish."

He chuckles. "Fuckin' limey then. C'mon, tell me. I won't give it up."

"Sully, if I knew, I'd tell you."

"You're lying. But that's okay. You're the one getting fucked here."

"You know where he is now? Your friend? A—— S——?" Wolfshein asks, using the Captain's real name.

"See," I tell Sullivan. "Wolfshein knows who he is. Wolfshein knows everything." And then to Wolfshein, "No. Where is he?"

"Not here. He's gone," Wolfshein says.

"Gone?"

"Yup. As in—he left. Some brass from the Defense Department came down here and waltzed him out. Big wigs. Know what I mean? Scrambled eggs on their shoulders. 'We're here for Captain A—— S——,' they told me. They even took his little bag of tricks. I got a call from my boss. 'Let him go,' he said. No charges. No nothing. Like it never happened. Like the guy doesn't exist."

I don't know what to say. "Sometimes the left hand doesn't know what the right hand is doing," is all I can come up with. But now I feel sure: the Captain set me up—or did he?

"I'll say one thing for you, Rich," Sully says. "You've got big balls."

Where have I heard that line before? Ah, Biff . . .

"Or," I say, "maybe I'm just crazy."

"So much for the nonviolent profile, huh?" Wolfshein muses aloud. "Hard to sell that when you're running around with plastic explosives and guys from Delta Force. What're you up to with that guy? His dad's a big man back in the old country, huh?"

"C'mon, I never bought it," Sully says when I don't answer. "I say: You tell a crook by the company he keeps. Jimmy Bulger," he laughs, "now there is a piece of work."

"Rich has got a lot of interesting friends," Wolfshein remarks. "I'm sure that, if he felt like it, he could tell one hell of a story." He turns and looks directly at me. "You should give it some serious thought, Rich. Because . . ." He nods and breaks off, turns to Sullivan, pushes his glasses back up his nose. "You know what I'm saying, Sully?"

"Of course. Rich is a good guy. And still a young man. Got a lot of life left in him. But I'm afraid he's gonna be an old man, a *very* old man by the time he gets out of prison."

They both nod and shake their heads as though pondering my bleak future. Two burly marshals come in with shackles and leg chains.

"We're not takin' any chances this time," Sully says as the men chain my ankles.

"Where're we takin' him?" Wolfshein asks Sullivan.

"Well," Sully looks at his watch, "it's too late to go to San Pedro."

"Hmmm," Wolfshein says, "and it's Friday night. We won't be able to get him in front of a judge until Monday morning."

Sully chuckles, shakes his head. "Shit," he says, "I hate to do that to another Boston guy."

"I don't see where we have any choice," says Wolfshein, another of his practiced lines.

They are talking about me as if I were not in the room. Then they both turn and smile at me. It feels like they rehearsed this little act.

"We've got a surprise for you, Rich," Wolfshein says. "Give you some time to think about what I've said."

EPILOGUE

IN CUSTODY

Oh, that magic feeling, nowhere to go . . .
The Beatles

Los Angeles, California, June 1982

Some surprise—a weekend in the LA City Jail, otherwise known as the
Glass House. Wolfman and Sully, those fuckers, I'm sure they had it all
planned. Bust him on a Friday night so he'll have the whole weekend to
cool his jets in arguably the worst jail in America. I'm also sure they're
getting their jollies out of my downfall. Be that as it may, for it shall
not end here. This is not the last I will see of those two. Indeed, it is
just the beginning of my enforced commingling with these federal law
enforcement types—the *über* Authorities. Fuck with me; I'll fuck with
you right back. It's all part of the journey.

Do I feel beaten? Curiously, I don't. My overriding fear that getting busted with no way out would make me feel weak and humiliated
and prove them right—thankfully that has not happened. Do I feel
sorry for myself? No, again. *Hell no*. On the contrary, I'm filled with an
encouraging, quiet confidence and grim acceptance of my fate. I feel
that I can handle this, whatever they come at me with—Wolfshein and
his colleagues in CENTAC and the Drug Enforcement Administration;
prosecutors and judges with the federal judicial system; the rats and

stool pigeons lining up to point their fingers at me; the prison guards who will stand over the years I see yawning ahead—I don't blame them and I accept it, because I know I deserve it. I brought it upon myself. It was inevitable, given the way I chose to live my life. I could have quit the smuggler's life a long time ago and retired rich. You push your luck, you go against everything you know you should be doing, and do everything you know you should not be doing, you keep upping the stakes, betting against the odds, and ultimately you will lose. You will take a serious fall.

Yes, they nailed my ass. But I still don't feel like an evil person, or even a very bad man or a criminal. A fuckup, maybe. A fool. And, yes, an asshole. A victim of unbridled hubris. Selfish! Jesus, yes—self-centered. I admit that, and it is my greatest sin: to believe that it is always all about me and my need to get my kicks. That's just stupid. It's bullshit, meaningless crap. Especially when I have had not one but many intimations that this life is never just about one's self; it's always about so much more. We're here today, gone tomorrow. When I think back to all the crazy shit I put myself through, and how I involved others in my insanity—for what? So I could feel like a big shot? Who cares that Stratton smuggled a lot of righteous weed and lived for a time like a rock star? Big deal. This life passes away; only our souls and good works endure. What have I done to honor creation and praise the Creator? Little else matters.

At least now I can stop running, and I can allay the fear of getting arrested. The worst has happened. They have my body, but they will never get my curiously deranged, THC-addled mind. I console myself with the thought that it's not over yet. There is still the final showdown with the Authorities to get me excited.

I know they are going to put a lot of pressure on me to roll over, lick my nuts, and become a rat. But fuck them. Even as the prison doors slam shut, I will not go gently into my cell. I'll fight these mindless bureaucrats with every ounce of resolve, every fiber of my being because I believe it's the right thing to do.

Follow me down as I go deep inside, take the inner journey, find and connect with my higher self to discover what I'm really made of. Then, God willing, I will survive this sojourn in the land of the living dead with body and soul intact.

Peace out.